true woman 201

interior design

ten elements of biblical womanhood

Mary A. Kassian

Nancy Leigh DeMoss

MOODY PUBLISHERS
CHICAGO

Unless otherwise indicated, all Scripture quotations are from the ESV® Bible (*The Holy Bible, English Standard Version*®). Copyright © 2001 by Crossway, a publishing ministry of Good News Publishers. Used by permission. All rights reserved.

Scripture quotations marked NKJV are taken from the *New King James Version*. Copyright © 1982 by Thomas Nelson, Inc. Used by permission. All rights reserved.

Scripture quotations marked NASB are taken from the *New American Standard Bible*®, Copyright © 1960, 1962, 1963, 1968, 1971, 1972, 1973, 1975, 1977, 1995 by The Lockman Foundation. Used by permission. (www.Lockman.org)

Scripture quotations marked HCSB are taken from the *Holman Christian Standard Bible*®, Copyright © 1999, 2000, 2002, 2003 by Holman Bible Publishers. Used by permission. Holman Christian Standard Bible®, Holman CSB®, and HCSB® are federally registered trademarks of Holman Bible Publishers.

Scripture quotations marked THE MESSAGE are from *The Message*, copyright © by Eugene H. Peterson 1993, 1994, 1995. Used by permission of NavPress Publishing Group.

Emphasis to Scripture has been added by the authors.

Cover Design: Julia Ryan | www.DesignByJulia.com
Interior Design: Julia Ryan | www.DesignByJulia.com
Edited by Lydia Brownback
Cover photo of pillows copyright © Blaz Kure / 2129374. All rights reserved.
Cover photo of green curtain © sumroeng chinnapan / 201378503. All rights reserved.
Cover photo of green wall texture © idea for life / 57419170. All rights reserved.
Cover floral graphic © LenLis / 81959941. All rights reserved.
Interior images: © Shutterstock, Photo of train wreck on page 92 © Sûreté du Québec's, used with permission.
Author photos: Photography by Katie

Library of Congress Cataloging-in-Publication Data

DeMoss, Nancy Leigh.
  True woman 201 : interior design: ten elements of biblical womanhood / Nancy Leigh DeMoss, Mary A. Kassian.
     pages cm
  Includes bibliographical references.
  ISBN 978-0-8024-1258-4
1. Bible. Titus, II--Textbooks. 2. Christian women--Religious life--Textbooks. 3. Women--Biblical teaching. 4. Women-
-Religious aspects--Christianity--Textbooks. I. Title.
  BS2755.52.D46 2015
  248.8'43071--dc23

                              2014044926

We hope you enjoy this book from Moody Publishers. Our goal is to provide high-quality, thought-provoking books and products that connect truth to your real needs and challenges. For more information on other books and products written and produced from a biblical perspective, go to www.moodypublishers.com or write to:

Moody Publishers
820 N. LaSalle Boulevard
Chicago, IL 60610

1 3 5 7 9 10 8 6 4 2

Printed in the United States of America

If you have ever wondered what biblical womanhood looks like here is your answer. Mary Kassian and Nancy Leigh DeMoss have written and designed a compelling study. Rooted in Titus 2, *True Woman 201 Interior Design* is refreshingly clear and understandable. The practical applications will cause these truths to wrap around the heart and bring hope and transformation. Thank you, Mary and Nancy. What a treasure!

Dr. Crawford W. Loritts Jr.
Senior pastor, Fellowship Bible Church, Roswell, Georgia

Nancy Leigh DeMoss and Mary Kassian are contemporary gurus when it comes to addressing the subject of biblical womanhood. This brand-new Bible study is based on sound teaching as well as rich personal experience, and culminates in meaningful life applications. Those women who will embrace this study opportunity, whether personally or in a group, will find helpful instruction and persuasive encouragement as they begin or continue a journey from sitting at the feet of the Savior and to all He has called them to be and to do.

Dorothy Kelley Patterson
Professor of theology in women's studies, Southwestern Baptist Theological Seminary

The need has never been greater for a practical, biblical, and faithful presentation of true biblical womanhood. Mary Kassian and Nancy Leigh DeMoss team up to write a work that will be immediately helpful to Bible studies and especially to the local church. As society grows ever more confused, the need for clarity and faithfulness among Christians looms even larger. This work will stand the test of time, and will serve as a most timely resource for women's Bible study.

Al and Mary Mohler
The Southern Baptist Theological Seminary

I am thankful for Mary and Nancy—for their character, courage, and commitment to Christ. Knowing who they are, I'm not surprised that this book is full of discernment, full of personal application, and full of the Bible. Women will not only hear a faithful and clear call to biblical womanhood in these pages, they will see why biblical womanhood is good and meet the One who calls them to it.

Kevin DeYoung
Senior pastor, University Reformed Church, East Lansing, Michigan

True Woman 201 celebrates women and the beautiful elements of design that make us female. Titus 2 is often referred to as the road map for woman-to-woman ministry, but few women have delved into the rich depths of this often quoted passage. Mary Kassian and Nancy Leigh Demoss provide a deep, biblically sound study with a modern design that will draw any woman to its message. *True Woman 201* fills a significant void in women's discipleship and will be a valuable resource for the church, small group, and individual study.

Terri Stovall
Dean of women's programs, Southwestern Baptist Theological Seminary

Few books have shaped my life and leadership like *True Woman 101* and now the sequel will no doubt drive me further in my spiritual journey. As a director of women's ministry for over twenty years, I agree these are a *must* for every Bible study program. They teach Truth. They emphasize not only the practical and useful but the biblical design and instruction God desires for women. These are powerful resources that will transform a woman's thinking and living in a culture that contradicts the true meaning of a woman.

Debbie Stuart
Director of ministry initiatives, Hope for the Heart

My first reaction to *True Woman 201* was simply the beauty of the artwork and design of the study. I was literally drawn into the study by its sheer appearance. But what I discovered is that this is not just a pretty design. It is the beauty of God's Word that is engrained into the fiber of every lesson. This study is not just nice words or stories from Kassian and DeMoss, but it is the divine revelation from God for women to live out their calling through the gospel.

Kelly King
Baptist General Convention of Oklahoma women's specialist

True Woman 201: Interior Design is an exciting ten-week study filled with solid biblical truth, insightful content, and opportunities for personal reflection—all presented in a beautiful format. Mary Kassian and Nancy Leigh DeMoss have provided an excellent resource for those who seek to understand how to glorify God through their womanhood. The women at my church can't wait to dig into this!

Kimberly Wagner
Author of *Fierce Women*

These are confusing times—times in which the very concept of gender is suddenly up for debate. Yet amid the confusion, the Bible stands firm, determining and defining biblical manhood and womanhood. The True Woman movement and books are a precious breath of fresh air that simply look to God's Word to gain God's perspective. By showing women what the Bible says about womanhood, Nancy Leigh DeMoss and Mary Kassian set women free to be true women—the women God has both designed and called them to be.

Tim and Aileen Challies

Extreme makeover programs are as popular as they are on TV because everyone loves to see dramatic change—whether it's weight loss, the clothes we wear, or a completely remodeled home. But the most powerful change of all is the transformed heart of a woman who has allowed herself to be completely "made over" by the Great Designer Himself. If you want to be such a woman, open the pages of this book and allow God to put fresh paint on the walls of your heart.

Janet Parshall
Nationally syndicated talk show host

contents

But as for you, teach what accords with sound doctrine. . . .

Older women . . . are to be reverent in behavior,

not slanderers or slaves to much wine.

They are to teach what is good,

and so train the young women

to love their husbands and children,

to be self-controlled, pure,

working at home, kind,

and submissive to their own husbands,

that the word of God may not be reviled.

Titus 2:1, 3–5

interior design
overview of lessons

Having a talented designer come in and create a new look for a home or restaurant is a popular topic of TV reality shows.

The shows follow a similar format. First, the designer and the owner take a look at the space and talk about how unsightly and dysfunctional it is. Then, the designer asks the owner to hand over the keys and trust him to do a renovation. Although she may be a bit nervous and doubtful, she agrees to let the designer take over and transform the space.

The designer comes up with a plan and quickly puts his team to work. They demolish and clear out everything old. They fix things that are broken, paint and paper the walls, lay new flooring, change the fixtures, bring in new furnishings, and choose just the right accessories to fit the new décor.

The highlight of the show is when the owner returns for the big reveal. The camera zooms in to capture the look of surprise, joy, and astonishment on her face as she takes in the change. The audience is shown "before and after" footage to demonstrate just how dramatic the transformation has been. The show ends with the happy owner giving a testimony about how much the metamorphosis means to her and how her life will change as a result.

These renovation shows are a great illustration for the object of this study. The Lord is the ultimate Designer. And He has a divine design for womanhood. He wants to come in and do a radical renovation of your heart. He wants to change you from the inside out. If you let Him, He'll give you an extreme makeover . . . a brand-new *interior design*.

The change won't take place overnight. But the outcome—a heart and character like His—will be grander than anything you could possibly have envisioned, better than anything you could have done on your own. And it all starts with trusting Him enough to hand Him the keys to your heart, asking Him to make a beautiful work of art out of your life.

And it doesn't end there. God wants to use you as part of His makeover team to help *others* experience His grand, interior design for their lives!

> "It is time for women of biblical faith to reclaim our territory. We know the Designer. We have His instruction manual. If we don't display the Divine design of His female creation, no one will. But if we do, it will be a profound testimony to a watching, needy world."[1]
>
> **Susan Hunt**

designing women

True Woman 201—Interior Design is a companion to True Woman 101—Divine Design. In 101, we examined the Bible's essential, foundational teachings on womanhood. We discovered that part of the grandeur of being created in the image of God is that He creates us either male or female.

God created man in his own image, in the image of God he created him; male and female He created them. (Gen. 1:27)

Contrary to what many claim today, God didn't create generic human beings. And gender is not interchangeable or fluid. God created male human beings and female human beings. And this is a marvelous thing!

Your womanhood is not a biological accident. It's not incidental to who you are or how you live. Our culture tries to minimize and neutralize the differences between men and women. It rejects the design God created for the flourishing of our lives together. It tries to convince us that male-female differences don't matter, and that each individual has the right to determine what gender means. But according to the Bible, the fact you were born female is profoundly significant. It's no minor or inconsequential detail. You are a woman to the depths of your humanity.

When you step into God's design for womanhood, you step into the great adventure of discovering who you were created to be. Dr. John Piper reminds us that "when it comes to human sexuality, the greatest display of God's glory, and the greatest joy of human relationships, and the greatest fruitfulness in ministry come about when the deep differences between men and women are embraced and celebrated."[2]

Embracing and celebrating God's design will help you thrive. All the things that make you "you"— your personality, talents, gifts, interests, intellect, emotions, and even your appearance—will mesh with who God created you to be as a woman. It won't look exactly the same for you as it does for your friends. Your womanhood will fit you like a custom-tailored outfit.

As we said in *101*, your womanhood isn't about fitting into a cookie-cutter mold. It's not about following a checklist of prescribed behaviors or a rigid division of labor. The Bible presents a design for True Womanhood that applies to all women—old, young; single, married, divorced, widowed; with children or without; gregarious, quiet, adventurous, reserved; whatever. Cookie-cutter patterns won't do. God's design for womanhood is much broader and more wonderful than that!

womanhood curriculum

In *True Woman 101* we studied the Old Testament record of creation and the fall to discover God's beautiful design for womanhood and to explore how that design has been damaged by sin. In *201*, we'll turn to the New Testament, to the book of Titus, to focus on some important elements of redeemed womanhood.

Titus was a young Gentile pastor on the island of Crete. Most of the Cretan believers hadn't been raised in the Jewish faith, so they were unfamiliar with the ways of God. Paul gave Titus some general instructions—things every believer needed to learn about the Christian life. He also gave sex-specific instructions, so they would know how Christianity was to impact their lives as men and women.

Pastor Titus was to teach these truths to the older women in the church, and they in turn were responsible to train the younger women. The apostle stressed that the women's response to this teaching could adorn the gospel of Christ and make it believable to a pagan culture. OR—it could cause unbelievers to reject the Word of God.

In Titus 2, we see a portrait of the countercultural Christian woman—a woman who honors God and reflects the heart of Christ. In the opening paragraph (verses 1, 3–5), Paul points us to ten essential elements of womanhood: discernment, honor, affection, discipline, virtue, responsibility, benevolence, disposition, legacy, and beauty.

These elements make up the "basic Christian womanhood" curriculum for the women of Crete. But they weren't just for those Mediterranean believers. Paul's instructions apply to women in every nation and every generation. They're just as relevant today as they were back then.

Each week of this *True Woman 201* study examines one of the ten "design elements" of womanhood drawn from Titus 2 and is divided into five lessons— it should only take you about fifteen minutes to complete each lesson.

To get the most out of this study, we suggest you go through it with a group of friends. At the end of each week, we've provided some questions to help you discuss what you've read and further explore and apply the Bible's teachings to your life. When you're done, encourage your friends to start their own groups. You'll find many additional resources, including companion videos and helps for group leaders, at TrueWoman201.com.

Together, *True Woman 101* and *201* encompass the foundational teaching of the True Woman movement. You can do *True Woman 201* without having completed *101*. But to get the whole picture about womanhood, we suggest you study both resources.

In these studies, we've tried to focus on timeless biblical principles rather than the specific application of those principles. Practical application is vital, and the Holy Spirit will help you apply these core truths to your specific life situation. But our goal is to provide teaching that is relevant for every woman in every season and circumstance of life, and that will be just as applicable to the great-granddaughters of our generation as it is to us.

Decades ago, the secular women's movement set out to spread its radical message and vision through small groups that met, multiplied, and eventually ignited a revolution. Our desire is that a new revolution will take root and spread in our day, as Christian women band together to ask, "How can we more fully reflect the beauty and gospel of Christ to our world, through the expression of our true, biblical design?"

the movement continues

True Woman 101 and 201 are a response to the many requests we have received for further biblical teaching and practical resources since the first True Woman conference in Chicago in 2008.

What a joy it is to see the message of True Womanhood being multiplied and to see Christ being put on display in a greater way through women's lives—not only in the US but in other countries around the world.

Thousands of women have attended True Woman conferences, signed the True Woman Manifesto, are following the True Woman blog, and are talking about the meaning of biblical womanhood with other women through various social media communities, small groups, and studies.

The goal of the True Woman movement is to help women . . .

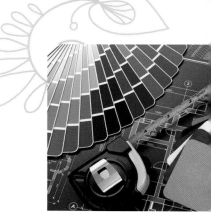

- *Discover and embrace* God's design and mission for their lives

- *Reflect the beauty* and heart of Jesus Christ to their world

- *Intentionally pass* the baton of Truth on to the next generation

- *Pray earnestly* for an outpouring of God's Spirit in their families, churches, nation, and world

When it comes to womanhood, many of us are tired of clichéd advice, shallow caricatures, and cookie-cutter solutions. It is our hope that this resource will shift the discussion to a better focus. We pray that it will

- enable you to explore God's timeless design for womanhood straight from His Word

- help you wrestle with how to apply God's design to your season of life

- encourage you to have grace toward women who differ in life circumstance and application

- equip you to pass on the message of True Womanhood to the next generation

Discovering and living out the meaning of True Womanhood will be a journey for you, as it has been (and is) for us. At points, you may find yourself disagreeing with what you're reading, or struggling with some of the implications of this teaching. We've had some of those same reactions ourselves! We would simply encourage you to turn to God's Word with an open, seeking heart. Ask His Spirit to teach you, to give you understanding, and to incline your heart to say "Yes, Lord!" to His Word and His ways.

every design has a purpose

C Charles Eames is a famous American designer who made major contributions to modern architecture and furniture design. He defined *design* as "a plan for arranging elements in such a way as to best accomplish a particular purpose."[4] We think his definition is appropriate for this study. God has a divine plan for womanhood. He has given us the elements that are necessary to accomplish that purpose. And what is that purpose? The goal is not just so our lives can be easier or work better. According to Isaiah 43:6–7, God created sons and daughters for the purpose of displaying His glory. His divine design reflects profound truths about His character and about the gospel of Christ.

You have a purpose. Your womanhood has a purpose. The Lord wants you to discover the beauty of His plan for manhood and womanhood, and to experience the joy and fulfillment of being exactly who He created you to be. He wants to arrange the interior of your heart and life so that you might best accomplish the purpose for which you were made. And He invites us to participate with Him in that grand undertaking.

Are you ready to start? Let's ask the great Designer to start renovating. And let's watch the amazing transformation as He gives us a beautiful, new *Interior Design*!

Mary   Nancy

discernment

Those who have met us know that we (Nancy and Mary) are almost as different as two friends can be. And those differences extend beyond our personalities and appearance into our interior decorating styles.

If we were to walk into a home décor store, Nancy would gravitate toward primary, winter colors—vibrant reds, blues, and greens. Mary would gravitate toward warm, bold, autumn tones—cinnamon, caramel, rust, chocolate, and teal. Nancy would like the floral patterns. Mary would like anything but. Nancy would be attracted to furniture that had light, clean, classic lines. Mary would be attracted to heavier, antique furniture with a funky modern twist. Nancy would be drawn toward serious and sophisticated accessories. Mary would be drawn toward quirky and artsy ones. One of the beautiful truths about women is that God created us all different.

*A True Woman is characterized by right thinking . . . She knows "**what accords with sound doctrine**."*

The two of us have different styles. And your style is likely different from ours. There are so many to choose from: contemporary, country, Victorian, Federal, St. Louis, Nordic, modern, French provincial, retro, eclectic. What's more, these styles can be combined with an endless variety of patterns, colors, textures, and accessories. As a result, our homes don't look exactly the same. They're all different.

But although styles differ, there are certain elements that all good designs have in common. Designers choose and arrange flooring, wall treatments, lighting, window treatments, furniture, and accessories according to their color, texture, line, form, and space. These are the critical elements of every design.[1]

This Bible study is about the critical design elements of womanhood. As we explained in the introduction, it's based on the passage in Titus chapter 2, where Paul outlines what the women in Titus' congregation needed to learn.

The first critical element of womanhood evident in the passage is discernment. A True Woman is characterized by right thinking . . . She knows "what accords with sound doctrine" (Titus 2:1).

"Wait a minute!" you may object; "isn't discernment something guys need too?" Absolutely. In this chapter Paul gives instruction tailored to several different groups of people in the church. In verse 2, he lists some things older men need to learn. In verses 3 to 5, he lays out the curriculum for older and younger women. In verse 6, he talks about the curriculum for young men. All these groups need to learn "what accords with sound doctrine." Obviously, both sexes need discernment. Men and women, young and old—all need to know sound doctrine.

But here's the thing. Though there's overlap, Paul's lists in Titus 2 suggest there's a different emphasis needed for each gender, in terms of how they apply and live out sound doctrine. Some traits are especially important to what it means to be a man, and some are particularly important to what it means to be a woman.

Paul gives certain traits a gender-specific emphasis. But that doesn't imply that they're *gender-exclusive*. For example, Paul instructs *women* not be slanderers; he exhorts *men* to be sound in faith. Obviously, that doesn't mean that men don't need to learn to control their mouths, or that women don't ever wrestle with doubt or doctrinal error.

Women are instructed to be reverent, to love their spouses and children, to exercise self-control, to be pure and kind, to be devoted to their homes, and to submit to God-ordained authority. Yet men arguably need to learn these things too! Men are instructed to be sober-minded, dignified, self-controlled, sound in faith, in love, and in steadfastness. Yet women need to learn these things too!

So why the sex-specific lists? Why not just lump everything together under one big category of "Important Stuff for Christians to Learn"?

The reason for the differing lists is that men and women are different. As we learned in *True Woman 101*, Paul's lists counteract our sex-specific sin tendencies and point us back to our divine design. So although "discernment" is important for both men and women, there are specific applications of "sound doctrine" that are particularly directed to and important for each gender to understand.

According to Paul, right thinking leads to right living. If what you think about womanhood isn't shaped by sound doctrine, chances are, you're not going to live in a way that pleases the Lord. Discernment, grounded in a clear understanding of God's Word, is the first critical element of true womanhood. →

a healthy mind

Not long ago, a nurse working at a hospital experienced a series of asthma attacks that flared up whenever she worked on the bone marrow transplant unit. Another nurse and nurse's aide also started to have chest tightness and wheezing, itchy eyes, and constant runny noses. All three complained to their supervisor about a dank, musty smell that seemed to emanate from the ward, but their complaints fell on deaf ears.

It wasn't until a six-year-old patient on the unit developed a fever and pneumonia and suddenly died, and an autopsy revealed that her lungs were filled with a fungus typically found in decaying organic matter, that management took the employees seriously. All of a sudden, their claim that the building was making them sick didn't sound so far-fetched.

Sure enough, an environmental investigation found that the air filters on the bone marrow transplant unit were clogged with a thick, greenish-black mold. The contaminants in the air were responsible for the employee sicknesses and the little girl's death. To deal with the problem, the hospital had to rip out its heating and air-conditioning system and renovate the entire bone marrow transplant unit.[2]

Some experts suggest that the lack of ventilation in newer buildings, combined with increased use of mold-friendly building materials, allows for severe mold infestations. The contaminated air results in "sick buildings," where large numbers of employees begin to experience similar health symptoms.

The apostle Paul wanted to make sure that the churches on the island of Crete provided a spiritually healthy environment for fledgling new believers. He wanted to make sure they were breathing spiritually healthy air.

Read Titus 2:1. What did Paul want Titus to be careful to teach?

Doctrine is a major theme in the book of Titus. Circle the word *doctrine* in each verse in the margin on the previous page.

What comes to your mind when you hear the word *doctrine*? How would you define it?

_____

_____

For some, the word *doctrine* undoubtedly conjures up images of old, coke-bottle-lensed theology professors using long, unfamiliar words and droning on and on in unintelligible languages. Perhaps the mere mention of the word makes you want to stifle a yawn, or bolt for the nearest exit.

It's important to understand that doctrine isn't something reserved for the theological elite. The word simply means "teachings." A doctrine is a set of beliefs. And everyone has one.

Atheists have a doctrine. For example, the famous evolutionary biologist Richard Dawkins believes the Bible should not be taught as reality. "It is fiction, myth, poetry, anything but reality."[3] That is his doctrine.

Oprah Winfrey used her multi-award-winning talk show to teach her doctrine of self-improvement, church-free spirituality, and guilt-free sexuality to millions of women each day.

In the space below, list some doctrines (teachings) about womanhood that are commonly expressed in popular media and contemporary culture:

The teaching you believe determines the way you live. Paul knew that believers in Crete would undoubtedly have and follow a doctrine. But he was concerned about what *kind* of doctrine they were going to teach, believe, and practice. Not any kind of doctrine would do. Paul was concerned that their doctrine would be "sound."

sound doctrine

Like the word *doctrine*, the word *sound* is also a recurring theme in the book of Titus. *Sound* essentially means "healthy." The Greek word for *sound—hugiainō—*is closely related to our English word *hygiene.* Sound doctrine is doctrine that is free from contamination. It's pure and wholesome. It is that which makes sick people well.

Our culture is obsessed with physical health and soundness. It advises us to avoid junk food, read labels, shop in whole-food stores, and pay more for organic foods. As a result, many people watch what they eat. But sadly, most are utterly unconcerned about their spiritual consumption. They are unaware that they are ingesting a lot of contaminated, unhealthy ideas.

Sound doctrine is healthy. It's pure, uncontaminated, and free from error. It's like breathing in clean, fresh air. Unsound doctrine is a mixture of truth and error. It's like breathing in air that's tainted with a dangerous contaminant. You may not smell or notice the toxin, but it's inevitable that it will negatively impact your health. Unsound doctrine leads to spiritually sick and weak believers, which leads to spiritually unhealthy churches.

In the verses in the margin, put a box around the word *sound.*

In the word cloud, cross out the three words that are antonyms (opposite meaning) of the word *sound:*

proven   healthy   solid
wholesome   infected   sick   true
safe   flawless   undamaged   reliable
proper   debilitating   secure

Why do you think Paul was concerned that the women in Crete know and believe sound doctrine?

> "He must hold firm to the trustworthy word as taught, so that he may be able to give instruction in sound doctrine and also to rebuke those who contradict it."
> **Titus 1:9**

> "But as for you, teach what accords with sound doctrine."
> **Titus 2:1**

> "...in doctrine showing integrity, reverence, incorruptibility, sound speech that cannot be condemned."
> **Titus 2:7–8 NKJV**

> "...so that in everything they may adorn the doctrine of God our Savior."
> **Titus 2:10**

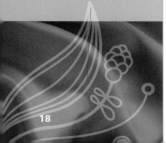

Do you know what your doctrine is? Do you care? Have you evaluated the doctrine of your favorite TV shows? Of the books and magazines you read? Have you evaluated what you're being taught about womanhood? Because every time you hear or see an advertisement, or watch a TV/computer/movie screen, or listen to the lyrics of a song, or read an article or book, or listen to your girlfriends chatter about their exploits, or catch up on the latest happenings on your Facebook or other social network, you are breathing in doctrine. And it's important to consider whether that doctrine is sound.

Check any statements below that are true of you:

- ☐ The teaching about womanhood I breathe in is generally sound.
- ☐ The teaching about womanhood I breathe in is generally unsound.
- ☐ I'm not sure if the teaching about womanhood I breathe in is sound.
- ☐ I don't think the unsound teaching in my environment affects me.
- ☐ I have strong filters in place so as to minimize the unsound teaching.
- ☐ I'm not convinced that my doctrine about womanhood matters.

Explain why you chose those particular statements:

_____

_____

In Titus 2, Paul outlines the Lord's expert design for womanhood. The basis for that design is sound doctrine. Sound doctrine is healthy, wholesome, and beneficial. Do you believe that? Do you believe that the Lord's design for women is not only right, but also beautiful and desirable? Do you believe that the instructions He gives you are truly "for your good" (see Deut. 10:12–13)?

→ **Close today's lesson in prayer, asking the Lord** to help you learn about and embrace His expert design.

"WHAT DOES THE LORD YOUR GOD REQUIRE OF YOU, BUT TO FEAR THE LORD YOUR GOD, TO WALK IN ALL HIS WAYS, TO LOVE HIM, TO SERVE THE LORD YOUR GOD WITH ALL YOUR HEART AND WITH ALL YOUR SOUL, AND TO KEEP THE COMMANDMENTS AND STATUTES OF THE LORD, WHICH I AM COMMANDING YOU TODAY FOR YOUR GOOD?"

Deuteronomy 10:12–13

the plumb line

$\mathcal{M}$ "Make sure to snap a line!" my (Mary's) handyman dad always reminds me when I embark on a decorating project. An accurate guideline is necessary to get the pieces set in the right place. Without one, the wallpaper, tiles, flooring, pictures, or moldings might not line up properly, and the decorating project may turn into a disaster.

Two tools are essential necessities for the decorating enthusiast: a plumb bob and a level. These tools ensure that a guideline is perfectly vertical or horizontal relative to the earth's true horizon.

You've probably seen a level (sometimes called a "spirit level" or a "bubble level"). It looks like a thick, metal ruler with embedded glass vials. The vials are incompletely filled with a colored spirit (alcohol), leaving a large bubble visible inside. The bubble moves with the angle of the ruler and indicates whether an object is "level"—that is, whether it is exactly *horizontal*, or true. To get a perfectly horizontal line, the decorator has to tilt the tool until the bubble is situated perfectly between the markings on the middle of the vial.

A plumb bob is a simple brass or metal weight with a point on one end. The bob is attached to a string (the plumb line), which is often coated in colored chalk. This tool uses the law of gravity to establish what is "plumb"— that is, what is exactly *vertical*, or true.

You can use a plumb bob to line up wall-paper, wall décor, or art, or to locate fixtures or decorations in relation to an object or surface above or below. You simply hold the end of the string near the ceiling and let the plumb bob hang free. When it stops swaying, the string is perfectly vertical. Depending on your project, you can then mark the top and bottom points, or snap the line to leave a chalk mark on a wall.

On one occasion, I tried to hang wallpaper without following my dad's advice. The walls looked straight to me, so I started papering in the corner. I didn't bother to check if the adjacent wall was plumb, and I didn't take the time to snap a line.

"Paul, a slave of God and an apostle of Jesus Christ, to build up the faith of God's elect and their knowledge of the truth that leads to godliness . . . "

Titus 1:1 HCSB

"He must hold firm to the trustworthy word as taught, so that he may be able to give instruction in sound doctrine and also to rebuke those who contradict it."

Titus 1:9

The first piece of wallpaper looked just fine. But I had to raise and tilt the second piece to get the edge and pattern to match. After that, each piece looked more crooked than the last. By the time I got to the middle of the wall, it was painfully obvious that the wall I had used as my starting line was slanted, and that things were going extremely wrong. The pattern was running uphill, and the bottom of the paper was getting farther and farther away from the floor. It was a disaster! I had to rip it all down and start over . . . Needless to say, I was careful to snap a line the second time around!

Paul knew that the ideas being promoted by some of the Cretan believers were a bit off. He wanted Titus to "snap a line" and put things in order by ensuring the lives and doctrine of the believers lined up plumb, level, and true with God's standard.

Read Titus 1:1–9 in your Bible. What do verses 1 to 4 point to as the standard for truth?

_____

_____

What would happen if the women in Crete increased in their knowledge of the truth (see verse 1)? Check all that apply:

- ☐ They'd all turn into mindless puppets.
- ☐ They'd demonstrate that Christian women are intelligent.
- ☐ Their increased knowledge would lead to increased godliness.
- ☐ Their right thinking would lead to right behavior.

What do you think it means to "hold firm to the trustworthy word" (v. 9)?

_____

_____

Scholars think that Paul wrote his pastoral letters of Titus and 1 Timothy shortly after being released from Roman imprisonment. Nero was the emperor on the throne (AD 54–68). Animosity against Christians was on the rise, and things were about to get a lot worse. The Roman government would soon take an official stand against Christianity. Paul would be imprisoned again, and eventually would be beheaded.

We don't know for sure if Paul yet sensed that his life and ministry were nearing an end. But these letters appear to have a sense of urgency about them. In light of the looming persecution, it was critical that the churches were strong and healthy and that they had solid, established, mature leaders. In his letter to Titus, just as in his first letter to Timothy, Paul warned against false teachers and issued instructions to various groups regarding proper Christian behavior. Paul wanted the churches to be "sound in the faith" (Titus 1:13) and to use the right plumb line to determine which ideas didn't line up with sound doctrine.

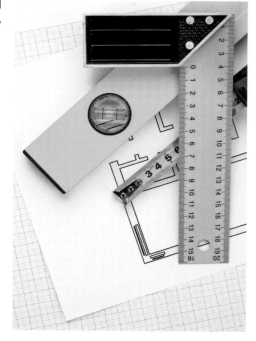

"Sanctify them in the truth; your word is truth."

John 17:17

In Titus 1:1–9 we learn that mature believers:

- Have a saving faith in the gospel of Christ Jesus

- Uphold the Bible as the standard for truth

- Regard the Word of God as trustworthy

- Honor the teachings of Christ and the apostles

- Know what accords with sound doctrine

- Are able to discern truth from error

- Exhibit godliness of character and godly relationships

Paul hoped that the men and women in Crete would hold firm to the trustworthy teachings of the faith. He anticipated that those who embraced sound doctrine would also be sound in faith, sound in love, sound in steadfastness, sound in speech, and sound in all sorts of other things too (1:13; 2:1, 2, 8).

A deeper knowledge of truth leads to deeper godliness. Healthy beliefs lead to healthy behavior. Right thinking, empowered by the Holy Spirit, leads to right living.

Read John 17:17 in the margin. How is truth instrumental in sanctifying us (making us more holy)?

_____

_____

Can you identify an instance in your life when unsound thinking resulted in unsound, unhealthy behavior?

_____

_____

Can you identify an instance in your life when the Word of God changed your thinking, and this resulted in sound, healthy behavior?

_____

_____

→ **Close today's lesson in prayer.**
Ask the Lord to show you if there are any areas in your thinking or lifestyle that are not "plumb," according to His Word.

discern the difference

In yesterday's lesson we learned that what we believe about the gospel and about the Bible is critically important.

According to Paul, the Word of God provides a plumb line. It establishes that there's a right way and a wrong way for Christians to think and behave. Some of its instructions are gender specific, so it also provides a plumb line for womanhood. There's a right way and a wrong way for us to think and behave *as women* . . . and the Word of God helps us discern the difference.

Read Ephesians 5:8–10 in the margin. Why do we need *discernment* in order to know what pleases the Lord?

_____

_____

"Walk as children of light (for the fruit of light is found in all that is good and right and true), and try to discern what is pleasing to the Lord."
Ephesians 5:8–10

"The wisdom of the prudent is to discern his way."
Proverbs 14:8

"It is the duty of every Christian to think biblically about all areas of life so that they might act biblically in all areas of life."[4]
Tim Challies

Discernment is the design element of womanhood that we're studying this week: A True Woman is characterized by right thinking . . . She is not swayed by every "wind of doctrine" (Eph. 4:14) that comes along. She has a heart for solid biblical teaching and has a growing knowledge of God's Word. She knows how to evaluate what she hears to see if it measures up to Scripture. And she knows how to live her life in a way that "accords with sound doctrine" (Titus 2:1).

The word "accords" (Greek: *prepō*) used here is significant. It means fitting, suitable, proper. A godly woman can sift through a multitude of options and identify which ones are proper—which "fit"— with sound doctrine. She can determine which choices suitably honor the Lord and figure out which one is best, given her particular circumstance.

Should you pursue higher education? Should you embark on a career? Should you marry George, or Frank, or forgo marriage altogether? How much should you work outside the home? Should you use birth control or family planning? Should you aim to have two kids or twenty-two? Should

you send your kids to public school? Private school? Or homeschool? Should you lead a Bible study or sing on the worship team? Should you spend your money on a trip to Disneyland or give it to rescue girls from the sex trade? Is it your responsibility to cook all the meals and his to cut the grass? Should you trade in all your pencil skirts for ankle dusters? Should you be listening to that band or going to that movie? For these and millions of other big and small questions, the Bible simply doesn't say.

Identify a current or past situation in which you weighed several options, and tried to discern what was "pleasing to the Lord."

_____

_____

Over the course of your lifetime you will be faced with a multitude of choices —some inconsequential, some good, some bad, some right, some wrong, some better, some best. That's why you need discernment. That's why you need the ongoing help of the Holy Spirit. That's why you need to wrestle with how to apply the Bible's precepts to your life.

You can't rely on a prescribed formula, or base your decisions on what your girlfriends are doing or on the standards set by our culture. You have a personal responsibility to figure things out. The Bible gives us guiding principles, but it doesn't specify exactly how to apply those principles. That's why each of us needs to *try to discern* how we can best please the Lord.

In the space below, write out a definition for the word *discern*.

_____

_____

If you peeked at a dictionary to help, you may have discovered that the English word, *discern,* comes from the French *discerner*, which means to distinguish or separate. It's based on the Latin *discernere: dis* (off, away) + *cernere* (distinguish, separate).

The concepts of *distinguishing* and *separating* are inherent in the Word. Discernment involves distinguishing the difference between two things and separating one from the other.

Spiritual discernment involves using God's Word as the standard for distinguishing and separating ideas and behaviors. It distinguishes and separates truth from falsehood, darkness from light, healthy from unhealthy, sound from unsound, and good from evil, based on the Bible's plumb line.

Author Tim Challies provides a helpful definition of spiritual discernment:

> Discernment is the skill of understanding and applying God's Word with the purpose of separating truth from error and right from wrong.[5]

Read 1 Corinthians 2:14 in the margin. Then, mark each statement below as true (T) or false (F).

_____ Spirit-filled women will discern things differently from women who walk according to the flesh.

_____ Any woman—regardless of whether or not she is a true believer—who reads the Bible has the ability to discern what pleases the Lord.

_____ There are many women who don't understand the Bible's precepts about womanhood and consider them foolish.

_____ Women who are spiritually discerning have a heightened ability to see and understand issues from God's perspective.

off color

A skilled decorator is discerning. She has an eye for what matches the décor of a room. She pays attention to the subtleties between various tints and shades. She knows when a particular color is "off" and doesn't fit with the design. She discerns differences that others may not notice or may shrug off as inconsequential. Spiritual discernment is much the same.

"So that you may approve [discern] what is excellent, and so be pure and blameless for the day of Christ."
Philippians 1:10

"Give your servant therefore an understanding mind ... that I may discern between good and evil."
1 Kings 3:9

"The natural person does not accept the things of the Spirit of God, for they are folly to him, and he is not able to understand them because they are spiritually discerned."
1 Corinthians 2:14

Members of the congregation at Crete were being deceived by teachers who were pushing doctrine that was politically correct, but theologically wrong (Titus 1:10). The reason they were fooled was that they didn't discern the subtleties between concepts that were true, and concepts that were only partially true. Falsehood often contains enough truth to mislead those who lack discernment. The idea is just slightly "off." If it were blatantly and utterly false, people wouldn't be taken in by it.

I (Mary) was in high school in the late-1970s, during the peak of the feminist movement. I remember asking my spiritual mentor, Diane, what she thought about women's lib. Diane, who was in her early twenties, was the adult sponsor of the Christian club I helped co-lead. Diane was a "go-getter"— extremely gifted, capable, and intelligent. I expected that she would enthusiastically support a movement that pushed for the equality of women.

When I asked for her opinion, she thoughtfully paused, and then said something like this: "Well . . . I can't say I know much about it, but from what I've heard, something seems 'off.' While I sympathize with many of the concerns, the clamoring for personal rights and the inciting of anger just doesn't sit right with me. It doesn't jibe with the character of Jesus."

Diane's words of discernment proved helpful for me over the following years as I completed a professional degree and embarked on a career in an educational and work culture that pushed feminist ideology. The red flag that Diane raised caused me to be cautious, and to pray for discernment about all the new and seemingly promising ideas that many were so quick to embrace.

In your own words, rewrite Challies' definition of spiritual discernment:

_____

_____

Read the verses in the margin on page 26. Summarize why it's important for you to be discerning about the opinions and ideas that come your way:

_____

_____

_____

→ **Close today's lesson** by personalizing Solomon's prayer from 1 Kings 3:9. Ask the Lord to help you become a more spiritually discerning woman.

always learning

*The fog was particularly thick as I (Nancy) drove to the *Revive Our Hearts* studio one morning. It was terribly difficult to see. People had clicked on their headlights, and everyone drove extremely slowly and carefully. Traffic crawled along at a snail's pace. In all that fog, I had to be careful to watch for the right turnoff. It took a lot more effort than normal to discern the difference between the right and the wrong turn, to avoid running into a car or pedestrian, and to stay on the road and avoid ending up in the ditch.

> *"For there are many who are insubordinate, empty talkers and deceivers . . . . They profess to know God, but they deny him by their works."*
>
> **Titus 1:10, 16**

There's a lot of spiritual "fog" out there these days . . . and not only in the world, but also in the church. There are all sorts of persuasive voices offering ideas about what we should believe and how we should live. And this is particularly the case with regard to "biblical womanhood." It can get quite confusing. Even disorienting.

The situation is not unlike the one facing the believers on Crete. They also had dissenting voices in the church telling them what they should believe.

Read Titus 1:10–16 in your Bible. List the traits and characteristics of the people pushing false ideas in the Cretan churches:

_____

_____

_____

_____

Crete is the largest of the Greek islands and is fifth largest in the Mediterranean. It lies at the junction of four seas: the Ionian, Aegean, Mediterranean, and Libyan. Its location put it at the center of the development of world culture and civilization. Crete was famous in Greek mythology as the birthplace of Zeus, and for the legends of King Minos, Theseus, and the Minotaur. It was the hub for the Minoans, Europe's first advanced civilization.

In approximately 67 BC, Crete was conquered by the Romans, who built luxurious Roman buildings, temples, stadiums, and baths on the island. By then, the Cretan population numbered about 300,000. Though most inhabitants were Greek, the cities also housed significant Jewish communities. Jews from Crete were in Jerusalem on the day of Pentecost (Acts 2:11).

Cretans were famed as daring sailors, prosperous traders, and fierce warriors. But they were also notorious for their character flaws. The Roman historian Titus Livius spoke of Cretan "avarice" (greed). The Greek historian Polybius wrote of their "ferocity and fraud" and "their mendacity"—which is the propensity to fabricate stories or bend the truth.

Another Greek historian, Diodorus Siculus, noted that Cretans tended to be stubborn and insubordinate. They were intent on doing things their own way. Paul quoted Epimenides, a Cretan poet/prophet, as saying "Cretans are always liars, evil beasts, lazy gluttons" (Titus 1:12). Things were so bad that in the ancient world the word "cretanize" was proverbial for telling a lie.

Paul was concerned because Cretan *mendacity* had spilled over into the Christian community. To accommodate Crete's Greek mythological culture, certain teachers were pushing elaborate myths in an attempt to make the Hebrew Scriptures more palatable for a better sell. They adopted new, speculative, and fanciful biblical interpretations, possibly based on Old Testament genealogies. Instead of adhering to the teachings and traditions passed down by the apostles, these upstart theologians promoted "cleverly devised myths" (2 Peter 1:16) that undoubtedly appealed to their first-century listeners' sense of political correctness.

"Most people—even Christians—have unthinkingly exposed themselves to so much deception that they do not even realize they are being deceived."[6]

Nancy

This problem was not limited to the church in Crete. Paul addresses similar issues in his letters to Timothy, a pastor in Ephesus.

Read the verses in the margin. What do you think Paul meant when he said these teachers "promote empty speculations rather than God's plan"?

_____

_____

"[Nor] to pay attention to myths and endless genealogies. These promote empty speculations rather than God's plan, which operates by faith. . . . Some have deviated from these and turned aside to fruitless discussion. They want to be teachers . . . although they don't understand what they are saying or what they are insisting on."

1 Timothy 1:4–7 HCSB

False teachers in the early church promoted new ideas that distracted people from pursuing godliness and got them caught up in controversial, speculative arguments (1 Tim. 1:4, 6; 4:7; 6:4, 20; Titus 1:10; 3:9; 2 Tim. 2:14, 16, 23).

Instead of encouraging believers to guard and cherish the deposit of truth they had received and to work at applying the Word, they fostered an attitude of irreverence toward Scripture and the apostles' teaching (1 Tim. 4:7).

The teachers tantalized believers with novel, progressive interpretations, which they confidently promoted as "knowledge" (1 Tim. 6:20). Their ideas were persuasive, yet subtly deceptive. These teachers confused rather than clarified the issues (1 Tim. 4:1–3; Titus 1:10–13; 2 Tim. 3). What's more, they advocated loose moral standards (1 Tim. 1:19, 20; Titus 1:15, 16; 2 Tim. 2:16, 19; 3:1–5). In essence, they encouraged believers to value and trust their own opinions more than they valued and trusted God's (2 Tim. 3:4).

Use the paragraphs above to make a list of the "red flags" (warning signs) that should have alerted the people in Crete that the teachings might be false:

"Have nothing to do with irreverent, silly myths. Rather train yourself for godliness."

1 Timothy 4:7

"Guard the deposit entrusted to you. Avoid the irreverent babble and contradictions of what is falsely called 'knowledge.'"

1 Timothy 6:20

weak women

W We can't be sure of the exact content of the false teaching, but it's clear that it was devoid of any true spiritual value and that it only led to further speculation, questions, controversy, and arguments. It's also clear that some women of that day were particularly susceptible to being deceived by it.

According to 2 Timothy 3:7, why do you think the women were taken captive by false teaching? Put a check [√] next to the statement(s) that apply:

_____ They were too feeble to stand against popular opinion.

_____ They weren't educated and hadn't studied the issues enough.

_____ The false teaching appealed to them because it validated their sinful tendencies and desires.

_____ Deep down, they didn't really want to change their behavior and turn from their sin.

Read 2 Timothy 4:3. Explain why and how Christian women in our day might reject sound teaching about womanhood:

_____

_____

The women mentioned in 2 Timothy 3 were always learning. The reason they were taken captive by false teaching—and were unable to "arrive at knowledge of the truth"—wasn't due to a lack of information. It was due to a lack of holy desires. You see, right thinking and right living go hand in hand. If you are unprepared to live the way God wants you to, chances are, you'll reject sound teaching and will simply gravitate toward teachers who will tell you what you want to hear.

→ **Close today's lesson in prayer.** Ask the Lord to give you the mind to discern sound doctrine and the heart to obey it.

"FOR AMONG THEM ARE THOSE WHO CREEP INTO HOUSEHOLDS AND CAPTURE WEAK WOMEN, BURDENED WITH SINS AND LED ASTRAY BY VARIOUS PASSIONS, ALWAYS LEARNING AND NEVER ABLE TO ARRIVE AT A KNOWLEDGE OF THE TRUTH."

2 Timothy 3:6–7

"FOR THE TIME IS COMING WHEN PEOPLE WILL NOT ENDURE SOUND TEACHING, BUT HAVING ITCHING EARS THEY WILL ACCUMULATE FOR THEMSELVES TEACHERS TO SUIT THEIR OWN PASSIONS."

2 Timothy 4:3

handling truth

"Teach me, O Lᴏʀᴅ, the way of your statutes; and I will keep it to the end. Give me understanding [discernment], that I may keep your law and observe it with my whole heart."

Psalm 119:33–34

In 2005, United States Secret Service agents began encountering a run of counterfeit bills unlike anything they had seen before. Except for identical serial numbers and tiny imperfections that casual observers were unlikely to notice, the cash almost looked and felt genuine. The funny money turned up everywhere from up-scale retailers to fast food stores in every state in the nation, and in nine foreign countries.

Despite the Secret Service's best efforts, the forger of these notes evaded capture for more than three years. By then, Albert Edward Talton, of Lawndale, California, had put more than $7 million in phony currency into circulation. And he'd made much of it using a computer, basic ink-jet printers, and supplies purchased from his local Staples.

Counterfeiting is considered such a threat to the fabric of the country that it is—along with treason—one of only two criminal offenses named in the US Constitution. According to the Secret Service, the best defense against it is to educate and train the public to discern the difference between genuine and fake currency. It encourages everyone to "Know Your Money!"[7]

"Knowing their money" is the process whereby the FBI trains its agents to spot counterfeits. Agents spend countless hours handling, examining, and intensely studying authentic currency. They are so familiar with the real thing that when a counterfeit is presented, its flaws are obvious to them. They can immediately tell that the texture, feel, and look aren't quite right.

False doctrine poses as serious a threat to the church as false money does to the economy. Paul wanted the believers in Crete to be so familiar with sound doctrine that they'd immediately discern if something was off. He wanted their thinking and lifestyles to display the pure, untainted truth of the gospel.

Read Psalm 119:9–16 in your Bible. According to the psalmist, how can we keep our thoughts and actions pure (healthy/sound)?

_____

_____

Discernment is the skill of understanding and applying the Word of God, with the purpose of separating truth from error and right from wrong. Familiarity with sound doctrine is what helped Diane (Mary's high school mentor) discern that certain elements of feminist doctrine were wrong. Diane was able to spot the falsehood because she had spent time handling the real thing. She knew her Bible!

According to Hebrews 5:14, how does a believer get better at the skill of spiritual discernment?

_____

_____

What do you think this "constant practice" involves?

_____

_____

> **"BUT SOLID FOOD IS FOR THE MATURE, FOR THOSE WHO HAVE THEIR POWERS OF DISCERNMENT TRAINED BY CONSTANT PRACTICE TO DISTINGUISH GOOD FROM EVIL."**
> **Hebrews 5:14**
>
> Deception was—and still is—crucial to Satan's strategy."[8]

I (Nancy) studied piano for years. Weekly lessons and daily practice were a regular part of the rhythm of life. While many of my peers were out socializing or having "fun" after classes and on weekends, I spent countless hours sequestered in a practice room, working on scales, arpeggios, and other technical exercises, playing through the same classical pieces over and over and over again, until they were mastered. There were no shortcuts or substitutes for "constant practice" if I wanted to become an accomplished pianist.

And there are no shortcuts or substitutes for "constant practice" when it comes to developing spiritual discernment—while others are whiling away their time with trivial pursuits, a woman who wants to be spiritually mature will devote herself to reading and mediating on God's Word and putting it into practice in her life. As we spend time in His presence, our minds are renewed, and we grow in our ability to discern truth from error, right from wrong.

Why is it important that you grow in discernment? Match each reason to the verse in which the idea occurs. Write an [H] in the blank for Hebrews 5:14 (on previous page), an [E] for Ephesians 4:14, and a [P] for Philippians 1:10:

_____ So you won't be tossed around by the latest new idea

_____ So you can figure out what the best choice is

_____ So you won't be fooled by clever but misguided people

_____ So you will get better at telling the difference between good and evil

_____ So you may be pure and blameless

_____ So you may grow up and mature spiritually

It's important that you strive to grow in discernment. Women who are discerning have the ability to see and understand issues from God's perspective. Empowered by the Holy Spirit, they strive for and are given an understanding of what pleases God and what doesn't. They do this by understanding God through his Word, and by applying the wisdom of sound doctrine to their lives.

> "So that we may no longer be children, tossed to and fro by the waves and carried about by every wind of doctrine, by human cunning, by craftiness in deceitful schemes."
>
> **Ephesians 4:14**

> "So that you may approve [discern] what is excellent, and so be pure and blameless for the day of Christ."
>
> **Philippians 1:10**

practice it

In his book *The Discipline of Spiritual Discernment,* Tim Challies points out that "discernment is a skill. It's not an inherent ability like breathing or chewing but a skill"—like playing an instrument—"that must be practiced and improved. There's not a person on earth who has been born with a full measure of discernment, or who has all of the discernment he will ever need. There's not a person who has attained a level of expertise that allows him to move on and to leave discernment behind. Like the master musician who practices his skills more as his acclaim grows, a discerning person will see with ever-greater clarity his need to increase in discernment. He will want to sharpen and improve this skill throughout his life."[9]

In the verses in the margin, circle the words *test* and *testing*.

The dictionary defines test as the means by which the quality or genuineness of something is determined. The Lord wants us to test the things we see and hear and not mindlessly accept them. He wants us to hold them up to the standard of Scripture and discern whether they line up with God's plumb line.

Every day you receive messages about how you should live—ideas about gender, relationships, love, marriage, morality, children, work, finances, possessions, leisure, attitudes, emotions, habits, and a host of other things that impact you as a woman. The ideas come from popular media, books, social networks, relatives, friends, and colleagues . . . and also from teachers and leaders in the church.

Are you testing those ideas? Are you familiar enough with Scripture to know what accords with sound doctrine? And to perceive when something is not quite right? A True Woman is characterized by right thinking. She applies herself to become a woman of discernment.

→ **In the space below,** write out Romans 12:2 as a prayer, personalizing it. Ask the Lord to help you become a woman who is grounded in the Word of God and who is able to discern His will.

_____

_____

_____

_____

"TEST EVERYTHING; HOLD FAST WHAT IS GOOD. ABSTAIN FROM EVERY FORM OF EVIL."

I Thessalonians 5:21–22

"DO NOT BE CONFORMED TO THIS WORLD, BUT BE TRANSFORMED BY THE RENEWAL OF YOUR MIND, THAT BY TESTING YOU MAY DISCERN WHAT IS THE WILL OF GOD, WHAT IS GOOD AND ACCEPTABLE AND PERFECT."

Romans 12:2

drawing it out,
drawing it in . . .

interior renovation

process

The video for Week One will help you process this week's lessons. You'll find this week's video, the leader's guide, and additional resources at TrueWoman201.com.

ponder

Think about the following questions. Discuss them with your friends, family, and/or small group:

1. Why is it so important for us to have sound doctrine?

2. Describe some characteristics of false teachers. How can we distinguish between true teaching and false?

3. Identify some beliefs or patterns of thinking in our culture that breed spiritual contamination. How can we guard ourselves against breathing in these spiritual toxins?

4. False teachers in Paul's day encouraged believers to value and trust their own opinions more than they valued and trusted God. How do you see that happening today when it comes to ideas about womanhood?

5. What is your "plumb line" for making decisions in those gray areas of life, situations for which Scripture doesn't provide a black-and-white answer?

6. What is involved in practicing spiritual discernment? Why is spiritual discernment vital to glorifying God with our lives?

7. What characteristics do you see in the women described in 2 Timothy 3:6–7? What made them weak, and how can we safeguard against living like they did?

8. How can you develop greater discernment in your home, your relationships, and in other areas of your life?

personalize it

Use this page to journal. Write down what you learned this week. Record your comments, a favorite verse, or a concept or quote that was particularly helpful or meaningful to you. Compose a prayer, letter, or poem. Jot down notes from the video or your small group session. Express your heart response to what you have studied. Personalize this week's lessons in the way that will best help you apply them to your life.

drawing it out,
drawing it in . . .

honor

The USS Arizona is a sunken World War II battleship and is the final resting place for 1,177 sailors and marines killed in the attack on Pearl Harbor, December 7, 1941. In 1961, an austere white monument was erected above the midsection of the ship. The deck of the Arizona lies just six feet below the surface of the water and is clearly visible from the memorial. A visit is a solemn and sobering experience.

A True Woman makes much of Christ . . . She is **"reverent in behavior."**

Prior to boarding the Navy-operated shuttle to the memorial, visitors receive a brief introduction and watch a twenty-minute documentary film that includes actual footage of the attack. They are reminded that the site is a tribute and a grave, and as such, deserves to be treated with the utmost respect and reverence. Men are to remove their caps. Cell phones must be turned off. Eating and drinking are prohibited. Conversation must be hushed and kept to a minimum. Children must be controlled and kept from running and playing. The memorial is to be honored as a place of learning, reflection, and quiet contemplation. Those who are loud, frivolous, or disrespectful will be asked to leave.

A somber hush falls over each group as it boards the shuttle. The chatter and laughter that characterize most tourist attractions are absent as visitors make the trip across the water. One can hear the humming motor and the water rushing past, but human voices are muted as the boat nears the brilliant-white, sloping structure. Even the children are quiet.

When the shuttle docks at the memorial, visitors solemnly disembark. The concrete structure seems to float astride the sunken battleship.[1] It actually stands on piers, and no part of it touches the ship. It's an open-air edifice, with large openings on either wall and in the ceiling above. There's a large opening in the floor near the far end, where one can lean on the railing and look down at the wreck.

Dominating the far end of the memorial is a room with a massive, gleaming white marble wall engraved with an alphabetical list of the sailors and marines who died aboard the ship that fateful morning. Upon my (Mary's) visit, I noticed a family standing there, quietly reading the long list of names. All at once, the young boy—who was about nine or ten years old—spontaneously snapped to attention with his hand to his forehead in a salute. He stood motionless in a salute in front of the memorial wall for a long while, with a tear rolling down one cheek. I was mesmerized by the gesture and by the venerable, resolute expression on his face. On the way out, I was close enough to overhear him say to his father, "Dad, when I grow up, I'm going to be a soldier. I want to be a man of honor like those guys."

Visiting the USS Arizona Memorial was a moving experience. But witnessing the effect it had on that young boy made it all the more memorable. His respect for the men who gave their lives for his freedom appeared to go far beyond a transient emotion. It translated into a resolve to become the same kind of man. His deep reverence evoked a personal response and commitment. I would not be surprised if one day that boy would cite his visit to the USS Arizona as his reason for enlisting in the service.

The second design element of biblical womanhood is honor. A True Woman makes much of Christ . . . She is "reverent in behavior." She's deeply respectful of the sacrifice that Jesus made on her behalf—and her profound reverence evokes a personal response and commitment.

Just as the reverence of that boy at the USS Arizona Memorial stirred him to commit to serve his country, so reverence for the Lord stirs a woman to dedicate herself to serving Christ. A reverent woman lives a God-centered life. She's wholeheartedly devoted to the Lord. She seeks to honor Him in every attitude, thought, and action. →

"Some people think that this kind of woman is joyless or dour, always somber. To the contrary, reverent women should be winsome. In His presence is fullness of joy!"

Nancy

mind your manner

Tourists to Paris rarely pass up an opportunity to visit the Notre Dame Cathedral. It's arguably the most stunning and remarkable masterpiece of Gothic architecture in the world, and among the largest and most famous churches ever built.

One of the fundamental characteristics of Gothic architecture was its height. New elements such as the flying buttress, pointed arch, and vaulted ceiling enabled architects to build structures of unprecedented elevation and grandeur. The light, airy, decorative interiors stood in stark contrast to the dark, heavy construction of Romanesque-style castles. For the average person of that era, entering a Gothic cathedral would have been a profoundly intense experience.

Notre Dame's elaborate portals, dramatic towers, magnificent spire, massive pipe organ, and regal statuary were built to impress. The architecture was meant to tell a story. It was designed in such a manner so as to *speak* to the viewer. Those medieval architects sought to present the idea of the smallness and insignificance of humanity in relation to the splendor and loftiness of God. They wanted the vertical emphasis of the building to evoke feelings of awe and reverence.

Notre Dame's interior achieves exactly this. The cathedral's long halls, enormous vaulted ceilings, and soft light filtered through intricate stained glass produce an ethereal atmosphere. There is no access to the cathedral's upper levels, obliging visitors to remain earthbound, gazing upward. The experience is breathtaking, especially on a first visit.

Reverence was an important virtue in the Gothic era. But Paul identified it as a critical virtue for women of every era. Paul tells Titus that older women "are to be reverent in behavior" (Titus 2:3).

Look up the word *reverence* in a thesaurus (If you don't have one, you can find one online at thesaurus.com). In the space below, jot down some synonyms for reverence:

_____

_____

Read the verses in the margin on the previous page. Which of the following words does the Bible use in conjunction with the word *reverence*?

☐ Respect   ☐ Honor   ☐ Fear   ☐ Esteem

Acts 10:2 tells us that Cornelius and his family "feared God"—that is, their lives were characterized by reverence for the God of Israel. Reverence, honor, and fear are closely related concepts. The biblical definition of *fear* embraces a much wider dimension than the common English one, which simply denotes some sort of dread or terror. The basic meaning of "the fear of God" is "reverential awe." It's a personal, jaw-dropping awareness of God's majestic greatness and holiness, reflected in a commitment to honor Him by turning from sin and faithfully obeying His Word.

Would those who know you identify you as a "God-fearer"? Why or why not?

_____

_____

temple-appropriate

In Titus 2, reverence is first in line in the list of virtues that stem from sound doctrine. The word translated "reverent" (Greek: *hieroprepēs*) is a compound word used only here in the New Testament. The first part, *hieros*, means "that which is holy or sacred" (from *hieron*, for temple), and the second part, *prepei*, means "that which is

fitting or proper." The basic idea is "conduct appropriate to a temple." *Hieroprepēs* refers to the type of attitude and conduct that befits holy people—the kind of conduct appropriate for priests and others who have dedicated themselves to temple service.

Priests who served in the temple needed to remember that they were performing sacred tasks in the presence of a holy God. They had to take care to follow the rules and exercise proper respect for the Holy Place and the Holy of Holies, the Ark of the Covenant, the Mercy Seat, the bread of the Presence, the sacrifices, the offerings—and all the great, eternal, invisible realities to which these visible symbols pointed.

Priests who were careless or profane risked judgment and even death (Lev. 22:9). As temple servants, they needed to conduct themselves with reverent fear. They needed to take God seriously, keeping Him in mind as they went about their daily tasks.

Given the definition of *hieroprepēs*, what do you think the apostle meant when he instructed women to be reverent in behavior?

_____

_____

> "The Christian must live as if all life was a sacred assembly."[2]
> **Clement of Alexandria**

The sacrificial system of the temple was no longer necessary after Jesus offered up His life as a single sacrifice for sins for all time (Heb. 10:12). Christ instituted a new covenant whereby we are saved by grace through faith (Eph. 2:8). We no longer need to go to the temple to be with God—rather, we ARE the temple of God (2 Cor. 6:16).

Read 1 Corinthians 3:16-17 and 2 Corinthians 6:16-17 in your Bible. What type of conduct is expected of the temple of God?

_____

_____

Just think: **YOU are the temple of God!** That's why the Lord wants your behavior to be holy and reverent.

Being reverent involves being profoundly mindful and respectful of God's abiding presence. A reverent woman knows that God's Spirit dwells in her, so she exhibits "temple-appropriate" behavior all the time—not just when she's in church or with Christian friends.

We're to live like we're in a temple because there's no division between sacred and secular. "Christianity" is not a category of life—but the whole of our lives. Whether we are out shopping with friends, balancing a spreadsheet, or changing a diaper, we must always remember that we are engaged in sacred things.

Put a check ✓ beside the attitudes and actions that are "temple-appropriate," and an "X" beside the ones that are not:

☐ Screaming   ☐ Blessing

☐ Malice   ☐ Encouragement

☐ Envy   ☐ Cussing

☐ Gossip   ☐ Generosity

Can you think of a recent instance in which your conduct was not "temple-appropriate"? How do you think greater reverence for God might have made a difference?

_____

_____

The beauty and grandeur of the Notre Dame Cathedral evoke feelings of awe and reverence in visitors, but those feelings normally pass when they exit the building. True reverence is more than a transient feeling. It involves being ever mindful of God's presence and honoring Christ by being "temple-appropriate" in everything you do.

→ **Close in prayer**, asking the Lord to help you be more aware of His abiding presence and more "temple-appropriate" in your attitudes and actions today.

giving precedence

O One of my (Mary's) favorite Christmas traditions is going to the local theatre to enjoy a performance of Handel's *Messiah*. This past year we took along two friends who had never before attended. Just before the famous "Hallelujah" chorus I leaned over to tell my girlfriend to be prepared to stand. I remembered how perplexed I was the first time I attended the oratorio, when the whole audience spontaneously rose to its feet for the song.

The tradition of the audience standing during the "Hallelujah" chorus goes back to the time of King George II (a contemporary of Handel's). Commoners were obliged to rise to their feet out of respect whenever the king entered a room or whenever he stood up. Apparently, when the

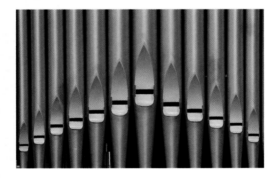

orchestra and singers broke into the "Hallelujah" chorus— "*And He shall reign forever and ever. King of kings, forever and ever! And Lord of lords, Hallelujah! Hallelujah!*— George II rose to his feet and stood for the rest of the song. And so did the audience.

Though we can't be certain, it's likely that the king of England stood out of respect for the King of kings. He probably felt it was appropriate for a mortal king to show deference and honor in the presence of the greater Monarch.

Read the verses in the margin. In the space below, explain why Scripture encourages us to revere the Lord.

The behavior of British monarchy is governed by a document entitled "The Order of Precedence," a complex set of rules that establishes the ranking of royal family members. It decrees where royals rank in the pecking order —who has preeminence and greater status—who must defer to whom.

"To the King of the ages, immortal, invisible, the only God, be honor and glory forever and ever. Amen."
I Timothy 1:17

"For who in the skies can be compared to the LORD? Who among the heavenly beings is like the LORD, a God greatly to be feared in the council of the holy ones, and awesome above all who are around him?"
Psalm 89:6–7

"Who would not fear you, O King of the nations? For this is your due; for among all the wise ones of the nations and in all their kingdoms there is none like you."
Jeremiah 10:7

It dictates the sequence in which the royals enter or leave official ceremonies and the order and position in which they are seated. Royals who are lower on the order must show deference in the presence of higher-ranking royals.

"The Order of Precedence" dictates, for instance, that although she is the future queen, the Duchess of Cambridge, Kate, who was a former commoner, must show reverence to the "blood princesses." This means that when her husband is not present, she is expected to curtsy to those born royal, such as Princesses Beatrice and Eugenie—both in public and in private. But when Kate and William are together, the princesses must curtsy to the both of them, to acknowledge William's greater status. All royals must bow in the presence of the reigning monarch.[3]

When a royal stands for or curtsies to another royal, she acknowledges that she understands her position in "The Order of Precedence." Her deferential behavior acknowledges, *There's someone here who is greater than I.* Propriety dictates that the lower-ranking person must demonstrate appropriate respect toward the higher-ranking party.

According to Deuteronomy 13:4, how do we demonstrate appropriate reverence for the Lord?

> "YOU SHALL FOLLOW THE LORD YOUR GOD AND FEAR HIM; AND YOU SHALL KEEP HIS COMMANDMENTS, LISTEN TO HIS VOICE, SERVE HIM, AND CLING TO HIM."
>
> **Deuteronomy 13:4** NASB

The Bible declares that the Lord God is the "most high" and "head above all"—the highest ranking being in the entire universe (Ps. 97:9; 1 Chron. 29:11). He is a great God, and a great King above all gods (Ps. 95:3). He is high above all peoples (99:2) and nations (113:4); "a God greatly to be feared in the council of the holy ones, and awesome above all who are around him" (89:7). As such, we owe Him our reverence and honor. This is His rightful due.

God is God and we are not. We are lesser beings, so it's appropriate that we acknowledge Him with deference and reverence. The "Order of Precedence" outlined in Deuteronomy 13:4 indicates that we do this by following, serving, and holding fast to Him. Our obedience is like a spiritual curtsy.

Underline the last sentence. Explain how obedience is like a spiritual curtsy.

_____

_____

reverent style

> "These people honor Me with their lips, but their heart is far from Me."
>
> **Matthew 15:8** HCSB

Titus 2:3 instructs women to be "reverent in behavior." The Greek word for behavior (*katastēma*) is much broader than our English word. *Katastēma* isn't just your actions. It refers to your entire attitude and conduct in all respects and on all occasions.[4] *Katastēma* is your "state" or "condition." It's your approach or style. It includes what you do and don't do, what you say and don't say, your countenance, attitude, manner, and entire demeanor. It includes your thoughts and emotions. It's how you react to your husband and kids, or to your boss, or that meddling relative. It's the outward expression of your inner character. *Katastēma* is the whole package!

Reverence is an attitude of the heart. It should permeate every aspect of a woman's life. It ought to change the way she lives: how she walks, talks, dresses, and carries herself, her countenance, how she thinks, feels, and acts.

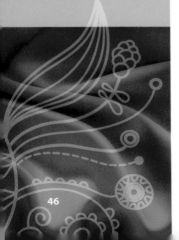

A reverent woman's life is markedly different from one who doesn't honor the Lord. A woman who conducts herself in a reverent manner:

- Reads and obeys the Bible (Deut. 28:58)
- Ensures that nothing in her life is more important to her than the Lord (Josh. 24:14)
- Serves the Lord in sincerity and faithfulness (Josh. 24:14)
- Is careful about her decisions (2 Chron. 19:7)
- Accepts correction (Zeph. 3:7)
- Is not wise in her own eyes (Prov. 3:7)
- Turns away from evil (Prov. 3:7)
- Treats others with gentleness & kindness (Lev. 19:14)
- _____ (Ps. 71:8)
- _____ (Prov. 3:9)
- _____ (Prov. 19:11)
- _____ (Rom. 1:21)
- _____ (Rom. 15:7)
- _____ (1 Cor. 6:20)

Complete the list above by summarizing what each verse indicates a reverent child of God is like.

How well does your life exemplify reverence? Circle two or three points on this list where you recognize a particular need to grow in reverence.

→ **Close in prayer.** Ask the Lord to help you develop true reverence for Him that is expressed in every area of your life.

me-first mistake

In 2014, Canada passed tougher legislation to protect war memorials and monuments.[5] The bill was proposed by a legislator who was livid when the monument in his home town was defaced—plastered with eggs—just before Remembrance (Veterans') Day.

> "Older women likewise are to be reverent in behavior, not slanderers or slaves to much wine."
>
> **Titus 2:3**

There have been numerous such cases. Vandals repeatedly defaced one prominent monument with graffiti. Another memorial was ravaged when someone scrawled "Canada will burn—Praise Allah" on it with heavy black permanent marker. Three young men were infamously photographed urinating on the National War Memorial, a revered site that includes the Tomb of the Unknown Soldier. Almost weekly, memorials are desecrated by vandals who spit, urinate, or defecate on them, or smash them, scrawl graffiti, steal plaques, or topple statues.

Previously, this kind of vandalism was met with an ordinary mischief charge. In most cases, the culprit was sentenced to community service. But the legislator argued that this was insufficient punishment for such acts of irreverence. A war memorial is "sacred" ground. As such, it ought to be respected, honored, and protected.

Under the new law, vandalism of war memorials and cenotaphs is regarded as more severe than other forms of public mischief. The offense now falls under the criminal code, and is punishable with stiff fines and even imprisonment. The Canadian government wants to send the message that it won't tolerate such sacrilege.

War memorials honor those who gave their lives to secure our freedom. Desecrating the memorial disrespects the sacrifice. It's irreverent behavior. The same sort of concept is present in Titus 2:3. After directing women to be reverent in behavior, Paul gives a couple of examples of irreverent behavior— two things that dishonor the One who gave His life for our freedom.

What two examples of irreverent behavior does Paul cite in Titus 2:3?

_____

_____

Explain why being a slanderer or a slave to much wine is irreverent:

_____

_____

dishonoring the sacrifice

W What is slander? Slander is a report meant to do harm to the good name and reputation of another. When we slander someone, we want that person to look bad and ourselves to look good. So at root, slander is self-promotion.

What about being a "slave to much wine"? Why did Paul talk about drinking? Were the older women coming to church tipsy? Commentators agree that alcohol addiction may indeed have been a problem in Crete. But we think Paul likely had in mind more than the intemperate use of wine, that he was concerned about the deeper heart issues involved.

Drinking in excess was symptomatic of an attitude of entitlement. The root problem was that of self-gratification and self-indulgence. If Paul were writing today, he might have also called women out for being "slaves to much shopping" or "slaves to much TV" or "slaves to much Facebook." Later in his letter, he points out that those who aren't walking under the control of the Holy Spirit are "slaves to *various* passions and pleasures" (Titus 3:3).

Read 2 Timothy 2:16 in the margin. How do you think a lack of reverence leads "people into more and more ungodliness"?

_____

_____

"BUT AVOID IRREVERENT BABBLE, FOR IT WILL LEAD PEOPLE INTO MORE AND MORE UNGODLINESS."

2 Timothy 2:16

Self-promotion, self-gratification, and self-indulgence—which are evidenced by behaviors such as slander and drunkenness—are the polar opposite of an attitude of reverence. An irreverent attitude says, "I am all that matters! It's all about me." A reverent attitude says, "Christ is all that matters! It's all about Him."

Irreverence is failing to value something of great worth. It's making little of something we should make much of. Whenever we make more of our opinions and desires than we make of the opinions and desires of Christ, we are guilty of irreverence. It is as though we deface and desecrate the memory of His sacrifice.

Read Hebrews 12:16 in the margin. Circle the word *irreverent*.

Jacob's twin brother, Esau, is upheld as a prime example of irreverence. Esau was the elder of Isaac's twin sons, so he was entitled to "primogeniture" —a larger share of his father's inheritance. But Esau forfeited his birthright to Jacob for the sake of a bowl of stew. He thus "despised" his birthright (see Gen. 25:29–34).

Why was exchanging his birthright for a meal irreverent? Check all that apply:

- ☐ The stew wasn't all that good.
- ☐ He put short-term gratification above long-term blessing.
- ☐ He based his choice on feelings instead of doing what was right.
- ☐ He failed to acknowledge the value of his inheritance.
- ☐ He had little regard for the consequences of his actions.

The incident with the birthright wasn't the only indication that Esau was irreverent. He married two Canaanite wives, godless women who made life bitter for his parents (Gen. 26:34–35). Finding a godly wife obviously wasn't a high priority for him. Esau had the same sort of cavalier "What's the big deal?" attitude toward dating pagans that he

---

Sidebar:

Irreverence is failing to value something of great worth. It's making little of something we should make much of.

"And make sure that there isn't any immoral or irreverent person like Esau, who sold his birthright in exchange for one meal."

Hebrews 12:16 HCSB

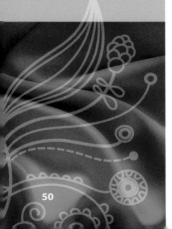

 had toward his birthright and ultimately, toward his relationship with the Lord. He was immoral and irreligious. God just wasn't a big priority in his life.

Esau symbolizes those who irreverently snub their nose at things of great value and embrace things of infinitely lesser value. In today's lesson, we learned that two ways in which women—and particularly older women—tend to be irreverent are in the way they speak ("slander") and by becoming self-indulgent ("slaves to much"). They are irreverent when they embrace a "me-first" attitude rather than a "Christ-first" one.

Is there any evidence of irreverence in the way you talk about others or in overindulgent habits?

_____

_____

What do you think is necessary for you to move from a "me-first" attitude to more of a "Christ-first" one?

_____

_____

→ **Take a moment** to confess any ways your speech or behavior is failed to honor the sacrifice of Christ. Ask the Lord to help you esteem and honor those things that are of great worth in His eyes.

"A SON HONORS HIS FATHER, AND A SERVANT HIS MASTER. IF THEN I AM A FATHER, WHERE IS MY HONOR? AND IF I AM A MASTER, WHERE IS MY FEAR? SAYS THE LORD OF HOSTS."

Malachi 1:6

"WHOEVER WALKS IN UPRIGHTNESS FEARS THE LORD, BUT HE WHO IS DEVIOUS IN HIS WAYS DESPISES HIM."

Proverbs 14:2

no sassy girls

A All this week we've been talking about the design element of honor: A true woman is reverent—she makes much of Christ.

In the first lesson, we learned that honor is a critical virtue that involves a deep, reverential fear of the Lord and an acknowledgment of His constant presence. It results in "temple-appropriate" behavior—not just on Sundays, but every hour of every day.

In the second lesson, we learned that reverence deferentially acknowledges the Lord's authority over us. Our obedience is like a spiritual curtsy. It's far more than just outward behavior. It involves our hearts, thoughts, demeanor, attitude, and actions—the entire package!

Yesterday, we saw that irreverence is failing to honor something of great worth. It's making little of something we should make much of. Whenever

we make more of our opinions and desires than we make of the opinions and desires of Christ, we are guilty of irreverence. It is as though we deface and desecrate the memory of His sacrifice.

To this point, we've been talking about honor and reverence in a general way—trying to understand what *honor* means and what it involves. But now, we're going to explore

why reverence is near the top of Paul's list of important traits for older women. Today and tomorrow we'll try to answer two questions:

1. Why is reverence a trait that's specifically important for the female sex?

2. Why is reverence particularly important for "older" women?

> "The godly woman, the woman of wisdom, honors her commitment all the days of her life, and she doesn't give in to fear."[6]
>
> —*Mary*

reverence and womanhood

E Every believer ought to honor the Lord and be respectful toward others. First Peter 2:17 says, "Honor everyone. Love the brotherhood. Fear God. Honor the emperor." The book of Romans commands, "Love one another with brotherly affection. Outdo one another in showing honor. . . . " and "Pay to all what is owed to them: taxes to whom taxes are owed, revenue to whom revenue is owed, respect to whom respect is owed, honor to whom honor is owed" (Rom. 12:10; 13:7).

The instruction to honor the Lord and to be respectful toward people is not restricted to women. Obviously, both genders ought to be reverent. But in the gender specific "curriculum" Paul laid out for the Cretan church, he identifies reverence as a trait that is of particular importance for women. And it's not the first or the only time that Scripture suggests that this is so.

Look up the following references and draw a line to match each reference to the thought it contains:

Proverbs 31:25   Older women are to be reverent in behavior, not self-promoting or self-indulgent.

1 Peter 3:1–2   A woman who reverences the Lord will be admired by those who know her best.

Proverbs 31:30   Strength and honor are a virtuous woman's clothing.

Titus 2:3   A husband may be won over without a word by the way his wife lives—when he observes her pure, reverent spirit.

Psalm 45:11   The king is enthralled by his bride's beauty; she must honor him, for he is her lord.

God created male and female and instituted marriage for a specific reason. Gender and marriage exist to tell the incredible story of Jesus. The Bible indicates there's a clear and corresponding parallel pattern between three relationships: husband/wife, Christ/church, and God/Christ.

You may remember the following illustration from *True Woman 101*. It illustrates the pattern. God is the head of Christ. Christ is the head of the church, and the husband is the head of his wife (1 Cor. 11:3). The husband-wife relationship is a physical, earthly symbol that helps us grasp the nature of Jesus' spiritual and eternal relationships.

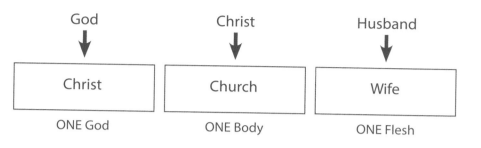

God →	Christ →	Husband →
Christ	Church	Wife
ONE God	ONE Body	ONE Flesh

God created two sexes so that we might shine the spotlight on the gospel from different angles. Even if a woman never marries, she is still uniquely qualified to be a "bride." A male cannot be a bride. Only a female can be a bride. Therefore, a woman has the capacity to display the "bride" part of the redemptive story in a way that a man cannot. What's more, she also has the capacity to reflect truths about Christ's relationship to God in a way that a man cannot.

So what does this have to do with Paul's admonition for women to be reverent? It has a great deal to do with it. Christ's disposition toward His Father is characterized by reverence. Reverence also character-izes the church's attitude toward Christ. Women have a unique responsibility to tell the Jesus story from the church ⟶ Christ and Christ ⟶ God angle. That's why reverence is a trait that's particularly important for women to exhibit.

"Jesus answered, '...I honor my Father.... I do not seek my own glory; there is One who seeks it, and he is the judge.'"

John 8:49–50

"During His earthly life, [Jesus] offered prayers and appeals with loud cries and tears to the One who was able to save Him from death, and He was heard because of His reverence."

Hebrews 5:7 HCSB

In the verses in the margins, underline the phrases that indicate that reverence / honor characterizes Christ's disposition toward God and the church's disposition toward Christ.

Explain in your own words why it's particularly important for you, as a woman, to cultivate a reverent spirit.

_____

_____

_____

Does our culture uphold reverence as a desirable trait for women? How does its view of reverence differ from that promoted in Scripture?

_____

_____

It's springtime as we're writing this chapter, and the start of "wedding season." I (Nancy) have been helping a sweet young woman I've known all her life, with plans for her wedding a few months from now.

Like most women preparing for their wedding, Jessica is paying special attention to getting the right dress, jewelry, accessories, makeup, and hairstyle for the big day. When the music starts, indicating it's time for her to walk down the aisle, she wants to look her absolute best. It's natural for a bride to want to honor her groom in this way.

Ultimately, the story of bride and groom points to the story of THE groom and THE bride—Christ and His church. How well are you displaying the bride part of the story? Do you struggle with an irreverent, crass, or rebellious attitude? Or do you honor Jesus by displaying a humble, respectful, reverent spirit?

Close in Prayer. Ask the Father to help you esteem and cultivate a humble, respectful, reverent spirit that is fitting for godly femininity.

"THAT ALL MAY HONOR THE SON, JUST AS THEY HONOR THE FATHER. WHOEVER DOES NOT HONOR THE SON DOES NOT HONOR THE FATHER WHO SENT HIM."

John 5:23

"IN YOUR HEARTS HONOR CHRIST THE LORD AS HOLY."

1 Peter 3:15

"MY COVENANT WITH HIM WAS ONE OF LIFE AND PEACE . . . IT CALLED FOR REVERENCE, AND HE REVERED ME AND STOOD IN AWE OF MY NAME."

Malachi 2:5 HCSB

growing reverent

"Those who honor me I will honor, and those who despise me shall be lightly esteemed."
1 Samuel 2:30

"The reward for humility and fear of the Lord *is riches and honor and life."*
Proverbs 22:4

"One's pride will bring him low, but he who is lowly in spirit will obtain honor."
Proverbs 29:23

"The wise will inherit honor, but fools get disgrace."
Proverbs 3:35

"When wickedness comes, contempt comes also, and with dishonor comes disgrace."
Proverbs 18:3

Bows are the traditional greeting in East Asia. Bowing is a gesture of respect. Bows are used to express deference, sincerity, remorse, or gratitude. Traditionally, the depth of the bow is related to the degree of respect or gratitude. Some bows are performed equally by two or more people, while others are unequal— the person of higher status either does not bow or performs a smaller bow in response.

When my (Mary's) son Matt was eighteen years old, he observed a young Asian man of about the same age greet his parents at the airport. The young man knelt down and touched his head to the ground at his father's feet before standing and embracing him.

I asked Matt what he thought of the custom. He said, "On the one hand, it was really weird to see him bow, since we don't do that here. But on the other hand, I was impressed by the deep respect he demonstrated for his father. Young people are so disrespectful—seeing respect is refreshing. I admired him for it."

Why was it admirable of the son to demonstrate respect toward his father?

_____

_____

It's interesting that it was the person demonstrating respect that gained Matt's respect. Respecting a parent is the right and proper thing for a son or daughter to do. It's the honorable thing to do. In humbly demonstrating honor, the young man gained honor.

Read the verses in the margins. What does a woman get by being reverent and respectful?

_____

_____

What about a contemptuous, mouthy, irreverent, disrespectful woman? What will she get?

_____

_____

What do you think it means to be honored by God?

_____

_____

Reverence for God impacts how we relate to people. Our respect for Him translates into a respectful attitude toward others. It causes us to demonstrate "temple-appropriate," honorable behavior in every aspect of our lives.

growing old & reverent

A According to Titus 2:3, demonstrating reverence is important for women, and particularly for women who are "older." How old is "older"? You may have heard it said that old age is always fifteen years older than you currently are!

According to 1 Timothy 5:9, widows had to be at least sixty years old in order to be put on the list to receive financial support from the church. But Paul doesn't specify how old you have to be to qualify as an "older" woman. The Greek word for "older women" is the only occurrence of that word in the Bible.

Though we can't specify an exact age, we think that "older" would generally be considered to be a woman who was past child-bearing/rearing years. Life expectancy at that time was shorter. So what Paul called an "older" woman would nowadays be a woman that we would call "middle-aged" or older.

"IF ANYONE SERVES ME, THE FATHER WILL HONOR HIM."

John 12:26

"FOR THE LORD GOD IS A SUN AND SHIELD; THE LORD BESTOWS FAVOR AND HONOR. NO GOOD THING DOES HE WITHHOLD FROM THOSE WHO WALK UPRIGHTLY."

Psalm 84:11

"WHOEVER PURSUES RIGHTEOUSNESS AND KINDNESS WILL FIND LIFE, RIGHTEOUSNESS, AND HONOR."

Proverbs 21:21

Older women are to be reverent. That's the aim of younger women too; it's just that it sometimes takes awhile to get there. A woman who has had more years of life under her belt has had her reverence tested, and hopefully refined. She's learned—in the school of hard knocks—how to stay ever mindful of God. She's learned that the purpose of her life is to make much of Christ. She's learned how to be humble and selfless, how to hold her tongue, how to be kind, and how to respect others.

Paul anticipated that chronological maturity would be accompanied by spiritual growth and maturity. That's why he associated the trait of reverence with older women. But we think he may have also done so because a sassy, contemptuous, cocky, irreverent older woman is particularly offensive and grating. Irreverence is a glaring blight on womanhood—and it becomes more unseemly the older you get.

When you're young, the character defect of irreverence can be covered up with youthful energy, good looks, natural abilities, and personality. But as you get older those things fade away, and the defect becomes more pronounced and visible. Women who have cultivated the inner beauty of a reverent spirit become more beautiful with age. But irreverent women get increasingly ugly as their physical beauty fades.

Read Psalm 92:12–14 in the margin. Using the author's analogy of plants, draw a picture of what a reverent versus an irreverent old woman might look like:

Reverent Older Woman Plant	Irreverent Older Woman Plant

"The righteous flourish like the palm tree and grow like a cedar in Lebanon. They are planted in the house of the LORD; they flourish in the courts of our God. They still bear fruit in old age; they are ever full of sap and green."
Psalm 92:12–14

"To keep the heart unwrinkled, to be hopeful, kindly, cheerful, reverent— that is to triumph over old age." [7]
Amos Bronson Alcott

When I was a girl, I (Nancy) knew two elderly sisters. One had a lovely, reverent spirit and was a joy to be around. The other was a cranky, crusty woman; she was miserable and she made everyone around her miserable. The stark contrast made a lasting impression on my young mind.

Thanks, in part, to the influence of those two sisters, ever since I was a little girl, I have aspired to someday be a "godly old lady"! But as I've grown older,

I've realized it doesn't just happen. (Well, the "old" part does, but not the "godly" part!) You don't just hit menopause and suddenly become a reverent woman. It takes time and attention to cultivate a truly godly, reverent spirit.

Sadly, most women drift through life. Days become weeks become months become years become decades and become a lifetime. If you are not intentional about becoming more spiritually mature, godly, gracious, and reverent, you will likely become more narrow, bitter, whiny, crusty, and petty as you age. Now is the right time to ask, "What kind of an old woman do I want to be?"

→ **Look at the two plants you've drawn on the previous page.** Circle the one you'd like to resemble in old age. Close in prayer. Ask the Lord to give you His enabling grace to become a reverent woman who honors Him.

drawing it out,
drawing it in . . .

interior renovation

process

The video for Week Two will help you process this week's lessons. You'll find this week's video, the leader's guide, and additional resources at TrueWoman201.com.

ponder

Think about the following questions. Discuss them with your friends, family, and/or small group:

1. What characteristics typically mark a woman who is reverent? How is the reverence in her heart reflected outwardly in her life and relationships?

2. What are some practical ways can we honor God above all other people and priorities in our lives?

3. As you consider your role in God's redemptive story, specifically as a woman, why is reverence such a critically important disposition? What does your disposition communicate to others about Christ's worth and value?

4. Paul gives two examples of irreverent behavior in Titus 2:3, one of which is slander. What lies at the root of slander?

5. What is the link between overindulgence and irreverence? As you assess your daily habits, where do you find a tendency to overindulge? Can you identify the heart attitude that tempts you in this way?

6. On Day 4 we read, "God created two sexes so that we might shine the spotlight on the gospel from different angles" (p. 54). What particular opportunity do we have as women to illuminate the gospel? How does reverence factor into how our light shines?

7. Why is the trait of reverence especially important for older women?

8. No matter your age, you are in the process of becoming an "older woman." How would others describe your character? What intentional efforts can you make to cultivate a godly and reverent spirit that will inspire others to stand in awe of God?

personalize it

Use this page to journal. Write down what you learned this week. Record your comments, a favorite verse, or a concept or quote that was particularly helpful or meaningful to you. Compose a prayer, letter, or poem. Jot down notes from the video or your small group session. Express your heart response to what you have studied. Personalize this week's lessons in the way that will best help you apply them to your life.

drawing it out,
drawing it in . . .

affection

*W*hat would you choose as "the essentials" for a curriculum on womanhood? In the first two design elements we studied—discernment and honor—Paul encourages us to adopt right thinking (sound doctrine) and a right heart attitude toward the Lord (reverence).

Then he lists several other things that are vital for women of God: loving their husbands and children, being self-controlled and pure, working at home, being kind, and being submissive to their husbands. These are things that older women ought to be competent to teach and younger women ought to be eager to learn.

A True Woman values the family . . . She "[loves her husband] and children."

Before we dive into these individual qualities, we'd like to make several general observations about the overall list: First, **this is a countercultural curriculum**! You're not likely to find these elements as part of many college women's-studies programs. This passage lays out the ways of the kingdom of God, which are radically different from those of this world.

The second thing that strikes us is **what is *not* on this list**. If you were going to disciple a younger woman, maybe a new believer, a single young career woman, or perhaps a newlywed—and you wanted to help her become spiritually mature and fruitful and live a life that is pleasing to God—what are the major subjects you would focus on?

Perhaps you'd say you'd want to teach her how to pray, how to study God's Word, how to witness. These are crucial subjects, and they are definitely part of the general educational curriculum for all believers. But it's interesting that none of those things appears on this list of required topics to get a major in biblical womanhood.

Another observation we would make is that the **qualities mentioned** have to be learned. "*Train* the young women . . . " (Titus 2:4). Women don't learn these things by osmosis or simpy by going to church and sitting under strong biblical preaching, important as that is. God says something else is needed as a part of the process of discipleship in women's lives—and that is other, mature women who come alongside and engage with them and teach them about womanhood in the context of the community of faith.

A fourth observation about this list is **the priority God places on the family and the home**. The majority of the elements relate specifically to marriage, motherhood, and the home. This passage assumes that young women need to know how to be wives and mothers. It assumes that marriage and motherhood are the norm and therefore the context in which most Christian women live out their faith.

At the same time, this passage is not just for wives and moms. The heart of Paul's instruction applies to *all* women, regardless of their family status.

Clearly God has gifted some women to be able to remain single for the purpose of serving Him in a more concentrated way. You read about that in 1 Corinthians 7. That's the case for me (Nancy). I've never married, and believe God has gifted and called me to serve Him as a single woman. Some women doing this study may be in the same situation.

What's more, given the realities of our culture, many women who desire to be married may never see that desire fulfilled. Remaining single is a reality that many Christian women face.

Further, some women who do marry are unable to bear children. So, it's possible you may never have a husband or children. Nevertheless, Paul's curriculum applies to you too. Why? Because marriage and family are vital to God's redemptive plan! As we learned in *True Woman 101*, the relationship between a husband and wife is powerfully linked to the story of Christ and His church-bride. God created male and female, marriage, sex, and procreation to foreshadow and testify about the amazing story of Christ and His church-bride.

The biblical story line of male and female (and marriage and family) has little to do with us; it has everything to do with God. Your womanhood is ultimately not about you. It's about displaying the glory of God and His powerful redemptive plan. Even if you never have a husband or children, it's crucial for you to understand the great, eternal realities to which your womanhood points.

The final observation to note about this passage is **the priority of love.** Where does Paul start? "Train the young women *to love*" (v. 4)—to love husbands, to love children, to love family . . . *to love what God loves*! A True Woman values and loves God's plan for the family. Married or not, she has a deep affection for family and does what she can to help families reflect the gospel story. →

dad's house

"For this reason I bow my knees before the Father [Patēr], from whom every family (patria) in heaven and on earth is named."
Ephesians 3:14–15

"Yet for us there is one God, the Father, from whom are all things and for whom we exist, and one Lord, Jesus Christ, through whom are all things and through whom we exist. However, not all possess this knowledge."
I Corinthians 8:6–7

"For the One who sanctifies and those who are sanctified all have one Father. That is why Jesus is not ashamed to call them brothers..."
Hebrews 2:11 HCSB

It's common practice for inventions to be named after their inventors. Have you ever enjoyed a ride on a Ferris wheel? It was named after the inventor George Ferris. Safety razor blades were invented by King Gillette. The Singer sewing machine was invented by Isaac Singer. Tupperware was invented by Earl Tupper. The diesel engine was invented by Rudolf Diesel.

The Jacuzzi brothers invented a portable hydrotherapy bath pump that was later used to build the first Jacuzzi hot tub. James Salisbury invented the Salisbury steak.

A notable political and military figure invented a handheld meal to eat during extended forays at the gaming table. The meal was named the "sandwich," after its inventor, the Earl of Sandwich.

You probably don't realize that the cardigan, nicotine, sideburns, shrapnel, bloomers, booze, a boycott, and even the comma were named after the people who brought them into existence or popularized their use.

In Ephesians 3:14–15, a play on words in the original Greek indicates that something common to humans was invented by God the Father and is named by Him. It's an incredibly important "invention" that He created and also defines:

> *For this reason I bow my knees before the Father [Patēr],*
> *from whom every family [patria] in heaven and on earth is named.*

According to this text, who is the "inventor" and what is the "invention"?

The inventor is _____

The invention is _____

Did you figure it out? The English word "father" is translated from the Greek word *patēr*, and "family" is translated from the Greek word *patria*. (The Latin *Pater* is the root from which we get our English word *paternity*.) God the *Patēr* (Father) invented the *patria*, the family.

In Israelite society, the basic family unit was called the "father's house" (Hebrew: *bet-ab* [*bet*=house, *ab*=father]). It usually consisted of several nuclear families that claimed descent from the same male ancestor. The eldest living male of a lineage and all his sons and grandsons and their wives and children were all considered part of the same household. Even though it was common for each nuclear family to have its own residence, they were still regarded as part of their father's house.

For us, the words *father* and *family* are related yet separate ideas, whereas in Greek and Hebrew, the concepts are inseparable. In Scripture, a family is a group of people associated with a common father. Paternity and family are so closely connected that some translators have suggested the association could be reflected in English by translating Ephesians 3:14–15: "I bow my knees before the *Father* from whom all *fatherhoods* are named."[1]

Nowadays it would be considered sexist to suggest that every family is part of a specific "fatherhood." Nevertheless, the language of the Bible demonstrates that from God's perspective, that's exactly what family is.

We know that human fathers and families are often broken and dysfunctional. Divorce, remarriage, and/or having children out of wedlock result in various contemporary family configurations. But that doesn't change the fact that fatherhood and family ultimately draw their existence, essence, and character from the fatherhood and family of God.

Read the verses in the margin on page 64. Based on the verses, mark the following statements true (T) or false (F).

_____ Family is created by God the Father.

_____ Family is named by God the Father.

_____ Family exists to testify of God the Father.

_____ Family is what the government defines it to be.

_____ Family is what the culture defines it to be.

What do you think it means for God to "name" the family?

_____

_____

_____

family name

In ancient thought a name is more than a label. It's more than just a means of distinguishing one person or thing from another. The act of naming indicates that the person giving the name has authority over that which he names (Ps. 147:4; Isa. 40:26). Furthermore, the assigned name reveals the person/thing's inner being or true nature (Gen. 25:26; 1 Sam. 25:25).

God the Father brought the family into existence. Naming it reinforces the fact that He has authority over it. He decides its structure. He decides its purpose. He decides its role.

But there's something else. Family contains individuals created in *God's own image and likeness* (Gen. 1:26). So when God names the family, it's different from His naming the stars (Ps. 147:4). The family is not only named *by* Him; it is also named *from* Him. Family (*patria*) derives its name from God's name (*Patēr*). This gives the family a unique and profound significance.

The meaning of "family" is based on God. He is the great original. Earthly families and fatherhoods are but copies of the heavenly one. They are signposts that point to a reality infinitely more amazing, more wonderful, and more eternal. God is all about family. And when all is said and done, "family" is more about Him than it is about us.

> "Blessed be the God and Father of our Lord Jesus Christ . . . he chose us in him before the foundation of the world. . . . In love he predestined us for adoption as sons through Jesus Christ."
>
> **Ephesians 1:2–5**

Refer to the verses in the margins to fill in the blanks of the sentences.

God the Father decided to have a spiritual family long before He

created human families. He chose us in Christ _____

the foundation of the world. When we believed, we were

_____ of God and became His children,

members of His _____, which is

overseen by His faithful Son.

Explain why the family is important to God.

_____

_____

_____

Do you think you love and esteem the family as much as God would like you to?
Explain your answer.

_____

_____

→ **Close in prayer.** Thank the Lord
that the concept of earthly families
was designed by Him to help us
understand what it means to be part
of His heavenly family.

"BUT TO ALL WHO
DID RECEIVE HIM,
WHO BELIEVED IN
HIS NAME, HE GAVE
THE RIGHT TO
BECOME CHILDREN
OF GOD, WHO WERE
BORN, NOT OF
BLOOD NOR OF
THE WILL OF THE
FLESH NOR OF
THE WILL OF MAN,
BUT OF GOD."

John 1:12–13

"BUT CHRIST WAS
FAITHFUL AS A
SON OVER HIS
HOUSEHOLD. AND
WE ARE THAT
HOUSEHOLD IF WE
HOLD ON TO THE
COURAGE AND
THE CONFIDENCE
OF OUR HOPE."

Hebrews 3:6 HCSB

family dwelling

*I*n yesterday's lesson, we learned that God the Father invented the family. He's the one who determines its meaning, purpose, and role. He's the one who instituted marriage as a lifelong covenant between husband and wife. He's the one who enables couples to be fruitful and multiply. He's the *Patēr* (Father) from whom every *patria* (family) in heaven and earth is named. Marriage and family were created by Him and exist *for* Him.

God created marriage and family to give us symbols, images, and language powerful enough to convey the idea of who He is and what a relationship with Him is all about. Even those whose families are broken and dysfunctional understand that an intact, healthy family is the ideal.

> *"Train the young women to love their husbands and children."*
>
> **Titus 2:4**

As God designed it to function, "family" helps us to understand what it means to have a heavenly Father and be part of a household of faith. It introduces us to the meaning of family resemblance, descendants, lineage, sonship, adoption, siblings, kinship, heirs, and 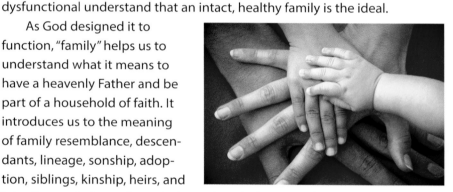 inheritance. As it was intended, marriage helps us understand concepts such as desire, love, commitment, fidelity, infidelity, loyalty, jealousy, headship, unity, intimacy, and covenant. In other words, the family was designed to point us to God and the gospel.

God gave us these images so we'd have human thoughts, feelings, experiences, and language adequate and powerful enough to understand and express deep spiritual truths. The visible symbols display and testify about what is unseen. That's why the symbols are so important.[2] And that's why family affection is at the top of Titus' list of "must-learns" for young women.

Look up Titus 2:4 in your Bible. What does Paul say is the "must-learn" for godly womanhood?

_____

_____

There are four Greek words that are all translated "love" in English. While the distinctions between these words are not always sharp or clearcut[3] and they are sometimes used interchangeably, in general they can be explained this way:

Storgē: Kinship and loyalty among family members—familial love

Phileō: Fondness, tenderness, affinity, or affection—friendly love

Agapē: Sacrificial, unconditional, principled love—commitment love

Eros: Erotic, intimate, romantic feelings—sexual love (this Greek word does not appear in the Bible)

Try to rank these four types of love as to how important you think they are to a good marriage, with #1 being the most important and #4 being the least important:

Explain why you ranked them the way you did:

_____ **Storgē**

_____ **Phileō**

_____ **Agapē**

_____ **Eros**

Did you have a hard time ranking them? All four types of love have their place in marriage! Let's focus on just two for the moment. *Agapē* is often used to describe a volitional love, the type of love that deliberately and selflessly decides to do what's right, choosing to act with goodwill and kindness. It's based on conviction, purpose, duty, and commitment. *Phileō*, on the other hand, is often used to describe more of an emotional response. *Phileō* means to deeply care about a person, to approve of him, to appreciate him, to welcome him, to treat him with affection.[4]

Agapē generally says, "I choose to love you," whereas *phileō* says, "I deeply like you and enjoy you." Titus 2:4 uses *phileō*—friendly love— to describe the type of love that women need to learn how to cultivate toward husbands and children. Paul's choice of words is interesting. He exhorts older women to:

sōphronizō . . . . . . instruct, discipline, teach, school

neos . . . . new, fresh, young, novices (young women)

eimi . . . . to be, to exist

philandros . . . . . . an adjective that combines the verb *phileō*, "to like," with "man" or "husband"—literally, *"husband-liker"*

philoteknos . . . . . an adjective that combines the verb *phileō*, "to like," with "child"—literally, *"child-liker"*

Confused yet?! In other words, Titus 2:4 says:

"School the newbies to be husband-likers and child-likers." Or . . .

"Teach the novices to deeply like/enjoy/appreciate/welcome husbands and children."

How might a marriage that has this kind of love be more satisfying than one without it?

_____

_____

husband-liker

Many years ago, I (Mary) hosted a women's event in my home. There were women of all ages present. As we munched on goodies, some of my young married friends began to complain about their husband's snoring habits. We doubled over in laughter and groaned in sympathy as one after another performed loud, boisterous imitations. It was all in fun, but the banter had a subtle undercurrent of female superiority and criticism of men for being so hopelessly . . . male.

After we had worn out the topic and the laughter had subsided, Judy, a sweet, middle-aged widow sitting in the corner, spoke up. Blinking back tears, she softly said, "I would give the world to hear Mike snoring beside me one more time. I really wish I would have appreciated him more." She said it with genuine regret and not a hint of condemnation. Ouch. Each young woman in the room knew she had just been schooled!

I lay awake in bed that night listening to Brent's soft snores and thought about Judy's words. Though it's been years, I still think of them often. Why is it so easy to focus on what I don't like about my husband rather than on what I do like? Why do I let the 10% that bugs me eclipse the 90% that doesn't? How can I remain deeply in love with him?—not just stay committed to him but truly like him, enjoy him, affirm him, welcome him, and appreciate him? What can I do to be a better friend to him? How can I be a better *husband-liker*?

Did you notice that little word "*eimi*" (to be, to exist) in the list of Greek words? Being a husband-liker is a state of being. It's a mindset that values and appreciates men and marriage. It's more of an attitude than an action. Oh, it certainly shows up in actions, but your attitude toward men and marriage is where it all starts. And that's something you can work on whether you're married or not.

Would you describe yourself as a "husband-liker"? Why or why not?

_____

_____

How can you cultivate a mindset that values marriage as God does?

_____

_____

→ **Take a moment to reflect on your attitude toward men and marriage** (and if married, toward your own husband). Ask the Lord to help you value marriage and family as He does.

It's official. In 2013, one of the world's leading dictionaries of the English language—Macmillan—revised the definition of marriage to include so-called marriages of same-sex couples.

Macmillan's definition of *marriage* now reads: "The relationship between two people who are husband and wife, or a similar relationship between people of the same sex."[5]

> "Let marriage be held in honor among all, and let the marriage bed be undefiled."
>
> **Hebrews 13:4**

Macmillan editor in chief, Michael Rundell, said the change suggests a future redefining of the terms *wife* and *husband* to reflect the fact that a wife isn't necessarily a woman and a husband isn't necessarily a man.[6] That's not entirely surprising, as we live in an era of pick-and-choose-your-own-blend-of-sexuality, where even the definition of *man* and *woman* and a person's gender are up for grabs.

The Bible flies in the face of such politically correct modern notions. It teaches that the Lord God created male and female, sexuality, marriage, husband, wife, and family. All of these draw their existence, essence, character, and meaning from Him. Though Macmillan and other dictionaries may come up with new, different definitions, it's not up to dictionaries—nor is it up to us—to define what *man*, *woman*, *husband*, *wife*, and *marriage* mean. God created these things. He dictates what they mean.

Dr. John Piper explains that "marriage is created and defined by God in the Scriptures as the sexual and covenantal union of a man and a woman in life-long allegiance to each other alone, as husband and wife, with a view to displaying Christ's covenant relationship to his blood-bought church."[7]

Marriage is a temporary, earthly, God-ordained institution that points to the eternal, heavenly union between Christ and His bride. Marriage is important. Marriage is good. And anyone who thinks or claims otherwise is not in sync with God's perspective on it.

Read Hebrews 13:4 in the margin. Who ought to hold marriage in honor?

☐ Women who are married ☐ Women who are divorced

☐ Women who are single ☐ Everyone!—including me

What do you think it means to hold marriage in honor?

_____

_____

False teachers in Ephesus were promoting a warped, gnostic view on sexuality and marriage. As we saw in the first week's lessons, their teachings particularly appealed to women (2 Tim. 3:6–7; see pages 30–31).

Gnostics viewed the physical, material world as evil. So they promoted "the abuse of the flesh." This could happen in two opposite ways: (1) shunning the flesh (abstinence), or (2) indulging it (sexual license).[8]

The gnostic heretics in the church in Ephesus upheld the celibate or single lifestyle as being more spiritual than marriage. This type of teaching undoubtedly influenced the women in that congregation to have negative and improper attitudes toward husbands, marriage, sex, and child-bearing.

Read 1 Timothy 4:1–4 in the margin. Circle the phrase that indicates the ultimate source of false teaching about marriage.

Why do you think deceitful spirits and demons promote beguiling, false ideas about marriage?

_____

_____

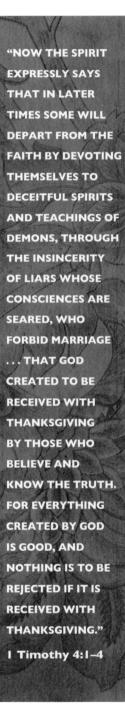

"NOW THE SPIRIT EXPRESSLY SAYS THAT IN LATER TIMES SOME WILL DEPART FROM THE FAITH BY DEVOTING THEMSELVES TO DECEITFUL SPIRITS AND TEACHINGS OF DEMONS, THROUGH THE INSINCERITY OF LIARS WHOSE CONSCIENCES ARE SEARED, WHO FORBID MARRIAGE . . . THAT GOD CREATED TO BE RECEIVED WITH THANKSGIVING BY THOSE WHO BELIEVE AND KNOW THE TRUTH. FOR EVERYTHING CREATED BY GOD IS GOOD, AND NOTHING IS TO BE REJECTED IF IT IS RECEIVED WITH THANKSGIVING."

1 Timothy 4:1–4

Paul valued the single life (1 Cor. 7). He saw it as allowing extra time for serving God. But he didn't view singleness as the norm. He acknowledged that God would give some believers the gift of singleness, but many more the gift of marriage. Paul took the false teachers to task for devaluing that which God had created as good. He upheld the husband-wife relationship as a vital symbol that displays Christ's relationship to the church (Eph. 5). Marriage is a holy, God-ordained institution that ought to be deeply honored by all.

Paul's letter to Titus was written at about the same time as his letter to Timothy. Both letters addressed the problem of false teachers. Titus' letter doesn't specify the content of the false teaching in Crete, but chances are it was similar to the false teaching in Ephesus.

Read Titus 1:11 in the margin. What was the result of the false teaching in Crete?

_____

_____

> "They must be silenced, since they are upsetting whole families by teaching for shameful gain what they ought not to teach."
>
> **Titus 1:11**

Upsetting means "overturning," "destroying," or "ruining."[9] It's Satan's goal to ruin and destroy entire families. Satan hates families. He hates God's definition of marriage. He hates the idea of husbands and wives faithfully bearing witness to the gospel. He hates holy, covenant marital sex. He hates children. Satan wants only to steal, kill, and destroy these things (John 10:10).

As was the case in Ephesus and Crete, wrong attitudes and ideas toward gender, sexuality, and marriage can creep into the church and be promoted by people who call themselves Christians. Scripture warns us to be careful and watchful about what we believe, how we think and act, because the devil prowls around (1 Peter 5:8), peddling deceptive ideas, seeking to deconstruct, devalue, and devour true womanhood, manhood, marriage, and family.

becoming husband-likers

W We hope you're beginning to understand why being a "husband-liker" is at the top of the must-learn attitudes for young women. Appreciating manhood and womanhood and honoring and supporting marriage is important for every woman, regardless of her age and circumstance of life.

On the chart below, jot down some practical ideas for how each type of woman could appropriately be a "husband-liker."

Profile	How this woman could be a "husband-liker"
Young teen girl	
Thirty-something single woman	
Divorced woman	
Married woman	
Older widowed or unmarried woman	
You	

→ **Do the exercise in the margin.** Do you have any attitudes toward men and marriage that the Lord wants you to correct? Close in prayer, asking Him to do so.

THINK ABOUT IT:

Are the following women husband-likers? Why or why not?

A college student who sleeps with her boyfriend

A bridesmaid who is envious and resentful that she's not the one getting married

A divorced woman who speaks negatively of her ex

A married woman who mocks her husband's shortcomings

A widow who refuses to be in a Bible study with married couples

A high school girl who objects when girlfriends start telling sarcastic "dumb boy" jokes

A woman who reads a book that glamorizes an affair

A girl who has a song about same-sex kissing on her playlist

A wife who chooses not to go to lunch alone with her male coworker

play room

The cover of the August 12, 2013 issue of *TIME* magazine featured a trim, attractive, early-to-mid-thirties couple in matching teal swimsuits, lying with arms leisurely entwined on a dappled sugar-white beach. Their serenity is due to the fact that they have chosen "The Childfree Life." The headline

explains that for many, "having it all means not having children."

Inside the magazine we see the same chic couple sitting coolly and comfortably under a beach umbrella clinking wine glasses, as a decidedly un-chic, unhappy couple trudges by with a tottering mountain of beach toys and kids in tow. The message could not be clearer: Life *without* kids is idyllic and fulfilling. Life *with* kids is chaotic and burdensome. The article cheerfully asserts that "women are inventing a new female archetype, one for whom having it all doesn't mean having a baby."[10]

We live in a culture that is increasingly hostile toward children-bearing. In 2007, Corinne Maier's saucy *No Kids: 40 Good Reasons Not to Have Children*

became a sensation in Europe. It was translated for American audiences two years later, and Maier's quips—"Breastfeeding is slavery," "Life with kids is life trivialized," "Family is an inward-looking prison," "Motherhood or success: Pick one"—were just as well-received here.

According to Maier, traditional ideas about femininity and motherhood damage the lives of women, keep them from being creative and intelligent, and prevent them from progressing in their careers. She encourages women to have the courage to say, "Me first."[11] "No kids, thanks. It's better that way."[12]

> "Older women . . . are to teach what is good, and so train the young women to love their husbands and children."
>
> **Titus 2:3–4**

Use the clues and refer to pages 68–71 to help you complete the crossword and see what Titus 2 teaches is the right attitude toward children.

ACROSS

1 A woman needs to learn how to be a husband-liker and _____ - _____.

5 A Greek word for "to deeply like, approve, welcome, and be fond of."

6 To train a novice to be a child-liker is to teach what is _____. (See Titus 2:3-4)

7 A type of love that women need to learn how to cultivate toward children.

DOWN

2 Love is both a decision of your head and a feeling of your _____.

3 *Phileō* says, "I deeply like and _____ you."

4 Being a child-liker is a state of being. It's a _____ that values and appreciates children.

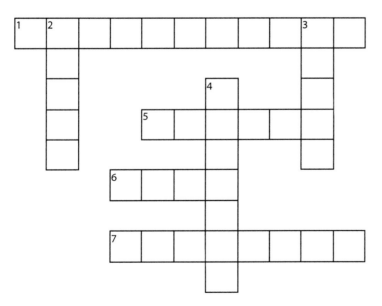

Would you characterize yourself as a "child-liker"? Why or why not?

_____

_____

Read Mark 9:36–37; 10:13–16 in your Bible. Contrast the disciples' attitude toward children with Jesus' attitude toward them:

The disciples' attitude: _____

_____

Jesus' attitude: _____

_____

Is your attitude toward children more like the disciples' or more like Christ's? Explain why.

_____

_____

becoming child-likers

Marriage and children used to go together like lightning and thunder. If a woman married, it was usually just a matter of time before children followed. But the birth control pill changed all that. Bearing children is now a woman's "choice," and completely separate from the choice to marry.

Popular wisdom dictates that a woman should choose to have children, if and when doing so is economically viable and contributes to her own sense of happiness and personal fulfillment. Sadly, this attitude is not limited to secular circles, as this Christian blogger illustrates:

> Why have I chosen not to have children? The simple answer is that I don't want them. It's not that I don't like kids, I just don't want my own. I don't want the responsibility of taking care of them. I don't want to be a parent or mother. Is that selfish? Maybe. But I'd rather run that risk than have a child and resent the child.[13]

How does this attitude line up with God's perspective on marriage and children?

_____

_____

"See that you do not despise one of these little ones. For I tell you that in heaven their angels always see the face of my Father who is in heaven."

Matthew 18:10

"The LORD was witness between you and the wife of your youth . . . she is your companion and your wife by covenant. Did he not make them one, with a portion of the Spirit in their union? And what was the one God seeking? Godly offspring."

Malachi 2:14–16

Read the verses in the margin on page 78. Circle the phrase in Malachi that indicates what God seeks through marital unions.

Which of the following statements BEST reflects why God wants married couples to produce godly offspring?

☐ The covenant union between Christ and the church produces godly offspring. Marriage, as a symbol of that union, is also intended to produce godly offspring. We "create" life because the act testifies of our life-giving Creator.

☐ Having babies is the most efficient and effective way to expand the kingdom and spread the gospel.

☐ Producing offspring is fun. Having kids is fulfilling and rewarding.

In response to *TIME*'s "The Childfree Life" article, blogger Stan Guthrie said:

Raising children, you see, isn't about you, and it isn't even about them. It's about Him—our heavenly Father, "from whom every family in heaven and on earth is named" (Eph. 3:15). We have children because we are made in His image, in the likeness of Him who told us to "be fruitful and multiply" (Gen. 1:28). We create because we are like our Creator. Among other good things, it is what we normally are called to do in this world, barring a special calling from God.[14]

Are you a child-liker? Does your attitude toward kids mirror Christ's attitude? Do you view children as precious gifts *from* God, to be nurtured and raised *for* God? Do you deeply like, welcome, approve of, appreciate, and enjoy them?

→ **How could you** cultivate a heart more like His toward children?

"BEHOLD, CHILDREN ARE A HERITAGE FROM THE LORD, THE FRUIT OF THE WOMB A REWARD."

Psalm 127:3

homestead

"Behold, everyone who uses proverbs will use this proverb about you: 'Like mother, like daughter.' You are the daughter of your mother, who loathed her husband and her children; and you are the sister of your sisters, who loathed their husbands and their children."

Ezekiel 16:44–45

"Whoever loves father or mother more than me is not worthy of me, and whoever loves son or daughter more than me is not worthy of me."

Matthew 10:37

I [Paul] wish that all were [single] as I myself am. But each has his own gift from God, one of one kind [singleness] and one of another [marriage].

I Corinthians 7:7

"I resent that the entire culture of this country is obsessed with kids," Rachel Agee told the author of "The Childfree Life" the day after her fortieth birthday.[15]

Rachel graduated from a Bible college where she was reportedly taught that "to be a godly woman, one must procreate for the kingdom."[16] "I just knew I couldn't trade my freedom for it," she said. She moved to Nashville to pursue her music career and stopped going to church because it was so "oppressively family-centric." Her wish for herself at forty is "to be who I've chosen to be and not to feel like I have to defend it."[17]

Rachel's story saddens us for two reasons. First, because she fails to understand and celebrate that God is all about family, and family is intended to be all about God. Church by its very nature is family-centric—church is a family!

The second reason it saddens us is that churches often fail to embrace un-married women as a vital part of the community. Women who don't have husbands or children can end up feeling like they don't fit in, or that they've somehow missed the mark.

Contrary to Rachel's perception, getting married and popping out babies is *not* a prerequisite for godliness. The apostle Paul extolled the single life as affording more time and energy for ministry (1 Cor. 7). The church *needs* singles who are dedicated to serving the Lord!

What's more, singleness reminds us that marriage and family draw their significance from that to which they point: Christ's marriage and God's family. The eternal is far greater than the temporal. As John Piper reminded us at the first True Woman conference, "In this world there are truths about Christ and His kingdom which can be more clearly displayed by womanhood in singleness."[18]

Pastor Piper explained that godly singles teach us that:

- *The family of God grows by regeneration through faith. It multiplies through spiritual birth.*

- *Relationships in Christ are more permanent and precious than relationships in families.*

- *Marriage will give way in the end to the relationship to which it was pointing all along.*

If you are unmarried and childless, it may be tempting for you to tune out the message that True Womanhood means being a *husband-liker* and *child-liker*. You may roll your eyeballs and think, "Not again. No more talk about husbands, kids, and families! . . . This just doesn't apply to me! I guess I'll never be a *true* woman." Like Rachel, you may resent the fact that the church is so obsessed with things you may or may not desire and may never have.

May we gently point out that EVERYBODY in God's household is in the "marriage," "kids," and "family" business? This teaching *does* apply to you. It applies to every woman, regardless of her life stage or circumstance.

I (Nancy) have not been given the gift of marriage or children of my own. Yet Titus 2 calls me to cultivate a love and deep appreciation for God's family plan. I need a heart for marriage and children as Mary does, though we live that out in different ways. For all of us, whether married or single, it looks like valuing, respecting, celebrating, prioritizing, and seeking to build up the marriages and children around us—whether our own, or others'. But that way of thinking requires swimming upstream—against our flesh and the culture.

"A True Woman is committed to upholding marriage and family as God's method of putting the gospel on display. Even if you are not married, you can still uphold marriage and family as valuable."[19]

Mary

Read the verses in the margin. What errors does the Bible warn of?
Check all the boxes that apply:

- ☐ Having a husband and children
- ☐ Not having a husband and children
- ☐ Disdaining husbands and children
- ☐ Idolizing husbands and children
- ☐ Picking up faulty attitudes about marriage and kids from others

Simone de Beauvoir, the mother of the modern feminist movement, taught that the institutions of marriage and motherhood were oppressive to women. She claimed that woman would only be liberated when she was "wrested away from the family."[20]

Betty Friedan, who launched the feminist movement in America in the 1960s, likened the home to a "concentration camp."[21] She claimed that in order to find fulfillment, women needed to get out of the home, get into the workforce, become economically independent, and reject traditional female roles. Full identity, freedom, and happiness for women would only come if we "changed the rules of the game" and "restructured" marriage, the family, and the home.[22]

Much like Ezekiel's day, in recent decades, our *mothers* and *sisters* have taught us to "loathe" husbands and children. In reaction to this, other voices have arisen that encourage wrong thinking on the opposite end of the spectrum. They encourage a woman to idolize marriage and family and make having the perfect husband, children, and home her god.

Describe an instance when you were exposed to faulty thinking about husbands or children being expressed or lived out.

_____

_____

Can you identify any ways that you have bought into faulty perspectives on marriage, children, or family?

_____

_____

"Love one another with brotherly [phileō] affection. Outdo one another in showing honor."

Romans 12:10

family affection

A According to 1 Corinthians 13, if we have amazing spiritual gifts, know all about the Bible, have incredible faith, and live utterly sacrificial lives—but we don't have love, what does it amount to? Nothing. We have nothing; we are nothing.

As Christian women, we reflect God's love when we love family, when we *like*, *enjoy*, and *delight* in

our family members. Don't claim to love God if you don't love your husband and your children. Don't claim to love God if you don't love your parents. Don't claim to love God if you don't love His family and don't have the heart toward marriage and children that He does.

How's your *phileō* quotient? It's one thing for people at work or in your church to think of you as a sweet, loving woman or friend. But what if we were to ask your family? What if we were to ask your husband, your children? What if we were to ask your parents, your siblings, or your roommates? Would they say your life is characterized by family affection?

→ **Look back over this week's lessons.** Ask the Lord to show you one main "take-away point" that you can apply to your life and write it down.

_____

_____

_____

_____

A PS for my (Nancy's) single sisters: As I'm editing this lesson, it happens to be Valentines Day. There are plenty of reminders that I'm not a "couple." And no one has sent me flowers today. But I realize how blessed I am to belong to God's family. And I'm grateful for opportunities to invest in others' marriages in meaningful ways and to show affection toward the many children God has placed in my life. In so doing, I can help tell the story of God's great, redeeming love!

Oh . . . I just got a text inviting me to join two families (eight children) for dinner. Think I'll take a break and go put this chapter into practice!

drawing it out, drawing it in . . .

interior renovation

process

The video for Week Three will help you process this week's lessons. You'll find this week's video, the leader's guide, and additional resources at TrueWoman201.com.

ponder

Think about the following questions. Discuss them with your friends, family, and/or small group:

1. What is the primary purpose for which God created marriage and family? How should this shape our own view of family?

2. At the beginning of the week we read an important, foundational truth: "Your womanhood is ultimately not about you. It's about displaying the glory of God and His powerful redemptive plan" (p. 63). In that light, what observations would you make about our culture's attempts to redefine gender, marriage, and family?

3. Why is Satan keen to promote unbiblical teachings about gender, sexuality, and marriage?

4. How would you describe what it means to have a "husband-liker" and "child-liker" mindset or attitude?

5. What are some practical ways you can protect marriage—both your own and that of others?

6. How did the disciples' attitude toward children differ from how Jesus viewed them? Which of those attitudes most closely matches yours? What has shaped your outlook?

7. At the first True Woman conference, John Piper said, "In this world there are truths about Christ and His kingdom which can be more clearly displayed by womanhood in singleness" (p. 80). What are some of those truths?

8. Discuss how Paul's teaching in Titus 2:4 could apply to all women, regardless of their marital or family status.

personalize it

Use this page to journal. Write down what you learned this week. Record your comments, a favorite verse, or a concept or quote that was particularly helpful or meaningful to you. Compose a prayer, letter, or poem. Jot down notes from the video or your small group session. Express your heart response to what you have studied. Personalize this week's lessons in the way that will best help you apply them to your life.

drawing it out,
drawing it in . . .

discipline

"Betcha can't eat just one!" was a slogan for Lay's potato chips that debuted in commercial advertising in the 1960s. The TV ad featured vaudeville actor Bert Lahr, who is best known for his role as the Cowardly Lion in the movie classic *Wizard of Oz.*

*A True Woman makes wise, intentional choices . . . She is "**self-controlled**."*

In the commercial, Lahr is tempted by a split-screen image of himself dressed up as the devil. "Betcha can't eat just one," says the red-horned, pointy-tailed demon, tempting Lahr with an open bag of Lay's. Lahr grabs the bag out of the devil's hand and wolfs down one chip after another. The taste is irresistible . . . *"No one can eat just one!"* The phrase becomes one of the longest-lasting taglines in American advertising.

Over the past fifty years, the public has watched as a parade of celebrities has taken the Lay's bet. Commercials have featured prominent athletes and a host of other well-known figures trying their best to stop after eating one potato chip. But guess what? They can't. The urge for another is so strong they just can't resist.

It's a clever slogan. And we think the reason it resonates with people is that it's true. It's tough to eat just one chip. You open the bag and, before you know it, you've eaten the whole thing.

And it's not just junk food that's difficult to resist. It's hard to put on the brakes in other areas of life, too. Like anger. Lust. Resentment. Self-pity. Addictions. Overspending.

The problem is not that we don't know these things are bad for us; the challenge is having the power to say "no" to things that aren't beneficial and "yes" to things that are. Many of our personal struggles and failures in the Christian life are related to a lack of self-control.

The design element we're going to study this week is discipline. A True Woman knows how to exercise restraint and how to make wise, intentional choices in her habits and daily routines. Those disciplines and choices flow out of a heart and mind that are under the Spirit's control. The grace of God and the work of Christ on the cross give her the *I-will-power* to say "yes" to the good, and the *I-won't-power* to say "no" to the bad.

The quality of self-control isn't just for women. It's mentioned in the book of Titus as a trait that's important for elders (1:7–9) and older men (2:2). It's the *only* characteristic that's mentioned in relation to younger men (2:6).

In Titus 2:12, Paul instructs *all* believers to live self-controlled lives. So why does he repeat the trait in his lists of what needs to be taught to various groups in the church. Wasn't he being redundant? Why didn't he save himself some space and time by leaving self-control off the gender-specific lists and just talking about it as something everyone needs to learn?

As we mentioned in the introduction to the first week's lessons, the reason for the differing lists is that men and women are different. Paul's lists counteract our sex-specific sin tendencies and point us back to our divine design. So although "self-control" is important for both sexes, there are certain aspects of it that are particularly challenging for women and other aspects that are particularly challenging for men.

There are aspects of self-control that a woman who's "been there" can teach another woman more effectively than a man can. For example, how to exercise self-control at "that-time-of-the-

month." Or during those years of exhaustion from getting up to nurse a baby. Or when our hormones are rewriting all our physical and emotional wiring.

As women, we can help each other handle challenges unique to womanhood. A girlfriend can tell you, "Honey, that's just your hormones talking!" You know she "gets" it. Many a husband has learned—the hard way—that it can be harder for his wife to receive input from him on these kinds of matters than from a mature, godly woman.

Self-control isn't *exclusive* to womanhood; but it does have a unique gender-specific application for women. That's why Paul instructed the older women to teach the *newbies* this important trait. →

say no to the marshmallow

Have you ever heard of the marshmallow test? In the late 1960s, researchers submitted hundreds of four-year-olds to an ingenious little test of willpower: the kids were placed at a table in a small room with a marshmallow and told they could either eat the treat now, or, if they could hold out until the researcher returned, they would get two.

Most children said they would wait. But some failed to resist the pull of temptation for even a minute. Many, like the child who stroked the marshmallow as if it were a tiny stuffed animal, struggled a little longer before eventually giving in. The most successful participants figured out how to distract themselves from the treat's seduction—by covering their eyes with their hands, turning around so they couldn't see it, kicking the desk, tugging on their hair, or singing songs, for instance—and delayed gratification for a full fifteen minutes until the researcher came back.

Follow-up studies on these preschoolers found that those who were able to delay gratification were significantly less likely than the kids who gobbled the snack in less than a minute to have behavioral problems, drug addictions, or obesity by the time they got to high school. The gratification-delayers also scored an average of 210 points higher on the SAT.[2]

Self-control is one of the fundamental character strengths emphasized by KIPP, a network of public charter schools across the US that are renowned for achieving dramatic improvement of inner-city students' behavior and academic achievement. The core feature of the KIPP approach is that character matters for success. It teaches children to restrain their impulses and exercise self-discipline for the sake of greater joys. The KIPP school in Philadelphia even gives its students a shirt that sports the slogan "Don't Eat the Marshmallow!"[3]

"Older women . . . are to teach what is good, and so train the young women to . . . be self-controlled."

Titus 2:3–5

"Strict exercise of self-control is an essential feature of the Christian's life."[1]

Dietrich Bonhoeffer

The trait of self-control isn't innate. Titus 2 emphasizes that it's something that requires training. What's more, it indicates that older women have a responsibility to teach younger women how to cultivate this quality in their lives. If you want to become the woman God wants you to be, it's vital that you learn self-control. And the best place to learn this is from an older woman who herself has learned and models godly self-control.

Read the verse in the margin on page 88. Circle the word self-controlled.

Mark the following statements as true (T) or false (F).

_____ The amount of self-control a woman has is primarily based on her personality type.

_____ Self-control is like a muscle—the more you exercise it, the stronger it gets.

_____ A self-controlled woman is rigid and joyless. She's more miserable than the woman who gives in to her impulses.

_____ Self-control is simply a matter of setting some goals and exercising your willpower.

_____ Self-control is first and foremost a heart issue.

Imagine you could toss a penny in a wishing well and immediately gain increased self-control in three personal behaviors, habits, thoughts, or attitudes. Which three would you choose?

1. _____

2. _____

3. _____

"Lack of self-control in one area of our lives makes us more vulnerable to lack of discipline in other, more major areas."[4]

Nancy

self-con·trol [**self**-*kuhn*-**trohl**] *noun*
Control or restraint of oneself or one's actions, feelings, etc.
Self-discipline, self-restraint, willpower, levelheadedness.

According to the American Psychological Association, Americans name the lack of willpower as the number-one reason they struggle to meet their goals.[5] People just can't seem to do what they set out to do. The number of New Year's resolutions that get made and broken each year is staggering. Only 8% of Americans successfully achieve their resolutions: 92% aren't kept. 80% fail in less than three weeks.[6]

Psychologists and life coaches advise us to come up with better strategies and more accountability to increase our willpower and odds of success. They suggest various techniques to help deal with temptation, distraction, procrastination, and impulsiveness.

Go into any bookstore and you'll find a wealth of information about impulse management, stress management, anger management, weight management, financial management, time management, communication, goal setting, and all the core competencies that women need to make life work.

Although this kind of advice can help modify behavior, it doesn't generally address the underlying issue. According to the Bible, self-control is more of a heart issue than a matter of personal management.

Read the verses in the margin. Where does self-control come from?

_____

_____

What characteristics go hand in hand with self-control?

_____

_____

How does the Bible's perspective on self-control differ from society's ideas about it?

_____

_____

_____

_____

"But the fruit of the Spirit is . . . self-control."
Galatians 5:22–23

"For the grace of God has appeared, bringing salvation for all people, training us to renounce ungodliness and worldly passions, and to live self-controlled, upright, and godly lives in the present age."
Titus 2:11–12

The Greek word for self-control is *sōphrōn*. Several different words are used to translate this one Greek word in our English translations of the Bible. For example, in Titus chapter 2, the King James Version of the Bible translates *sōphrōn* as "temperate" (v. 2), "discreet" (v. 5), and "sober" (v. 12). Self-controlled. Temperate. Discreet. Sober. Why so many words? What exactly does *sōphrōn* mean?

Sōphrōn is hard to capture in just one English word. It's derived from two Greek words. The first part of the word, *so*, comes from *sōzō*, which means "safe,"[7] or from *sōas*, which means "sound."[8] The second part, *phrēn*, means "mind." It's sometimes written as "fren" and is found in the English language in words like schizophrenia, phrenitis (inflammation of the brain), frenzy, and frenetic. *Phrēn* likely comes from the ancient Greek word *phrao*, which means "to rein in or curb."

Essentially, *sōphrōn* means having a *safe (saved), reined-in mind*, or a *sound mind*. It's a person who acts like they're in their right mind, spiritually speaking. *Sōphrōn* is an adjective. It describes what a person IS—one's mindset—more than one's behavior. *Sōphrōn* enables us to have self-controlled behavior, but it all starts with a self-controlled mindset —with a saved, safe, reined-in, sound mind.

Write your own definition of *sōphrōn*.

_____

_____

_____

We'll be talking more about the definition of *sōphrōn* throughout the rest of this week. We think you'll agree that all of us could benefit from having a *sōphrōn* mind.

→ **Do you want to exercise more self-control?** Close today's lesson in prayer. Ask the Lord to train you by His grace to have a *sōphrōn* mind and life.

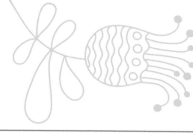

The lone engineer on duty had one last task before he caught a cab down to the quaint tourist town in the valley to turn in for the night. He had to "tie down" the train: apply its airbrakes, set the handbrakes on all five locomotives, and engage enough handbrakes on the railcars to secure the roughly 10,000-ton load.

Applying the handbrakes was a labor-intensive process, especially for this train, whose load of crude-oil tankers stretched almost a mile up the track. The engineer had to clamber up each consecutive tanker and manually crank a large wheel for two to three minutes until the mechanism was tight.

> "Self-control and discipline are gifts we can use to constrain sin and promote holiness. They are gifts we can use to hinder old habits and promote new, better patterns." [9]
>
> **Tim Challies**

Technically, on a track with a grade that steep, he should have engaged at least thirty of the seventy-two railcar brakes.[10] But the handbrakes were just for backup. The locomotive's airbrakes were plenty strong enough to secure the train on their own. They had faithfully held the train in place night after night for as long he could remember. So after setting just eleven railcar handbrakes, the engineer went to his hotel, crawled into bed, and fell fast asleep.

Shortly after midnight, on July 6, 2013, the unthinkable happened. The airbrakes failed, and the handbrakes were insufficient to hold back the weight of the load. Unmanned, the train began to roll down the seven-and-a-half-mile slope toward the tourist town, picking up speed along the way. Witnesses at the outskirts saw the out-of-control string of railcars roar past in the dark, fireworks of sparks wildly spewing from shrieking metal wheels.

The train derailed and crashed in the heart of Lac-Mégantic, Quebec, beside the Musi-Café, a popular restaurant and bar still buzzing with patrons and staff. A river of oil spilled into the street and exploded into a blazing inferno. Half of the town's center was incinerated. Forty-seven people were cremated alive. A few months later, a friend of mine (Nancy) visited the site while on a business trip; he said it still looked as though a bomb had gone off.

The horrible, horrible tragedy at Lac-Mégantic illustrates what can happen when brakes fail. In today's lesson, you'll see that "failed brakes" are an apt metaphor for a lack of self-control.

Yesterday, we learned that *sōphrōn* means having a saved, safe, *reined-in*, sound mind. *Sōphrōn* contains the idea of restraint. The last syllable, *phrēn* or *fren*, likely comes from the ancient Greek word *phrao*, which means "to rein in or curb."

Interestingly, modern Greek uses the word *phrena/frena* for *car brakes*. What's more, *handbrake* in Spanish is *freno de mano*. In each instance, the word for *brake* stems from the same ancient Greek root as the second syllable of *sōphrōn*. It's a powerful word-picture: self-control (*sōphrōn*) involves *putting on the brakes*.

putting on the brakes

Fractured relationships. Affairs. Broken marriages. STDs. Addictions. Abortions. Debts. Eating disorders. We often hear heartbreaking stories from women who've crashed and burned. And usually, it's because they've had some sort of "brake failure" in their lives.

Unlike the train crash in Lac-Mégantic however, the crashes in our lives generally aren't caused by a major, one-time brake failure. More often, they're a result of a series of small failures along the way.

A relationship doesn't grow cold and ugly overnight. It happens gradually. The couple repeatedly fails to put on the brakes with their attitudes, words, and actions. Hundreds of small, seemingly insignificant failures accumulate to sour the relationship. Often the pair can't even identify when it was they got off track.

A woman doesn't just wake up one morning and decide to have an affair. No. The affair happens when day after day she fails to put on the brakes with her thoughts, fantasies, and sexual boundaries.

Without self-control, we have little or no defense against sin and temptation. Like a city without walls, and like the failed brakes on the Lac-Mégantic train, there's nothing to prevent an impending disaster.

On the following chart, look up each reference and draw a line to match it with the area in which it indicates the need to exercise self-control:

	Area requiring self-control
Proverbs 16:32	friendships
1 Thessalonians 4:3–5	body
1 Corinthians 9:27	emotions
Colossians 4:5	appearance
1 Timothy 2:9–10	speech
Proverbs 13:3	possessions
Luke 12:15	sexuality
Proverbs 1:15	time

Can you identify an instance when someone's failure to put on the brakes in one of the above areas caused them to crash and burn?

_____

_____

Read Proverbs 25:28 in the margin. Explain how a lack of self-control is "like a city broken into and left without walls."

_____

_____

"A man without self-control is like a city broken into and left without walls."

Proverbs 25:28

Ancient cities were protected by walls and towers. Proverbs 25:28 presents a picture of an attacking army making a breach or opening in a city's defensive system. As a result, the city is left without protection. Losing self-control is like that. Self-control serves a protective function in our lives. A lack of self-control gives the enemy opportunity and leaves us vulnerable to attack. Without self-control, we have little or no defense against sin and temptation. Like a city without walls, and like the failed brakes on the Lac-Mégantic train, there's nothing to prevent an impending disaster.

gaining self-control

What about you? How are you doing in the area of self-control? Be honest with yourself. Are you off track with your mouth? Do you need to restrain your use of foul language? Coarse jokes? Cutting sarcasm? How about gossip or criticism? And what about your thought life? Do you need to rein in your daydreams and imaginations? How about the amount of time you spend on Facebook? Or TV? Or texting? Do you need to exercise more self-control in your media habits? And how about your eating or spending habits?

We think you'll agree that we all need more *sōphrōn*! It's a *sōphrōn* state of mind that enables us to "put on the brakes" and curb fleshly, unhealthy desires. A *sōphrōn* state of mind will help you gain more self-control in every area of your life—your tongue, your behavior, your habits, your sexual life— all of this will flow out of a *sōphrōn* mind.

What are one or two areas of your life in which you need greater *sōphrōn*?

_____

_____

Choose a verse from the previous page or visit TrueWoman201.com to pick a verse that applies to your situation. Write the verse down in the space below. Work on memorizing it each day this week.

_____

_____

→ **Close in prayer.** Ask the Lord to bring this verse to mind and to help you apply it the next time you need to put on the brakes in this area of your life.

pulling out all the stops

You've likely heard the phrase "pulling out all the stops." For example, "Jane pulled out all the stops for her daughter's wedding." Pulling out all the stops means to be fully invested, to hold nothing back. But do you know where the expression comes from?

I (Nancy) learned about "pulling out the stops" when I took a semester of organ lessons in college. The knobs on a pipe organ are called "stops."

When these knobs are pushed in, they restrict air from flowing through the pipes. The reduced air dampens or completely shuts off the sound each pipe can make. Conversely, "pulling out all the stops" allows each pipe to be filled with the maximum amount of air, causing the organ to produce its richest, fullest, and most vibrant sounds.

Yesterday, we learned about the need for brakes in our lives . . . about the need to "put ON the stops," so to speak. Today, you'll see that the most powerful and effective way to *put on the brakes* in your thoughts and actions is to *pull out all the stops* in your relationship with the Lord.

At the root, self-control and self-discipline problems are spiritual issues. As such, they require spiritual solutions. You probably don't need another popular, flavor-of-the-month, self-management technique in order to conquer that habit you've been battling all these years. Chances are you already know what and how you need to change. You just need the power to follow through and actually do it.

Read the verses in the margins on this and the next page.

What does the indwelling Spirit of God provide for us? Check all that apply:

- [ ] Power
- [ ] Self-control
- [ ] Excellence
- [ ] Everything we need to live self-disciplined lives

Why do we fail to exercise self-control? Check all that apply:

- [ ] We're not religious enough
- [ ] We haven't yet found the right technique
- [ ] We just don't have enough willpower
- [ ] We deny the power of God

denying His power

P Paul prayed that we might understand the immeasurable greatness of God's power. He wanted us to realize that this power is not only vast, but that it is also accessible. It is at work IN us.

If you believe in Jesus, the very same power that raised Christ from the dead is at work in YOU! Just ponder that for a moment. Do you believe it? It's hard to comprehend, isn't it? But the Bible says it's so.

If we're followers of Christ we already have all the power we need. We have the power to make right choices. We have the power to say "yes" to what's right and "no" to what's wrong. We have the power to resist temptation. We have the power to exercise self-discipline and self-control. Because we have God's Spirit, we have EVERYTHING we need to succeed at life and godliness. We don't need to beg God for more willpower. The power we need is already at our disposal.

In his second epistle to Timothy, Paul described certain people as self-absorbed, money-hungry, self-promoting, arrogant, profane, coarse, contemptuous, unbending, slandering, abusive, undisciplined, lustful, and wild. They lacked self-control. They did all the right religious stuff, like going to church and Bible studies. But they showed no evidence of spiritual progress or growth.

They were enslaved to bad habits. They demonstrated no success in reining in their attitudes, their mouths, and unhealthy personal appetites. They weren't any different from the previous year, or the year before that. If anything, things had gotten worse. They were more impatient, more critical, more argumentative, more resentful, more back-stabbing, more self-justifying, more unloving, more out-of-control. Over time, their lives had become increasingly chaotic and unkempt. (See 2 Tim. 3:2–7.)

These people claimed to have a relationship with Christ, but their lives demonstrated that they had no such thing. They had the outward trappings of godliness, but no real spiritual life. Their problem was that *they denied the power of God*, the only source of true life and godliness.

What do you think it means to deny the power of God?

_____

_____

> "Over-indulgence blinds us to the truth, turning us inward, making us slaves to our own insatiable desires."[11]
> **Don W. King**

denyer or relyer

The Greek word translated "deny" means to refuse, disregard, decline to agree with, and pay no attention to.[12] A true believer does not deny the power of God in the ultimate sense that Paul describes in 2 Timothy 3. But at some level, we deny His power when we ignore it or don't appropriate it to change our lives.

A woman who denies the power of God may appear to be godly. She may request prayer at her weekly small group for her temper or the challenge of loving her difficult husband or her struggle with an unhealthy habit. Perhaps she laments her lack of willpower or self-discipline. But deep down, she doesn't truly think that God's power is adequate for her particular need. In her battle against the flesh, flesh always seems to win.

Every true child of God has at his disposal all the power he or she needs to please God. Denying the power of God is the opposite of having faith in the power of God. When it comes to self-control, you can either DENY or RELY. You can deny that you have enough power, or you can rely on His power that is always enough.

A DENYer ignores/forgets about the Spirit.—A RELYer is attuned to the Spirit.

A DENYer experiences limited power.—A RELYer's power supply is unlimited.

A DENYer indulges the flesh.—A RELYer denies the flesh.

A DENYer suspects she'll never change.—A RELYer has faith that she can.

A DENYer gives up trying.—A RELYer perseveres.

A DENYer depends on self to change—A RELYer depends on God to change.

What about you? With regard to the three self-control challenges you identified on page 89, are you more of a DENYer or RELYer? Explain your response.

_____

_____

On the list above, circle which "RELYer" trait you would like to see more of in your life.

Read Galatians 5:16–25 in your Bible. What might it look like for you to "pull out all the stops" and walk in the Spirit? Do you believe this is really possible?

_____

_____

→ **Close in prayer.** Ask the Lord to help you pull out all the stops and rely on His Holy Spirit to give you self-control.

battlefield of the mind

This week we've been studying the element of self-discipline. A True Woman makes wise, intentional choices . . . she is "self-controlled." God's grace gives her the *I-will-power* to say "yes" to the good, and the *I-won't-power* to say "no" to the bad. Through the indwelling power of the Spirit, she exercises restraint, governs her desires, emotions, and behavior, and is disciplined in her habits.

In the first lesson we examined the Greek word for self-control, *sōphrōn*. *Sōphrōn* is sound-mindedness that results in self-controlled, sound living.

In the second lesson, we continued talking about the definition of *sōphrōn*, picking up on the fact that it contains the idea of restraint. Self-control involves *putting on the brakes* and curbing fleshly, unhealthy desires.

In Day 3, we learned that self-control requires the power of the Holy Spirit. The most powerful and effective way to put on the brakes in your thoughts and actions is to *pull out all the stops* in your relationship with the Lord.

Today, we want to focus on the fact that self-control requires sound thinking. The fight for self-control takes place on the battlefield of your mind.

Underline the definition of *sōphrōn* in the second paragraph above.

Explain what you think it means to be sound-minded:

_____

_____

"Not being able to govern events, I govern myself."[13]

Michel de Montaigne

Irrational behavior, compulsive behavior, impulsive behavior, unstable behavior, fleshly behavior—all these things are evidence of a mind that is not sound, "for as [a man] thinks in his heart, so is he" (Prov. 23:7 NKJV). That means **the battle begins in the mind**. And that's why God says you must have a sound mind. You must learn how to think straight.

An unstable mind will result in unstable behavior. A self-indulgent mind will result in self-indulgent behavior. A sound mind will result in sound behavior. A disciplined mind will result in disciplined behavior. A godly mind will result in godly behavior.

Sometimes we focus too much on trying to change or stop the behavior, when what we need to do is go back and find out what kind of thinking produced that kind of behavior in the first place. It's easier to fix the "what" if we understand the "why."

Why did you lash out at your husband?

"Because *he* made a cutting, sarcastic comment."

No. What happened is that your husband acted in such a way that it brought to the surface and revealed your unsound thinking.

Why did you scream at your child?

"Well, if *she* hadn't drawn a mural on the wall with her magic markers . . ."

No. What happened is that your three-year-old acted in such a way that it brought to the surface and revealed your unsound thinking.

Why did you blow your budget and buy those shoes you didn't really need?

"Because they were a really great deal."

No. What happened is that the slashed price tag brought to the surface and revealed your unsound thinking.

What were you thinking? Here are some examples of the type of false beliefs that may have accounted for your behavior:

> I have a right to return tit for tat.
> Life should be easy.
> He's the problem, not me.
> I deserve to be happy.
> I just can't handle it!
> Indulging is better than holding out.

Do you see how wrong thinking leads to wrong behavior? What if you paused to recalibrate your mind with truth? When your husband made that cutting remark, what if you had told yourself, "*Do not be overcome by evil, but overcome evil with good*" (Rom. 12:21)? Or "*Let no corrupting talk come out of your mouths, but only such as is good for building up, as fits the occasion, that it may give grace to those who hear*" (Eph. 4:29)?

When you saw the mess your child made on the wall, what if you had thought, *"Be strengthened with all power, according to his glorious might, for all endurance and patience with joy"* (Col. 1:11)?

When that cute pair of pumps started calling your name, what if you had countered with, *"Whoever trusts in his riches will fall, but the righteous will flourish like a green leaf"* (Prov. 11:28)?

Would your behavior have been different? We suspect it would have been.

Read the following case study:

> Jen felt flattered when Brad, her handsome, married boss, stopped her in the hallway and praised her for her work. His eyes had lingered for a moment and had set her heart aflutter. After that day, she couldn't get him off her mind.
>
> Getting ready for work in the morning, she spent extra time on her appearance. She went out of her way to bump into Brad more often, inventing reasons to drop by his office with a question. Unlike her caustic husband, Brad truly appreciated her.

> It started off innocently enough. But it wasn't long before the compliments were augmented by flirtation, business lunches, heart-to-heart talks, texts, emails, and ever-deepening emotional attachment. It was on a business trip to Chicago that they consummated their illicit affair.

What was Jen thinking? What are some false beliefs that likely led to her moral failure?

_____

_____

The Bible teaches that we have a mortal enemy named Satan, who is "the father of lies" (John 8:44). He specializes in false beliefs and corrupt thinking. You need *sōphrōn* because your adversary the devil prowls around, peddling unsound ideas. He actively works against you, to mess up your thinking.

"Be sober-minded [self-controlled]; be watchful. Your adversary the devil prowls around like a roaring lion, seeking someone to devour."

I Peter 5:8

"Do not be conformed to this world, but be transformed by the renewal of your mind, that by testing you may discern what is the will of God, what is good and acceptable and perfect."

Romans 12:2

What are you thinking? Identify the false beliefs that lie behind the self-control challenge you identified on page 94.

_____

_____

_____

_____

According to Romans 12:2, how can you combat unsound thinking?

_____

_____

_____

right thinking and right praying

P eter exhorts readers to be self-controlled and sober-minded "for the sake of your prayers" (1 Peter 4:7). Think about that connection for a moment. It's obvious that sound, clear-minded thinking can help us combat false beliefs and make wise decisions. But it does more than that. Peter's primary expectation is that sound thinking will result in more praying, and more sound praying. Thinking right helps me pray right.

Right thinking helps me see things from God's perspective. Praying helps me call upon and submit to God in light of that perspective, and to obtain the guidance and power I need to exercise self-control in the situation. Right thinking and prayer are key to winning the battle over destructive habits.

→ **Ask the Lord to** help you renew your mind with right thinking "for the sake of your prayers." Make it a habit to turn to Him to obtain the guidance and power you need for self-control.

cultivating *sōphrōn*

Self-control (*sōphrōn*) is the ability to choose wise actions. When we know what we ought to do, but fail to do it . . . we lack self-control.

When we've already had more than enough to eat, but have another serving anyhow . . . we lack self-control. When we stay up late to surf the Internet, knowing full well that we have to be up early the next morning . . . we lack self-control. When we procrastinate doing our taxes, leaving ourselves in a last minute panic to get them done . . . we lack self-control. When we spend, spend, spend and never save . . . we lack self-control. When we have time for hours of Facebook and TV each day, but can't find time for Bible study and prayer . . . we lack self-control. When our emotions are controlled by circumstances . . . we lack self-control. When we speak rashly without thinking . . . we lack self-control. When we choose the fleeting pleasures of sin, forfeiting the long-term, eternal blessing of living in obedience to Christ . . . we lack self-control. When we're big on intent, but small on follow-through . . . we lack self-control.

None of us can read the above paragraph and claim to have arrived. I (Mary) think about that handful of chocolate chips I just mindlessly threw in my mouth when I walked into the kitchen to take a break from writing. I (Nancy) think about how I procrastinated with answering emails this morning and surfed some blogs instead.

Like you, we've had many self-control challenges over the years: getting to bed and getting up at a reasonable hour, having a regular quiet time, keeping our houses tidy, exercising regularly, eating temperately, managing our emotions, thinking the best of others, having patience, watching our words . . .

Fighting for self-control is an ongoing challenge. We make gains in one area, and then notice another that requires attention. Every day we win some battles and lose others. Some self-control issues are tough. They may last for years. Nevertheless, we can both testify to the Lord's faithfulness.

Looking back, we can see that we have grown in this area. By His grace, we are more disciplined now than when we were younger. And we are committed to press on!

Self-control/discipline requires training and effort. Titus 2 indicates that women have a responsibility to teach other women how to cultivate this quality in their lives. In your small group meeting, you'll have an opportunity to seek out some specific advice for one of your current self-control challenges. But we'd like to give you some general steps that will help you get started.

six steps to cultivate *sōphrōn*

Through the gospel of Christ and His work on the cross on our behalf, our fleshly, sinful choices can be overcome and we can walk in the freedom and victory of His resurrection life. Here are some practical steps to develop self-control (*sōphrōn*), which begins in the heart and the mind and ultimately manifests itself in our behavior and choices.

1: **REFLECT** on the situation

"Be sober-minded; be watchful. Your adversary the devil prowls around like a roaring lion, seeking someone to devour." (1 Peter 5:8)

- In which area of your life do you need more self-control/personal discipline? (E.g., *I become impatient and irritable when I visit my mom.*)

- Identify the circumstance that usually triggers a lack of self-control. (E.g., *I snap when she tells me what I should do. I get defensive and angry when she gives me advice about my friends and job.*)

- Take some time to evaluate the faulty thoughts and motivations behind your lack of self-control. Identify unsound attitudes, thoughts, and beliefs. (E.g., *I believe she doesn't have my best interests at heart. I feel like she's judgmental. I'm too arrogant to consider her advice.*)

2: **READY** yourself for action

"Prepare your minds for action, keep sober in spirit [self-controlled]."
(1 Peter 1:13 NASB)

- Recognize that your lack of self-control is a spiritual issue and as such will require a spiritual solution.

- Counter your unsound thinking with sound, biblical thinking. What is true? What does the Lord want you to think, feel, and believe? (E.g., *I can't know her heart. The Lord wants me to think the best about her, to be humble, patient, and to honor her.*)

- Choose an applicable verse to memorize and meditate on.

- What else will you do to ready yourself for action? (E.g., *I will have my roommate pray with me before I go for a visit.*)

3: **REMEMBER** your commitment

"Ponder the path of your feet; then all your ways will be sure." (Prov. 4:26)

- Most of us act and react without thinking. We disengage our minds and operate on impulse. To change a wrong pattern, it can help to put a *"sōphrōn* comma" between the circumstance and our reaction.

- The *"sōphrōn* comma" is a slight pause to "ponder the path of our feet," to consider whether our next action is sound. Is that bag of cookies calling your name? Don't just mindlessly dive in. Ponder the path of your feet with a *sōphrōn* comma. Ask yourself, is this wise? Is this taking me a step closer or a step farther away from being pleasing to the Lord in this area of my life?

4: **RELY** on the Holy Spirit

"Walk by the Spirit, and you will not gratify the desires of the flesh." (Gal. 5:16)

- During your *"sōphrōn* comma" you determined the right course of action. Now you need the power to follow through. The indwelling Holy Spirit will enable you to say no to the demands of your flesh and yes to that which honors God.

- Peter expected that right thinking would lead to right praying. Pray and ask the Lord for His grace and help; then step out in faith and obedience.

"For the grace of God has appeared ... training us to renounce ungodliness and worldly passions, and to live self-controlled, upright, and godly lives in the present age, waiting for our blessed hope, the appearing of the glory of our great God and Savior Jesus Christ."

Titus 2:11–13

5: **REPLACE** wrong patterns with virtuous ones

"Put off your old self . . . and put on the new self." (Eph. 4:22–24)

- When we leave a void in our lives, another sinful behavior is just waiting to rush in if we don't purposely fill the void with something better (see Luke 11:24–26). Whenever we "put off" a sinful or non-self-controlled behavior, we need to "put on" a virtuous behavior.

- Proactively identity and cultivate good habits that could replace bad habits in your life. For example, it's not enough to stop spending four hours a day on Facebook; what will you put in its place? How can you use that time wisely—by reading Scripture, spending one-on-one time with your children or friends, writing encouraging notes, inviting guests over for dinner, etc.?

6: **RESOLVE** to keep pursuing a *sōphrōn* life

"Every athlete exercises self-control in all things. They do it to receive a perishable wreath, but we an imperishable." (1 Cor. 9:25)

- Don't beat yourself up when you fail. God's grace is sufficient for all your shortcomings. Reevaluate. Perhaps you need to change how you ready yourself for action, or perhaps you need input from someone who has fought and won the same battle. Don't give up. Press on toward the prize—for His glory!

- Remember the kids waiting for the researcher to return so they could have two marshmallows instead of just one? We're waiting for something more wonderful than our minds can comprehend—the return of Christ! And that's what ultimately motivates us to "make every effort" to be sound-minded and self-controlled.

Use the Six Steps to Cultivate *Sōphrōn* to complete the "My *Sōphrōn* Worksheet" on page 109. You can use the self-control challenge you identified earlier, or choose a different one.

drawing it out, drawing it in . . .

↓

interior renovation

process

The video for Week Four will help you process this week's lessons. You'll find this week's video, the leader's guide, and additional resources at TrueWoman201.com.

ponder

Think about the following questions. Discuss them with your friends, family, and/or small group:

1. What is the benefit of gender-specific instruction—older women teaching younger women—when it comes to living a disciplined life?

2. From a biblical perspective, how is self-control different from behavior modification?

3. Explain the meaning of the Greek word *sōphrōn*. What role do our thoughts play in the development of self-control? Give some examples of how our mindset determines our behavior.

4. What is the most effective way to "put on the brakes" in areas where you find yourself out of control? On the flip side what would it look like to "pull out all the stops" in your relationship with God?

5. We learned on Day 3 that we don't need to beg God for more willpower. Why is that true?

6. Describe the difference between a DENYer and a RELYer (see p. 99). How can we move from being DENYers to RELYers?

7. As you consider where in your life self-control is a struggle, can you identify the false beliefs that underlie your struggle? What specific truths can you apply to dislodge those false beliefs?

8. Review the Six Steps to Cultivate *Sōphrōn* (pp. 105–107). Where in your life will you begin today to step out in faith and apply these steps?

personalize

Refer to the Six Steps to Cultivate *Sōphrōn* on pages 105–107 to complete the following worksheet and personalize this week's lessons on self-control. Use the self-control challenge you identified earlier (see page 94), or choose a different one. You can use the questions again in the future, to help you work through other self-control/discipline challenges.

my *sōphrōn* worksheet

STEP 1: Reflect on the situation
Circumstance that normally triggers my lack of self-control/discipline: _____

_____

_____

My unsound attitudes, thoughts, and beliefs: _____

_____

_____

STEP 2: Ready myself for action
What does the Lord want me to think, feel, and believe? _____

_____

_____

Applicable verse(s): _____

_____

STEP 3: Remember my commitment
How I will remember my commitment: _____

_____

_____

Ask the Lord to help you put a *"sōphrōn* comma" between the circumstance and
your reaction.

STEP 4: Rely on the Holy Spirit
Am I depending on my own willpower or the power of the Spirit to cultivate self-control?

Step 5: Replace wrong patterns with virtuous ones
What sinful or non-self-controlled areas of my life need to be "put off"?

_____

_____

What wise, godly habits can I "put on" in their place?

_____

_____

STEP 6: Resolve to keep pursuing a *sōphrōn* life
Do I need to adjust my strategy? How can I keep making "every effort" to
develop self-control in this area?

drawing it out,
drawing it in . . .

virtue

A ccording to Roman folklore, soap was first discovered by a group of women who went to wash their clothes in the Tiber River, beneath Mount Sapo, where priests regularly sacrificed animals. The previous night's rain had washed the animal fat and wood ashes from the altar down into the river. To their surprise, the women found that the fat and ash in the water made it easier to get their laundry clean.

*A True Woman cultivates goodness . . . She is "**pure**."*

The Romans mixed goat tallow with beech tree ashes to produce soap for cleaning. They also used soap for medicinal purposes, to treat skin ailments. The demand for soap was apparently substantial, because a soap factory—complete with neat stacks of bars— was discovered in the ruins of Pompeii, one of the cities buried by the volcanic eruption of Mt. Vesuvius in AD 79.

However, as much as the Roman Empire would like to take credit for inventing soap, history indicates that soap making actually dates back to the Babylonians. Their inscriptions contain the earliest known written soap recipe, which also called for a mixture of animal fat, wood ashes, and water.

The ashes of certain trees and plants contain a high concentration of potassium carbonate salt. This highly alkaline substance is also called "potash." When water is filtered through potash, the resulting liquid is called "lye." Lye is a strong corrosive, valued for its cleaning and grease-dissolving abilities.

The Israelites used saltwort as their source of lye. This alkali-bearing plant abounds on the shores of the Dead Sea and the Mediterranean. To make soap, the Israelites mixed lye derived from the saltwort with olive oil. The Bible indicates that they used soap to wash their hands (Job 9:30), bodies (Jer. 2:22), and clothes (Mal. 3:2).

It's interesting that the Hebrew words for lye (*bor*) and soap (*borit*) are both derived from the root word for "purify."[1] The word is used by King David, for example, in Psalm 18:20: "The LORD dealt with me according to my righteousness; according to the cleanness [*bor*] of my hands he rewarded me."

David equated "clean hands" with "righteousness." This association is made throughout Scripture. Physical cleanliness is often used as a metaphor for spiritual purity and goodness.

This week we're studying the design element of virtue. A True Woman is "pure." (Virtue and purity are two sides of the same coin: the presence of goodness and the absence of defilement.) Using the Bible's metaphor, we could say that she has a clean heart and life.

Purity appears in Titus' sex-specific list for women. It's also commanded of women elsewhere in Scripture (1 Peter 3:2). Purity is an important element of womanhood. As we pointed out earlier, that's not to say that purity is unimportant for men. It's equally vital that men aim to be pure (cf. Ps. 119:9; 1 Tim. 4:12; 5:2). But as Paul writes to Pastor Titus under the inspiration of the Holy Spirit, he specifically challenges women to be pure. In the broader context of this epistle, where he is dealing with how the church can successfully shine the light of the gospel in a dark world, this seems to suggest that Christian women can point to the meaning and significance of purity in a special way.

The New Testament refers to the church as Christ's "pure virgin" (2 Cor. 11:2). Christ cleanses His Bride "by the washing of water with the word" so that she might present herself to Him "in splendor, without spot or wrinkle." She and her clothes are clean . . . "holy and without blemish"

(Eph. 5:25–28). When the apostle John caught a glimpse of Christ's future heavenly marriage, he observed that the Bride readies herself for it by clothing herself with fine white linen, "bright and pure" (Rev. 19:7–8). The Bride gives attention to her appearance; she wants to be sure that both she and her dress are spotlessly clean and beautiful for her Groom.

God wants His daughters to shine a spotlight on the beauty of the gospel by exhibiting a joyful, bride-like desire to present ourselves to Christ dressed in spiritual splendor, without spot or wrinkle, holy and without blemish, bright, clean, and pure. In this week's lesson you'll find out more about why virtue is a critical element of true womanhood and discover how you can cultivate it in your life. →

more than 99⁴⁴ᐟ¹⁰⁰% pure

The Ivory soap slogan "99⁴⁴ᐟ¹⁰⁰% Pure" was first used by Proctor & Gamble in 1882. At the time, the use of soap for personal hygiene was not widespread in America. Imported European Castile soap made of olive oil was a luxury too expensive for everyone but the wealthy. Proctor & Gamble sold a soap made of tallow, but it was hard and yellowish and had an unpleasant aroma.

> "Older women . . .
> are to teach what is
> good, and so train
> the young women
> to be . . . pure."
>
> **Titus 2:3–5**

After years of experimentation, James Gamble developed a formula for a palm-and-coconut-oil-based white soap. It could be produced with inexpensive ingredients, and its fragrance was much more

appealing. The search for a name ended when Harley Proctor had a sudden flash of inspiration at a Sunday church service. The Scripture reading was from Psalm 45: "*All thy garments smell of myrrh, and aloes, and cassia, **out of the ivory palaces**, whereby they have made thee glad*" (v. 8 KJV). The first bar of "Ivory" was sold in 1879.

It was fortunate for Proctor & Gamble that the invention of Ivory coincided with Louis Pasteur proving that germs existed. Pasteur demonstrated that bacterial contaminants and microbial pathogens invisible to the human eye were responsible for sickness and disease. Cleanliness served a higher purpose than merely looking and smelling good. A clean body was essential to good health.

With the public's focus on Pasteur's scientific discoveries, Harley Proctor decided on a new angle to hawk Ivory soap. He figured if he could come up with a lab test showing Ivory was "purer" than other soaps—containing fewer unnecessary ingredients and no contaminants—he'd win sales. There wasn't a standard for purity in soap, so Harley hired a scientist to concoct one.

The consultant concluded that 100% pure soap would consist of nothing but two ingredients: fatty acids and alkali.

With the definition for soap purity thus established, Harley sent Ivory soap and Castile soap, commonly considered to be the best soap on the market, to chemists for analysis. To his delight, they concluded that Ivory soap was purer. Only about half of 1% of the total ingredient list didn't qualify as a fatty acid or alkali. Ivory was $99^{44/100}$% pure.

Proctor & Gamble promoted "purity" as the soap's distinguishing feature, and even linked outer to inner purity. For example, one ad proclaimed, "Free from *impurities*, Ivory soap is the product with which good mothers maintain their children's purity."[2]

Highlight the word *pure* in Titus 2:3–5 in the margin.

How would you define the word *pure*? You can use a dictionary or come up with your own definition.

If you looked at a dictionary for help, you may have discovered that the English word *pure* comes from the Latin word *pūrus*, which means clean, unmixed, uncontaminated. The Latin meaning is quite similar to the Greek.

The Greek word for pure is *hagnos*. It comes from the same root as *hagios*, holy. It means "faultless; uncontaminated; immaculate; clean." It signifies moral purity, innocence, and chastity. In ancient Greek, the word originally meant "that which awakens awe" or "that which excites reverence."[3]

Complete the chart by identifying which words/phrases and references from the verses in the margin match the definition of *pure*. (Some answers may be repeated.)

Definition of *Pure*	References	Equivalent Word (s) & Phrase(s)
Faultless	Job 33:9; Philippians 2:15	Blameless
Clean		Without spot
Uncontaminated	2 Peter 3:14; Daniel 12:10	
Immaculate	Daniel 12:10	
Awe-inspiring		Shine as lights

"You say, 'I am pure, without transgression; I am clean, and there is no iniquity in me.'"
Job 33:9

"Be diligent to be found by him without spot or blemish."
2 Peter 3:14

"That you may be blameless and innocent, children of God without blemish. . . [shining] as lights in the world."
Philippians 2:15

"Many shall purify themselves and make themselves white and be refined."
Daniel 12:10

perfectly pure

Ivory soap's standard of 99⁴⁴/₁₀₀% pure seems impressive. Most students would be happy to get 99⁴⁴/₁₀₀% on a test. Therapists would be happy if they managed to get patients 99⁴⁴/₁₀₀% better 99⁴⁴/₁₀₀% of the time. A woman would be happy to get a 99⁴⁴/₁₀₀% flawless diamond. But although 99⁴⁴/₁₀₀% might seem extremely good, it's still not perfect.

God is 100% pure. 100% good. 100% clean. 100% perfect. His character is morally excellent. In Him is no spot, stain, imperfection, or contamination —not even 1/10,000th of a percentage point. His righteousness is immaculate, illustrious, and absolute. He is holy, holy, holy (Rev. 4:8).

God wants His people to understand what holiness is all about. And He wants them to understand that sin—of every kind, in any form, to any degree—is an infinite affront to His holy character and that there can be no fellowship between a holy God and sinful people. But He also wants them to know that He is a merciful God who has made provision for unholy people to be purified and reconciled to Himself.

In the Old Testament, these foundational truths were communicated and pictured through laws God established for ritual purity. In the court of the tabernacle, a large bronze basin (a "laver") was placed between the altar and the entrance to the inner temple. The priests needed to wash their hands and feet before entering the Holy Place and before serving at the altar (Ex. 30:17–21). They needed to be ceremonially spotless in order to approach a spotless, holy God.

One of the priests' main duties was to teach the Jews the difference between clean/pure and unclean/impure (Ezek. 22:26; 44:23). Ceremonial purity qualified one to participate in worship, an activity central to the life of ancient Israel. Being ceremonially unclean was a serious matter. It meant you couldn't fellowship with God.

Jews became ceremonially unclean through contact with mildew, infection, disease, death, blood, or bodily discharge, all of which pictured the contamination of sin. An individual who had become defiled in this manner could only be restored to a pure, clean condition through ritual washings and the offering of sacrifices specified by God. Likewise, any sins God's people committed made them impure and had to be atoned for by the shedding of the blood of innocent animals offered up as substitutes for their own lives. Only then could they approach a holy God.

Read Hebrews 9:13–14; 10:19–23 in your Bible. How can we be clean before a holy God?

When Jesus died to pay the penalty for our sins, He provided a "once for all" means of purification. Ceremonial washing is no longer needed. We don't have to clean ourselves up in order to approach God. Jesus has justified us before a holy God—i.e., He has granted us *positional* purity. This is vital. Before we move on to discuss how we can grow in *personal, practical* purity (sanctification), we want to make sure you understand that purity is not a *prerequisite* to gaining God's favor. You don't have to work at becoming "good enough." The sacrifice of Jesus covers all your sin and makes you 100% spotless and pure in God's eyes.

→ **Take a few minutes to meditate** on the amazing truth that the shed blood of Jesus is the "soap" that makes us 100% pure in the eyes of God—that those who believe in Jesus are forgiven and are considered spotlessly pure and clean. Have you experienced that cleansing? What difference would it make in the way you think and live if you were always mindful of this truth?

> "WHO SHALL ASCEND THE HILL OF THE LORD? AND WHO SHALL STAND IN HIS HOLY PLACE? HE WHO HAS CLEAN HANDS AND A PURE HEART . . ."
>
> Psalm 24:3–4

> "FOR BY A SINGLE OFFERING HE HAS PERFECTED FOR ALL TIME THOSE WHO ARE BEING SANCTIFIED."
>
> Hebrews 10:14

love canal

*L*ove Canal was supposed to be a dream neighborhood.[4] It was located in the city of Niagara Falls in Upstate New York, near one of the most spectacular natural wonders in North America. But all was not well in Love Canal. In the early 1970s, some residents noticed a black sludge seeping through the basement walls of their newly built homes.

Over the next few years, a woman who ran a beauty salon in her basement developed a debilitating illness. The leukemia rate skyrocketed. Schoolchildren developed strange rashes and vague, unexplained allergies. Women suffered a high rate of miscarriages. Babies suffered birth defects, deformities, and chromosomal abnormalities. Baby Sheri was born with a hole in her heart, a deformed nose and ears, and mental retardation. Her teeth came through in a double row on her lower jaw. Between 1974 and 1978, defects occurred in 56 percent of Love Canal births.

Residents had no idea that their homes had been built on top of 21,000 tons of buried toxic industrial waste. When heavy rains in the mid-1970s caused groundwater levels to rise, the waste was pushed up closer to the surface. In some areas, old, rusted barrels broke through the surface into backyards and even lifted swimming pools. Puddles of noxious chemicals

bubbled up in schoolyards, gardens, and basements. Toxic streams trickled down the streets.

The federal government was called in to intervene. In response to the Love Canal disaster, it launched the Environmental Protection Agency (EPA) Superfund in 1980, and poured millions of dollars into toxic waste cleanup efforts.

> *"You blind Pharisee! First clean the inside of the cup and the plate, that the outside also may be clean."*
>
> **Matthew 23:26**

Read Matthew 23:25–28. The outside of the Pharisees' "cups" looked sparkly clean. But what was on the inside? On the cup to the right, list what their cups contained.

The Jewish religious leaders prided themselves on how well they followed Old Testament ritual purity laws. What's more, they had come up with all sorts of extra cleanliness rules for people to follow. The importance they placed on ceremonial washings is reflected in the fact that a major section of Jewish rabbinical writings (*Mishna*) is entitled "cleanness" (*Tohoroth*).

The rabbis stipulated that in order to be clean, you had to wash your hands with a volume of 1½ eggs worth of water, hold your hands in just the right position, and let the water flow in the right direction. Your cleanliness and your spirituality depended upon perfectionistic attention to such details.

Read Mark 7:1–7, 20–23. Explain why Jesus wasn't satisfied with the Pharisees' squeaky clean behavior.

_____

_____

Read Matthew 23:26 in the margin. What did Jesus say the Pharisees needed to do?

- ☐ Buy some new coffee cups
- ☐ Get a refill at Starbucks
- ☐ Focus on cleaning the inside
- ☐ Buy a new brand of detergent

What implications does this have for a woman who wants to grow in virtue?

_____

_____

_____

purity starts in the heart

The religious leaders' excessive concern about external appearances had resulted in an inauthentic spirituality. They had reduced their relationship with God to a massive list of *dos* and *don'ts*. Outwardly, they got it right. In modern terms, they didn't sleep around, cheat on their taxes, exceed the speed limit, or come in late for work. They went to church regularly, read and memorized their Bibles, had an active prayer life, led small group studies, gave tithes and offerings, and had a playlist full of worship songs on their iPods. But according to Jesus, though their behavior appeared good, they had totally missed the point.

A relationship with the Lord isn't about following a list of dos and don'ts. It's not about merely *appearing* to be good. It's about opening up the depths of your heart to Him and cooperatively embarking on a lifelong cleanup project—becoming in practice what He has made you positionally.

Though the analogy is imperfect, it's like the difference between a Love Canal resident who pries a rusty barrel out of her backyard and is satisfied to let it go at that, versus one who contracts with the EPA to keep digging until every hidden toxin is exposed and removed. The former is proud of how clean her yard looks, while the latter knows that more impurities lie hidden beneath the surface, and that without ongoing help, the dangerous toxins will continue to produce negative results. (See Luke 18:9–14.)

"All the ways of a man are pure in his own eyes, *but the LORD weighs the spirit.*"
Proverbs 16:2

"There are those who are clean in their own eyes but are not washed of their filth."
Proverbs 30:12

"Prove me, O LORD, and try me; test my heart and my mind."
Psalm 26:2

"Search me, O God, and know my heart! Try me and know my thoughts! And see if there be any grievous way in me, and lead me in the way everlasting!"
Psalm 139:23–24

Put a check in the box to indicate who you are more like:

☐ I'm more like the woman who's just concerned about surface appearance.

☐ I'm more like the woman who invites the expert to dig up my yard.

Read the verses in the margin. Mark the following statements as true (T) or false (F).

_____ My inward attitudes and thoughts are a better indicator of my level of purity than my outward actions.

_____ My heart is deceptive. I can be sinful and wrong even when I feel blameless and right.

_____ An impure thought is not sin unless I act on it.

_____ I need to continually ask the Lord for help to test my motives and thoughts for any impurity.

The Bible teaches that purity relates to *who you are* (the inside) as much as *what you do* (the outside). Sexual immorality, adultery, sensuality, coveting, deceit, envy, slander, pride, foolishness, and all sorts of other sins come from within (Mark 7:21–23). They start with your heart.

Personalize and pray Psalm 139:23–24. Ask the Lord to search and test your heart and thoughts and to point out any specific "spots" of impurity that are keeping you from enjoying full fellowship with Him. Record anything the Holy Spirit brings to mind.

_____

_____

_____

→ **Take a few moments** to confess and repent of what God has shown you. Ask Him to forgive you, and to lead you in the way everlasting.

it's your vice talking

*J*The element of womanhood we're studying this week is virtue—moral excellence, goodness, or purity. A virtue is the opposite of a vice. A vice is a habit or practice that's immoral or evil. It's sinful. Some people use the word *vice* to refer to a minor, undesirable action—like drinking too much soda, or biting one's nails, for example. But a vice is more serious than that.

The modern English word that best captures the nature of a vice is the word *vicious*, which means "full of vice." A vice is an unholy habit or practice that is detrimental to a person's spiritual well-being. King Solomon identified seven vices:

> *There are six things that the L*ORD* hates,*
> *seven that are an abomination to him:*
> *haughty eyes, a lying tongue,*
> *and hands that shed innocent blood,*
> *a heart that devises wicked plans,*
> *feet that make haste to run to evil,*
> *a false witness who breathes out lies,*
> *and one who sows discord among brothers.* (Prov. 6:16–19)

The New Testament contains several lists of vices. Three of those lists are shown on the chart below.

Mark 7:21–22	Romans 1:24–31	Colossians 3:5–10
Evil thoughts	Lust/Sexual impurity	Sexual immorality
Sexual immoralities	Dishonorable sexual	Impurity
Thefts	passions	Lust
Murders	Evil	Evil desires
Adulteries	Greed	Greed
Greed	Envy	Idolatry
Wickedness	Murder	Anger
Deceit	Quarrels	Rage
Sensuality/	Deceit	Malice
Promiscuity	Malice	Slander
Envy	Gossip	Abusive speech
Slander	Slander	Filthy talk/
Pride	Insolence	Obscenities
Foolishness	Arrogance	Lying
	Boastfulness	
	Disobedience to	
	parents	

"Let all bitterness and wrath and anger and clamor and slander be put away from you, along with all malice."

Ephesians 4:31

"So put away all malice and all deceit and hypocrisy and envy and all slander."

1 Peter 2:1

As you can see, there are plenty of vices—so many that we can't begin to address them all. But one in particular appears to be uniquely pertinent to women. It's cited in the sex-specific instruction Paul gave to Titus.

Which vice from Titus 2:3 appears in each list on the chart?

_____ _____ a _____ _____ _____ _____

Circle all the vices on the chart that pertain to speech.

Why do you think Paul includes a "speech vice" in his Titus 2 curriculum for women?

_____

_____

speak no evil

It's interesting to note how often faulty speech appears as a vice in Scripture. The contaminants in our hearts frequently bubble out through our words. Gossip, quarrelling, boastfulness, and deceit are obviously speech issues. But foolishness, malice, lust, and immorality can also show up in the way we talk. Our vices often "speak."

Titus 2:3 says that women "are to be reverent in behavior, not slanderers." The NASB translation says they should not be "malicious gossips." The KJV says "false accusers." These are all translations of the Greek word *diabolos*, the word from which we get our English word *diabolical*. Thirty-four of the thirty-eight times *diabolos* is used in the New Testament, it's used as a name for Satan, the devil. He's the great slanderer (John 8:44; Rev. 12:10). When we slander, we are "devil-like"—our speech resembles his!

Two of the three times when *diabolos* refers to slander, it's speaking specifically to women. God created women as relators and gave us an amazing capacity for verbal communication. Unfortunately, Satan likes to turn this strength into a weakness. He likes to twist virtue into vice.

Read Proverbs 6:16–19 on the previous page. What phrases in this passage relate to the sin of slander?

How does the Lord feel about these "speech vices"? Do you view slander the same way He does? Explain why or why not.

_____

_____

What is slander exactly? Legally, it's defined as an untruthful statement about a person that harms or defames their reputation. But the Bible's definition is broader than that. Slander means to speak critically of another person with the intent to harm . . . even if the information is correct. That's why _diabolos_ has been translated "malicious gossip" as well as "false accuser."

One commentator suggests that slander means "purveyor" (supplier) of intrigue or scandal.[6] A closely related Greek word, _blasphēmia_, which is also translated _slander_ means "to revile; to hurt the reputation or smite with reports or words; [to] speak evil of."[7] In the Bible, all manner of false and/or malicious talk about others qualifies as "slander."

Answer the following questions to see if the vice of slander needs to be uprooted from your heart:

1. Are you a "whisperer" (Prov. 16:28; 26:20, 22)? Do you say things about others behind their backs that you wouldn't say to their faces?

☐ never ☐ seldom ☐ occasionally ☐ often ☐ habitually

2. Are you a backbiter (Prov. 25:23)? Do you share personal injuries or resentments with the intent to harm or damage someone's reputation?

☐ never ☐ seldom ☐ occasionally ☐ often ☐ habitually

3. Are you a talebearer (Lev. 19:16; Prov 11:13; 18:8 NKJV)? Do you share juicy bits of information that cast others in less than a positive light?

☐ never ☐ seldom ☐ occasionally ☐ often ☐ habitually

4. Do you listen to or share reports that assume the worst about someone's motives (1 Cor. 13:7; Prov. 15:26; Lam. 3:62)?

☐ never ☐ seldom ☐ occasionally ☐ often ☐ habitually

5. Do you malign (Prov. 30:10 NKJV; Titus 3:2 NASB)? Do you speak harmful untruths or evil about others so as to make them look bad?

☐ never ☐ seldom ☐ occasionally ☐ often ☐ habitually

Slander is diabolical. There is no acceptable degree of malice or slander or evil speaking for Christian women. If we wish to grow in virtue, we need to have zero tolerance for this vice.

→ **Pray and repent of the sin of slander.** Read the verses in the margin and Proverbs 8:6–8 in your Bible. What characteristics of pure speech do you see? Ask the Lord to purify your heart and your speech.

_____

_____

_____

"AND ALL SPOKE WELL OF HIM AND MARVELED AT THE GRACIOUS WORDS THAT WERE COMING FROM HIS MOUTH."

Luke 4:22

"LET NO CORRUPTING TALK COME OUT OF YOUR MOUTHS, BUT ONLY SUCH AS IS GOOD FOR BUILDING UP, AS FITS THE OCCASION, THAT IT MAY GIVE GRACE TO THOSE WHO HEAR."

Ephesians 4:29

If you ask a group of Christians what first comes to mind when they think of the word *pure*, many will likely mention sexual purity. As we pointed out in the first lesson, the Greek word for pure comes from the same root as the word *holy* and means "faultless; uncontaminated; immaculate; clean." To be pure simply means to be "clean"—that is, to be filled with virtue and not vice. The Lord wants us to be pure in every aspect of our lives.

> "Do you not know that the unrighteous will not inherit the kingdom of God? Do not be deceived: neither the sexually immoral, nor idolaters, nor adulterers, nor men who practice homosexuality . . . will inherit the kingdom of God."
>
> **I Corinthians 6:9–10**

The perception that *purity* means "sexual chastity" isn't unwarranted though. That's an important part of purity. We are sexual beings. Therefore, the battle between virtue and vice is often fought on the sexual front.

On the chart of vices on page 120, highlight or put a box around any sexual vices.

Chastity is a word you don't hear a lot today. It refers to sexual virtue. It means "refraining from sexual acts that are contrary to morality." Unfortunately, the word *chastity* hasn't always had a great reputation.

Perhaps you've heard of the "chastity belt"—the iron-clad underwear that a jealous medieval knight supposedly locked on his young wife to guarantee her fidelity until he returned from a Crusade.

We did some research on chastity belts, and guess what we discovered? These Renaissance chastity devices are a myth, a hoax! In fact, most of the metal chastity belts once on display in museums have been removed to avoid further embarrassment because of their lack of authenticity.[8]

That's not to say that chastity belts didn't exist. They just weren't the instruments of female gender oppression they've been made out to be.

The chastity belt was first mentioned in poetry metaphorically, as a promise of fidelity. Historians say that in the middle ages, a simple cord tied around the waist was a symbol of fidelity. The cord around the waist of a monk, for example, represented his vows of abstinence. Similarly, a woman might wear a velvet cord under her clothing as a pledge of her faithfulness.

Cloth and leather chastity belts were developed in the Victorian era. In the late 1800s, during the Industrial Revolution, some women wore this type of undergarment to work. They usually worked in a factory with close quarters and little supervision. These women wore the chastity belt as a rape-deterrent, to help protect against sexual abuse.[9]

Sadly, our culture views female chastity in the same light as the mythical chastity belt: It's from the dark ages . . . outdated, oppressive, and harmful to women. But the Bible presents a radically different picture. It indicates that sexual fidelity for those who are married and sexual continence for those who are unmarried puts the gospel of Jesus Christ on display. It's a beautiful, powerful, and profound symbol of covenant union and faithfulness.

In your Bible, read 1 Corinthians 6:12–20, and fill in the blanks to complete the sentences below:

In the covenant of marriage, a man and woman become _____ flesh (v. 16). The husband-wife sexual union illustrates a profound spiritual truth: Everyone who enters into a covenant relationship with Jesus becomes _____ spirit with Him (v. 17). Faithful, *no-sex-outside-of-marriage* / Joyful, *sex-inside-of-marriage* conduct bears witness to the covenant relationship between Jesus and the church. Ultimately, sex is not about me: I am _____ my own (v. 19). Whether unmarried or married, my sexuality is meant to _____ God (v. 20).

Explain how sex outside of marriage between a man and a woman is an assault against the story of Christ's covenant relationship with the church:

How is withholding sex within marriage also an assault against the story?

Apparently there was a saying that was common in Paul's day: "*Food is meant for the stomach and the stomach for food*" (1 Cor. 6:13). Absorbing the slogan from the pagan culture, some believers in Corinth believed that because the appetite for food was natural and God-created, it was therefore acceptable to indulge those appetites by eating and drinking to their hearts' content.

They further claimed that their freedom to indulge their culinary appetites extended to sexual appetites. Eating and sex were both natural bodily functions. "Food for the stomach and the stomach for food" was a typical Greek way of arguing by analogy that the body was for sex and sex for the body. Sexual appetites should be fulfilled, not frustrated.

Paul countered that only those actions that respect and reflect the believer's relationship with the Lord are "helpful," and therefore permissible. Covenant sex between a man and wife tells the right story about the gospel. It testifies to the legal and spiritual union that occurs when we enter into a covenant with Jesus. Sex outside of a marriage covenant is incongruent with this storyline. It violates the gospel and is therefore not permissible.

In the act of sex, a husband and wife physically bear witness to the spiritual, supernatural, and legal joining that took place when they made their covenant. Sex bears witness that God has made two one. That's why God restricts sex to marriage. If unmarried individuals are physically intimate, they tell a lie with their bodies. They testify that a joining has taken place, when in fact it hasn't.

Paul argues that sexual sin is a serious sin unlike any other, for it involves telling a lie about God with every part of your being (1 Cor. 6:18). Sexual sin is such an offense against the Lord that we should abhor even a "hint" of messing around.

Read Ephesians 5:3–5 in the margin. Circle the phrase "Should not even be heard of among you," which could also be translated "there must not even be a hint of it." Given this standard, how would you rank the following behaviors for God's people? Mark them as "proper" (+), "improper" (-) or "it depends" (+/-).

_____ Using off-color humor   _____ Reading a romance novel

_____ Dressing seductively   _____ Texting sexual innuendo

_____ Imagining romantic encounters   _____ Watching TV reality shows

_____ Group of guys/girls going   _____ Looking at provocative images
                     out for the evening

How do you determine whether something is proper or improper?

_____

_____

Practically speaking, what must you stop doing (or get rid of) to eliminate every hint of sexual impurity from your life?

_____

_____

Read 1 Thessalonians 4:1–12 in your Bible. What insights do you see in this passage to help believers deal with sexual temptation and replace sexual vice with virtue?

_____

_____

Paul concludes 1 Corinthians 6 with both an earnest exhortation and a compelling motivation: *"Flee from sexual immorality. . . . Glorify God in your body"* (vv. 18–20)!

→ **Ask the Lord** to help you flee every hint of sexual immorality so that what you do with your body will glorify Him.

like pure silver

"He will sit as a refiner and purifier of silver, and he will purify [them] and refine them like gold and silver, and they will bring offerings in righteousness to the LORD."

Malachi 3:3

"And I will put [them] into the fire, and refine them as one refines silver, and test them as gold is tested. They will call upon my name, and I will answer them. I will say, 'They are my people'; and they will say, 'The LORD is my God.'"

Zechariah 13:9

There's a familiar story in Christian circles about a group of women that met for a Bible study. While studying in the book of Malachi, chapter 3, they came across verse 3 that says: "He will sit as a refiner and purifier of silver." This verse puzzled the women and they wondered how this statement applied to the character and nature of God. One of the women offered to find out more about the process of refining silver and to get back to the group at their next meeting.

That week, the woman called a silversmith and made an appointment to watch him at work. She didn't mention anything about the reason for her interest beyond her curiosity about the process of

refining silver. As she watched the silversmith, he held a piece of silver over the fire and let it heat up. He explained that in refining silver, one needed to hold the silver in the middle of the fire where the flames were the hottest, so as to burn away all of the impurities.

The woman thought about God holding us in such a hot spot; then she thought again about the verse that says: "He [sits] as a refiner and purifier of silver." She asked the silversmith if it was true that he had to sit there in front of the fire the whole time the silver was being refined. The man answered yes, he not only had to sit there holding the silver in the fire, but he had to keep his eyes on the silver the entire time it was in the fire. If the silver was left a moment too long in the flames, it would be destroyed.

The woman was silent for a moment. Then she asked the silversmith, "How do you know when the silver is fully refined?"

He smiled at her and answered, "Oh, that's easy—when I see my image reflected in the silver."[10]

Over the past few lessons, you may have felt the Lord holding you in a "hot spot" as He revealed some impurities in your life. Be assured that He doesn't do this to judge and condemn you. No. "There is therefore now no

condemnation for those who are in Christ Jesus" (Rom. 8:1). So don't be burdened with guilt—be overwhelmed at His amazing grace! Take joy in the fact that though you struggle with sin, Christ has already secured the victory. You stand 100% pure and clean before God (Eph. 1:4)!

The reason the Lord holds you to the fire is not to punish you, but to reveal the splendor of Christ through your life. It's not so that you might *earn* God's favor; it's because you've *already received* God's favor. The great "refiner and purifier of silver" wants to reveal His beauty in you and make you shine.

Read the verses in the margin. What happens when you put your faith in Christ's promises?

_____

_____

Being a "partaker of the divine nature" means that . . . (check all that apply)

- ☐ Jesus lives in me.
- ☐ I have the power to overcome vices.
- ☐ I am god of my own life.
- ☐ I have everything I need for godliness.
- ☐ I can reflect the image of Christ.
- ☐ I no longer have a human nature.

Why should being a partaker in Christ's nature motivate us to "make every effort" to grow in virtue? How does being a partaker in His nature enable us to live a pure life?

_____

_____

"HE HAS GRANTED TO US HIS PRECIOUS AND VERY GREAT PROMISES, SO THAT THROUGH THEM YOU MAY BECOME PARTAKERS OF THE DIVINE NATURE, HAVING ESCAPED FROM THE CORRUPTION THAT IS IN THE WORLD BECAUSE OF SINFUL DESIRE. FOR THIS VERY REASON, MAKE EVERY EFFORT TO SUPPLEMENT YOUR FAITH WITH VIRTUE."
2 Peter 1:4–5

"EVERYONE WHO THUS HOPES IN HIM PURIFIES HIMSELF AS HE IS PURE."
1 John 3:3

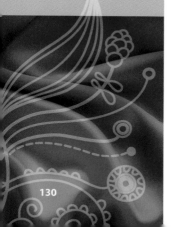

"Even if some do not obey the word, they may be won without a word by the conduct of their wives, when they see your respectful and pure conduct."
1 Peter 3:1–2

"Virtue is beauty." [11]
Shakespeare

"Since we have these promises, beloved, let us cleanse [purify] ourselves from every defilement of body and spirit, bringing holiness to completion in the fear of God."
2 Corinthians 7:1

To be a partaker means to be a partner; to participate or share in something. The Greek word is similar to the word for *fellowship* or a close mutual relationship. When God's Holy Spirit comes to dwell in us, we become a partner of Christ's divine nature—we begin to share in it.

The word *nature* means one's natural condition. An individual, by birth, has a human nature. God makes it possible for humanity to also partake in His nature. This doesn't mean that we become part-God. It simply means that besides having a human nature, the divine nature also dwells in us.[12] *"But we have this treasure in jars of clay, to show that the surpassing power belongs to God and not to us"* (2 Cor. 4:7).

Christ-in-us gives us the power and desire to change positively, and for more and more of His character to be demonstrated in our lives. We seek to keep our hearts clean and white not because we *have* to, but because we *want* to. Desiring virtue is part of our new nature. Our Bridegroom's amazing love, grace, and holiness motivate us to make every effort to be spotlessly clean for Him.

No impurity is acceptable in the Christian life, however small it may be. Peter urges us to "make every effort" to increase in virtue. Paul echoes this sentiment. He wants us to work at purifying ourselves from every defilement and every vice, "bringing holiness to completion" out of respect for God. Our holiness won't be completed until we see Jesus. Bringing it to completion simply means "to advance it toward its intended goal"—it's Paul's way of saying, "Keep making every effort to grow in virtue!"

Circle or highlight the phrase "bringing holiness to completion in the fear of God" in 2 Corinthians 7:1 in the margin. What do you think this means?

_____

_____

How can you continue to grow in virtue? Draw lines to match each verse with its corresponding statement.

By guarding my way with God's Word	Philippians 1:10
By obeying the truth	Psalm 119:9
By confessing and forsaking sin	1 John 1:9
By drawing near to God	1 Peter 1:22
By approving what is excellent	James 4:8

Getting rid of vice and growing in virtue isn't easy. It takes work. That's why the Bible says, "Make every *effort* to add to your faith virtue" (2 Peter 1:5). That's right: love-motivated, Spirit-enabled, Christ-glorifying effort.

How will you "make every effort" this week to grow in virtue?

We mentioned in the first lesson that in ancient Greek, the word *pure* originally meant "that which awakens awe" or "that which excites reverence." Purity is ravishingly beautiful. It makes the gospel attractive and believable. When you make every effort to cultivate virtue in your life, the great "Refiner and Purifier of silver" will reveal His beauty in you, and others will be drawn to love and worship Him!

drawing it out,
drawing it in . . .

interior renovation

process

The video for Week Five will help you process this week's lessons. You'll find this week's video, the leader's guide, and additional resources at TrueWoman201.com.

ponder

Think about the following questions. Discuss them with your friends, family, and/or small group:

1. Review 2 Corinthians 11:2; Ephesians 5:25–28; and Revelation 19:7–8. What link do you see in those passages between purity and the Bride of Christ?

2. God is 100% pure, which is another way of saying that He is perfectly holy. How does this aspect of His character shed light on some of those Old Testament ceremonies that may seem so strange to us today?

3. Through Jesus, God has granted us "positional purity." What does this mean, and why is grasping this truth vital to our walk with God?

4. Life is sometimes easier when we can make it about following a list of dos and don'ts, but how can that be a spiritual danger? What lies at the heart of a pure, thriving relationship with the Lord?

5. List some of the ways that the words we speak can flow out into vice. Why is slander particularly vicious, and why must we as women be on special guard against it?

6. How do sexual chastity and marital sex each express the truth of the gospel?

7. Identify some types of sexual impurity that are widely practiced and tolerated in the "Christian" world today. What effect does that have on our witness in the world?

8. What is accomplished by the process of refining silver? What does that metaphor in Scripture tell us about God's intentions in the difficulties we go through? You may be going through a hard time right now. If so, how does understanding the refining process change your outlook?

personalize it

Use this page to journal. Write down what you learned this week. Record your comments, a favorite verse, or a concept or quote that was particularly helpful or meaningful to you. Compose a prayer, letter, or poem. Jot down notes from the video or your small group session. Express your heart response to what you have studied. Personalize this week's lessons in the way that will best help you apply them to your life.

drawing it out,
drawing it in . . .

responsibility

"Should women work?"

As proponents of biblical womanhood, we've often been asked this question. Personally, I (Mary) think it's a silly question. Whenever I'm asked, I have to fight the urge to bang my hand against my forehead and retort, "DUH . . . Of course women should work!!!"

I was too forthright and blurted it out once (thankfully minus the "DUH" and the head-banging gesture). The young, single college student standing in front of me conceded, "Naturally, a woman who stays at home with kids works too . . . that's not what I meant."

Though I inquired, I had a hard time pinning down exactly what she meant. Did she want to know if I thought single women should get an education? Or embark on a career? Or quit school if they got engaged? Or whether marriage meant a woman couldn't have a paying job—that gainful employment and marriage are lifelong either/or propositions? Or whether it's okay for a woman to be an entrepreneur? Or a CEO? Or whether women should hold down jobs only in cases of financial necessity? Or maybe whether moms should work outside the home only if their children are a certain age?

*A True Woman maintains the right work priorities . . . She values "**working at home.**"*

In the end, I concluded that, whether she realized it or not, this girl was hoping for a one-size-fits-all template. The Bible affirms the principle that there's a unique responsibility for the home that goes along with biblical womanhood and a unique responsibility for provision that goes along with biblical manhood. But the Bible simply doesn't give us a one-size-fits-all template for how to apply that when it comes to women and work.

What's more, those of us who have walked the path of career, marriage, and motherhood, and who've faced the economic realities of raising a family, know that the answers aren't always simple. The factors that impact a woman's decisions about work are often competing and complex—they're highly dependent on her individual circumstances, her season of life, her capacity, and her calling. Our lives come in different "shapes and sizes," so the pattern for work and biblical womanhood is definitely not "one-size-fits-all."

We are saddened by the "married-is-better" wars, the "mommy-wars," the "my-life-is-more-biblical-than-yours" wars, and the competition and general lack of grace that often plague Christian women. In this week's lessons, we hope to elevate the discussion about work to a different level. We pray that studying the Bible's teaching about work, productivity, womanhood, and the home will help you make wise decisions regarding your particular situation and lead you to extend grace toward women whose lives look different from yours.

I (Nancy) have worked full-time in vocational ministry for my entire adult life. As a single woman, my challenges and issues related to work have looked different from Mary's. What it means for each of us to have a "heart for home" has also varied according to our changing life seasons.

As a married woman with children, I (Mary) have experienced numerous marketplace-work, stay-at-home-work, and ministry-work combinations. After graduating with a professional degree in rehab medicine, I worked full-time in the secular marketplace. After the birth of my first son, I returned to hospital work two mornings a week, leaving baby with grandma. After my second child was born, I stayed home, and started a small home-based business to supply contract rehabilitation workers in homecare and rural settings. My third son had special needs. I closed down the business and focused on home-educating him and my other children. During those years, I sporadically did some consulting work.

I have constantly had to weigh my decisions about marketplace and ministry work with my commitment to manage my home well, and to be a good wife, mom, daughter, sister, and friend. I want to be a faithful steward of all the gifts and relationships the Lord has entrusted to me.

In our minds, the question isn't "Should women work?" but rather "What is God's view of work?" "How do I choose which work receives the most time and attention at this stage in my life?" "Am I giving my home the focus and priority God wants it to have?" And "am I determining the value of my work based on earthly or heavenly economics?"

These are some questions we'll try to address as we consider how to be women who faithfully steward God's gifts by being fruitful, creative, industrious, productive workers . . . and who fulfill our responsibility to be "working at home." $\rightarrow$

it's off to work we go

One of the best-known songs in Walt Disney's classic 1937 movie *Snow White and the Seven Dwarfs* is a song about work. It's sung by the group of seven dwarfs as they dig in the diamond mines: *"Heigh-ho, heigh-ho / It's off to work we go! / We'll keep on singing all day long / Heigh-ho, Heigh-ho . . ."*

Snow White, who stayed behind at the seven dwarfs' house, spent all day washing laundry, cleaning house, cooking, and baking pies, but she didn't sing "Heigh-ho, heigh-ho" . . . presumably because she didn't go "off to work."

The fact that only those cartoon characters who were employed at non-home-based paid jobs were portrayed as truly "working," identifies some ideas about work that are relatively new, historically speaking:

- the idea that work and home are separate spheres

- the idea that "work" only encompasses those activities for which you are financially compensated

- the idea that traditionally, women's *only* work was to cook, clean, and look after children

> "Our homes are supposed to point people to Christ and give them a taste for their home in heaven. They're supposed to be glimpses of heaven here on earth."[1]
>
> *Nancy*

the family business of work

Up until the 19th century, the home was the center of production and the small business unit of the local economy. Most families ran a "family business," which generally involved everyone in the household—husband, wife, and children. If the family raised sheep, everyone was expected to pitch in with the work of shearing, sorting, scouring, bundling, and selling the wool and lanolin by-products. If the family worked in the textile industry, it was "all hands on deck" for dyeing, carding, spinning, and weaving. Tradesmen, such as blacksmiths and carpenters, set up shop where they lived and undoubtedly enlisted help from their families. Merchants who sold goods had their living quarters situated above their retail spaces.

The family was a single economic unit that worked together for the common good of its members. Certainly, there was a division of labor in which the husband's focus was predominantly on provision, and the wife's predominantly on household management. But work was a family affair. There wasn't a big chasm between "home" and "work"—the two spheres overlapped. Everyone in the home was productive. Everyone worked.

The "*Heigh-ho, heigh-ho, it's off to work we go*" phenomenon didn't occur until the Industrial Revolution in the early 1800s. At that point, the home stopped being the place of economic production. People left their homes for employment in factories. Their income was no longer associated with the family business. Instead, the money they earned was theirs and theirs alone.

The perception of what qualified as "work" also changed. Work became paid employment outside of the home. Work in the home had no quantifiable economic value, and therefore didn't really qualify as "work." The *public* marketplace became the valued sphere and the sphere associated with men. The *private* sphere, the place of non-monetary return, became the devalued sphere and the sphere associated with women. This profound cultural upheaval had enormous implications for our modern perceptions about work, economics, and women's labor and productivity.[2]

This week, we're going to study Paul's instruction to Titus about women "working at home" (2:5). But first, it's important to note that women in the Bible performed and were valued for many different types of profitable work.

Read Exodus 35:25–26; Jeremiah 9:17; Acts 16:14–15. Complete the chart by writing down the missing references beside the kinds of jobs women performed.

Type of work/industry performed by women	Scripture
News casting (heralds)	Psalm 68:11; Proverbs 9:3
Special events (professional mourners)	
Producing military equipment (tentmaker)	Acts 18:1–3
Medical & health care services (midwives)	Exodus 1:15
Nanny & child care services (wet nurse)	Exodus 2:7–8
Art & interior design (curtain weavers)	
Agriculture (wheat gleaners)	Ruth 2:8–9
Musician (composers/lament singers)	2 Chronicles 35:25
Financial planner (inheritance manager)	Job 42:15
Sales & marketing (seller of purple goods)	
Fashion design (tunics and garments)	Acts 9:39
Charitable work (workers in the Lord)	Romans 16:12
Real estate deals (buys a field)	Proverbs 31:16
Wholesaler (profitable merchandise)	Proverbs 31:18, 24
Entrepreneurial ventures (plants a vineyard)	Proverbs 31:16

Exodus 35:25–26 and Jeremiah 9:17 use a word to indicate that the women were highly competent at their trades. What's the adjective the verses use to describe these women?

_ _ _ _ _ f u l

paul's female friends

The apostle Paul had numerous female coworkers and friends, among them those who engaged in various types of income-generating work. In Corinth, he worked alongside a female tentmaker, Priscilla, and her husband.

You just read about Lydia, the seller of purple goods. Lydia was from Thyatira, a city in the province of Lydia in Asia Minor. She was a successful businesswoman who apparently possessed considerable wealth, for in addition to the house she likely maintained back home, she had a residence in Philippi large enough to lodge Paul and his companions and serve as the meeting place for a fledgling church.

Paul's friend Phoebe was a Greek patroness, who used her wealth for the benefit of the church in Cenchreae.[3] When Phoebe traveled to Rome on business, Paul asked her to deliver a letter to the Roman church. In the letter, Paul commended Phoebe for the valuable service she had provided for him and other believers in the region (Rom. 16:1–2).

Luke reports that numerous women of prominent influence and social standing were members of Paul's church in Thessalonica (Acts 17:4, 12). Some of these women held public positions and others were likely wives of city officials.[4]

As we consider what Paul meant by women "working at home," it's important to understand that he did not prohibit women from working in other contexts outside the home.

In Romans 16:3–16 Paul greets twenty-eight friends, nine of whom are women: Prisca, Mary, Junia, Tryphaena, Tryphosa, Persis, Rufus' mom, Julia, and Nereus' sister. What did Paul commend about these women and what was his attitude toward them?

_____

_____

Did you notice how often Paul commended these women for their hard work? Paul respected and appreciated the diverse contributions of women. And he praised them for their hard work—in whatever sphere the Lord placed them.

What are your spheres of responsibilty in this season of your life?

_____

_____

→ **Ask the Lord** to show you in this week's lessons how you can best glorify Him in each of those arenas.

nine to five

W "*Working 9 to 5, what a way to make a living!*" is a phrase from the hit song from a 1980 comedy film starring Jane Fonda, Lily Tomlin, and Dolly Parton. The plot revolves around three working women who overthrow their "sexist egotistical lying hypocritical bigot" male boss. They don't want to be "a step on the boss man's ladder." They want to get more recognition, more position, and more money for the work they do.

The movie *9 to 5* was released at the height of the feminist movement and is full of negative, derogatory messages about men. Nevertheless, it illustrates our culture's underlying view about the nature and meaning of work. Work is simply a means to an end. We're in it for what we get out of it—be it money, prestige, affirmation, personal satisfaction, or a cushy retirement. So if the effort we put in doesn't provide enough return, then it's time to overthrow the boss or look for a new job.

Our ideas about work impact our decisions about working in the marketplace versus the home. A proper theology of work—that is, an understanding of what the Bible teaches about it—is vital to help us make wise choices about what, why, where, when, and how to work.

Describe your opinions about work by indicating how strongly you agree or disagree with the following statements:

1. It's important for a woman to feel fulfilled in her chosen work.

1	2	3	4	5	6	7	8	9	10
strongly agree			disagree		neutral		agree		strongly agree

2. A successful woman has a successful career.

1	2	3	4	5	6	7	8	9	10
strongly agree			disagree		neutral		agree		strongly agree

> "*Jesus answered them, 'My Father is working until now, and I am working.'*"
>
> **John 5:17**

> "*My food is to do the will of him who sent me and to accomplish his work.*"
>
> **John 4:34**

3. A married woman needs to have a back-up plan for financial independence.

1	2	3	4	5	6	7	8	9	10
strongly agree		disagree		neutral		agree		strongly agree	

4. Menial and/or trivial work is a waste of a woman's potential.

1	2	3	4	5	6	7	8	9	10
strongly agree		disagree		neutral		agree		strongly agree	

5. The goal of work is to get enough money to retire from work.

1	2	3	4	5	6	7	8	9	10
strongly agree		disagree		neutral		agree		strongly agree	

6. Economics plays the biggest factor in work decisions.

1	2	3	4	5	6	7	8	9	10
strongly agree		disagree		neutral		agree		strongly agree	

7. The value of work is determined by how much money the worker gets paid.

1	2	3	4	5	6	7	8	9	10
strongly agree		disagree		neutral		agree		strongly agree	

8. It's a valid option for a husband to stay home with the kids if the wife earns more.

1	2	3	4	5	6	7	8	9	10
strongly agree		disagree		neutral		agree		strongly agree	

You'll be discussing popular opinions about women and work in your small group session. For the remainder of this lesson, we want to begin to address some important points the Bible makes about work in general.

1. Work was created to put the nature and character of God on display.

Leonardo da Vinci once said, "Make your work to be in keeping with your purpose."[6] The first thing you need to know about work is that it exists because we've been created in the image of the great worker, God. We work because He works. Work is a God-ordained activity. Honest, diligent, attentive, productive, innovative, creative, faithful, fruitful, conscientious, hard work bears witness to God's nature and character.

Work does not primarily exist for the purpose of financial gain (though we may get paid). Its primary purpose is to glorify God. "*Whatever you do, do all to the glory of God*" (1 Cor. 10:31). So the question, when weighing work options, is not which option will make you the most money, or be the most satisfying, or interesting—but which will bring God the most glory.

2. All legitimate work is an extension of God's work.

Medical work is an extension of the work of the God who heals. Construction work is an extension of the work of the God who builds. Design work is an extension of the work of the God who creates. Tidying a room reflects the work of the God who brings order to chaos. Rocking a screaming baby reflects the God who comforts. Cooking a meal reflects His work of providing our daily bread. All legitimate work (work that's not illegal or immoral)—whether it's paid or unpaid—has value insofar as it is done for the glory of God.

What are one or two chores or responsibilities that you find particularly unpleasant and/or difficult?

_____

_____

"Whatever you do, work heartily, as for the Lord and not for men, knowing that from the Lord you will receive the inheritance as your reward. You are serving the Lord Christ."
Colossians 3:23–24

"No matter what my work is, it matters. It matters because my work is a stage to bring glory to my God."[5]
Tim Challies

"And whoever gives one of these little ones even a cup of cold water because he is a disciple, truly, I say to you, he will by no means lose his reward."
Matthew 10:42

Read Colossians 3:23–24 in the margin. How might the awareness that you're working for Christ change the way you do these tasks and/or your attitude toward them?

_____

_____

3. Your work has eternal significance.

No legitimate work, undertaken for the glory of God, is menial or meaningless. Hard physical labor wasn't beneath the dignity of the Son of God. Jesus worked as a carpenter for about seventeen years and only about three years doing itinerant ministry. Carpentry was a lowly, ill-paying profession. Yet Jesus was doing God's work when pounding a nail just as much as He was doing it when preaching on the hillside—because He was doing what God wanted Him to do when God wanted Him to do it.

What you're doing is not "just a job," or a series of insignificant, repetitive tasks. Before you even existed, God uniquely, purposefully designed your gifts and abilities. He determined that you would do work for His glory. Your work matters to God. It has eternal kingdom significance. What matters in eternity is that you are faithful here on earth with the resources, responsibilities, and relationships God has entrusted to you. When you work—whether at home, in the church or community, or in the marketplace—you're ultimately working for the eternal paycheck.

Think about your current work responsibilities at home and/or the marketplace. Explain how you can do this work "for the eternal paycheck."

_____

_____

→ **Close today's lesson in prayer.** Thank the Lord for the gift of work and for the specific types of work He has given you to do. Ask Him to help you see your work from His perspective and to show you how to glorify Him in those tasks that seem least significant or glamorous.

everyone's got a job

Yesterday we addressed some important points the Bible makes about work. First, work was created to put the nature and character of God on display. Second, all legitimate work is an extension of God's work. Third, your work has eternal significance.

Today we want to cover three more points: God wants you to make strategic decisions about how to allocate your available time and energy. Christians are called to glorify God through doing "good works." And finally, you need to take God's gender-specific emphasis of work responsibility into account when making work decisions.

4. God wants you to be strategic in your allocation of time and energy.

Women have different skills, interests, and responsibilities; we face different circumstances. But one thing we all have in common is that our time is limited. We only have twenty-four hours each day. For most of us, that means we simply can't do all the things we'd like to do. We have to determine how to best allocate our time and energy. Often, this means trying to figure out which is the best option from among several competing good options—saying "no" to one type of "good work" so we have the time and energy to excel at another.

Thankfully, the work of survival has been simplified by the advent of appliances, grocery aisles stocked with food, vehicles, retail stores, and the availability of ready-to-wear clothing. Can you imagine how much time it would take to drive a horse and buggy into town to buy some salt, and then return home to mill grain, bake bread, and catch and pluck the chicken before it went into the pot for supper? Or how much time it would take to card the wool, spin the thread, weave the fabric, and stitch together the pieces for that skirt you're wearing?

"Do not work for the food that perishes, but for the food that endures to eternal life, which the Son of Man will give to you. For on him God the Father has set his seal."

John 6:27

"And do not seek what you are to eat and what you are to drink, nor be worried. For all the nations of the world seek after these things, and your Father knows that you need them. Instead, seek his kingdom, and these things will be added to you."

Luke 12:29–31

We have so much more discretionary time on our hands than the women who came before us. And you can be certain we'll be accountable to God for what we do with it.

It takes prayer and intentionality to make strategic choices—to spend our time and energy wisely, with the aim of making the greatest contribution possible in light of eternity. And it takes a willingness to swim against the tide.

For example, these days many Christian women are choosing to go back into the marketplace full-time after their children are out of the nest—or, in some cases, they're whiling away their days playing bridge or golf.

While there's nothing inherently wrong with those activities, we have to ask *why* this is the pattern. Are these women mindlessly marching to the world's drumbeat? Or are they prayerfully considering how they might invest more of their time in acts of mercy or in discipling and encouraging younger women?

Women's ministry leaders have shared with me (Nancy) their frustration that the empty nesters in their churches—who are greatly needed and have so much they could offer—have so little time and availability to invest in younger women.

In every season of life, whether married or single, our decisions and the way we use our time ought to be based on kingdom values rather than personal comfort or financial gain.

Read Matthew 6:19–33 in your Bible. What should you take into consideration when making decisions about how to invest your time and energy?

"THE LORD GOD TOOK THE MAN AND PUT HIM IN THE GARDEN OF EDEN TO WORK IT AND KEEP IT."

Genesis 2:15

"MAN GOES OUT TO HIS WORK AND TO HIS LABOR UNTIL THE EVENING. O LORD, HOW MANIFOLD ARE YOUR WORKS! IN WISDOM HAVE YOU MADE THEM ALL."

Psalm 104:23–24

God expects us to invest the resources He has entrusted to us—time, talents, and money—in things that will last. Jesus doesn't condemn business success or economic prosperity. Jesus and Paul both benefited from the generosity of independently wealthy women (Luke 8:2–3; Acts 16:13–15). The Lord is simply challenging us to examine the motives of our hearts to see if we treasure Him and His kingdom above temporal things.

Our goal is to arrive on heaven's doorstep and be exuberantly greeted with the words, "Well done, good and faithful servant! You have been faithful with what you were given . . . Come enter into my joy!" (see Matt. 25:21–23).

How intentional and strategic are you being in investing your time, talents, and money for the kingdom of God?

_____

_____

5. Women who have been redeemed show it through "good works."

"Good works" is a theme that's repeated several times in the book of Titus. Paul urged his young pastor friend to *"show yourself in all respects to be a model of good works"* (2:7). He pointed out that Jesus died *"to purify for himself a people for his own possession who are zealous for good works"* (2:14). Good works cannot save us; but they are an inevitable evidence and expression of true faith and godliness.

> "Likewise also that women should adorn themselves . . . with what is proper for women who profess godliness— with good works."
> **I Timothy 2:9–10**

> "And having a reputation for good works: if she has brought up children, has shown hospitality, has washed the feet of the saints, has cared for the afflicted, and has devoted herself to every good work."
> **I Timothy 5:10**

> "[Dorcas] was full of good works and acts of charity. . . . All the widows stood beside him weeping and showing tunics and other garments that Dorcas made while she was with them."
> **Acts 9:36–39**

Read the verses in the margin. Make a list of the kinds of "good works" that godly women are encouraged to practice and for which they are praised.

_____

_____

_____

How do women who are devoted to good works glorify God and make the gospel believable to both believers and unbelievers?

_____

_____

6. Scripture promotes a gender-specific emphasis on work-responsibility.

We see this in Genesis, as God puts Adam in the garden of Eden "to work it and keep it" (2:18) and as the consequences of sin affect Adam and Eve in different realms of responsibility. We see it in Proverbs 31, where husbands and wives are honored for different types of work.

And did you notice that one of the "good works" for which widows are recognized in 1 Timothy 5:10 is "bringing up children"? Bringing up children is a "good work." Obviously, childrearing is a responsibility that's shared by both parents (Prov. 22:6). However, the Bible indicates that the division of labor that goes into maintaining a home and raising kids isn't identical.[7]

As we saw in *True Woman 101*, the husband bears the primary burden of responsibility for *economic provision* while the wife bears the primary burden of responsibility for *family nurturance*.[8] We need to take this into consideration as we make decisions about where to allocate our time and energy.

Being responsible for family nurturance is not to say there may not be situations or seasons when it would be appropriate for a mom to have a job or career

outside the home. Being responsible for provision is not to say that the husband can't look after the kids, cook, or help keep the house clean. It just means that God has determined who's ultimately responsible for what. Male-female roles are neither identical nor interchangeable.

How have culture, your upbringing, and/or Scripture influenced your thinking about work? How do you feel about the fact that Scripture promotes a gender-specific emphasis on work-responsibility?

→ **We know we've touched on some really sensitive areas today.** And it's not possible to cover all the bases in this limited context. Ask the Lord for wisdom to know what choices would be most pleasing to Him for your life. Ask Him to show you if you need to make any adjustments in your thinking about your responsibilities and the time you allocate to them.

working where?

Recently, I (Mary) asked my son to run to the grocery store for me to pick up some items. As he walked out the door, I called after him, "Don't forget the milk!" The fact that I told him to remember the milk didn't mean it was the only thing I wanted him to buy. He was going to bring back all sorts of groceries—things on my list—and other staples, fruits and vegetables at his discretion. But the milk was particularly important to me. I was all out and needed some badly. I didn't want to eat my Cheerios dry.

The list Paul gave to Titus is kind of like that. It's not a comprehensive list of everything a Christian woman keeps in her "pantry"—it's more like a don't-forget-the-milk reminder about items that are particularly important  for biblical womanhood. It's important to understand that the emphasis on a woman's responsibility to work "*at home*," doesn't indicate that she doesn't work in other locations too. At different seasons in her life, she may also work at the church, at the soup kitchen, at the school, at the hospital, at a friend's house, and at the office downtown. To follow our analogy, 2% milk is what the family normally drinks; but she may also have chocolate milk, almond milk, and buttermilk in her fridge.

In the first lesson, we saw that Paul valued women who worked in the marketplace and who served the church. Marketplace, church, and home can all be viable locations for work. But in deciding how to allocate our time and energy among these options, Paul challenges Christian woman to be sure they don't neglect their families and homes. Doing a good job of managing her home is one of the most important "good works" the Lord wants a woman to do.

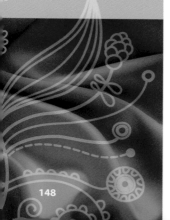

In the margin, circle the phrases "working at home" and "manage their households." Look up Proverbs 31:27 in your Bible and rewrite it in the space below:

_____

_____

What do you think it means to look well to the ways of your household?

_____

_____

_____

household responsibilities

T The NKJV translates Proverbs 31:27, "She watches over the ways of her household," while the HCSB says, "She watches over the activities of her household and is never idle."

This woman who is praised for looking well to the ways of her household by no means leads a dull or trivial life. To the contrary, her life is full and varied. She imports exotic food ingredients, makes meals for a house full of people, looks after kids, spins wool, weaves cloth, makes bed coverings, invests in real estate, plants a vineyard, designs and manufactures her own clothing, manages a small business, and cares for the poor, all while looking like a million bucks!

Now that could be a bit intimidating for the most energetic, gifted woman. But the thing that stands out in this passage is not so much all this woman's

"SHE SEEKS WOOL AND FLAX, AND WORKS WITH WILLING HANDS."
Proverbs 31:13

abilities or all the things she *does*. What makes her extraordinary is the fact that she is so utterly un-self-centered and that she consistently demonstrates a heart to serve her family and others—all grounded in her reverence for God.

Proverbs 31 is actually a poem that a mom used to teach her young prince his A-B-C's. Each verse sequentially starts with a letter of the Hebrew alphabet. Besides learning his alphabet, this mom hoped that the memorized acrostic would one day influence the young prince's choice of a bride.

In essence, the queen mom wanted this message to sink in:

Don't marry a lazy, self-indulgent woman of leisure. Look for a girl who is multi-faceted, capable, and industrious—one who isn't marrying you for your money. Make sure she has a serving, compassionate spirit, and isn't afraid to get her hands dirty. And make sure she's the kind of woman who'll make her God, husband, kids, and home a priority!

"Besides that, they learn to be idlers, going about from house to house, and not only idlers, but also gossips and busybodies, saying what they should not. So I would have [them] ... manage their households, and give the adversary no occasion for slander."
I Timothy 5:13–14

"For among them are those who worm their way into households and capture idle women burdened down with sins, led along by a variety of passions."
2 Timothy 3:6 HCSB

The Old Testament praises the woman who "looks well to the ways of her household" while the New Testament instructs her to be "working at home." The idea is essentially the same. In Greek, "working at home" is a unique compound word that combines the word *home* or *house* with the word *work* or *keep/guard*.

Each English translation handles the word a little differently: "working at home" (ESV); "workers at home" (NASB); "homemakers" (NKJV); "keepers at home" (KJV).

In essence, "working at home" indicates *"an efficient management of household responsibilities."*[9] It's the same concept as, "she watches over the activities of her household and is never idle" (Prov. 31:27 HCSB). A woman's job of running the home is not to run herself ragged doing everything herself, but to ensure that what needs to be done actually gets done.

Scripture teaches that women ought to give priority to the work of their home. With its emphasis on the dignity of work it's no surprise that it also warns against the sin of idleness.

Read the verses in the margin. Why did Paul think that young widows with no proven track record of good works should be omitted from the list of widows officially supported by the church?

Paul's concern about idleness extended to men as well:

We hear that some among you walk in idleness, not busy at work, but busybodies. Now such persons we command and encourage in the Lord Jesus Christ to do their work quietly and to earn their own living. (2 Thess. 3:11–12)

the sin of idleness

To be idle is to "not be working or active," to habitually avoid one's responsibilities, or to fill one's time with things of no real worth or significance. Idleness is not the opposite of busyness. Idle people are often extremely busy. Take the woman of Proverbs 7, for example: "*She is loud and wayward; her feet do not stay at home; now in the street, now in the market, and at every corner she lies in wait*" (Prov. 7:11–12). Though this woman was busy, she was actually being idle; for she wasn't doing the "good work" she was supposed to do.

One of the reasons Scripture commands women to be *working at home* is that the Lord doesn't want us to be *idle at home* . . . or anywhere else for that matter. His main concern isn't our physical location. It's that we keep ourselves

busy doing the "good works" for which He created us. For wives and moms, that means not neglecting the practical needs of the home and family. For all women, it means being a diligent worker in whatever sphere(s) He has placed us for the blessing of others and the glory of God.

Do you struggle with idleness, busying yourself with time-wasting activities, or competing activities that keep you from "working at home" and "looking well to the way of your household"? Explain.

_____

_____

→ **Take a moment to examine your heart.** Ask the Holy Spirit to point out if/how you engage in time-wasting activities, and which responsibilites you may be neglecting as a result. Ask Him what changes you need to make in order to diligently put first things first.

important work to do

"Women's work within the home gives her no autonomy; it is not directly useful to society, it does not open out on the future, it produces nothing."[10]
Simone de Beauvoir

"Women who adjust as housewives, who grow up wanting to be just a housewife, are in as much danger as the millions who walked to their own death in the concentration camps ... they are suffering a slow death of mind and spirit."[11]
Betty Friedan

In the classic children's fantasy book *The Phantom Tollbooth*, a young boy drives his toy car through a tollbooth that mysteriously appears in his bedroom and finds himself in the Kingdom of Wisdom. The Kingdom is in chaos because Rhyme and Reason—the Kingdom's two princesses—are missing. To restore order, the young boy, Milo, must go on a quest to rescue them.

Milo travels to the Mountains of Ignorance, where he and his faithful companions must dodge and outwit various villains to save the princesses. Here, they come across a pleasant, faceless gentleman, dressed in an elegant black business suit. The gentleman hires them to do three jobs: move a huge pile of sand grain by grain using tweezers, move a well of water drop by drop using an eye dropper, and dig a hole through a cliff using a needle.

The three friends toil hour after hour after hour after hour. After days of hard work, they have little to show for their efforts. Milo calculates how long it will take to finish.

"Pardon me," he said, tugging at the man's sleeve and holding the sheet of figures up for him to see, "but it's going to take eight hundred and thirty-seven years to do these jobs."

"Is that so?" replied the man, without even turning around. "Well, you'd better get on with it then."

"But it hardly seems worthwhile," said Milo softly.

"WORTHWHILE!" the man roared indignantly.

"All I meant was that perhaps it isn't too important," Milo repeated, trying not to be impolite.

"Of course it's not important," he snarled angrily. "I wouldn't have asked you to do it if I thought it was important." And now, as he turned to face them, he didn't seem quite so pleasant.

"Then why bother?" asked Tock, whose alarm suddenly began to ring.

"Because, my young friends," he muttered sourly, "what could be more important than doing unimportant things?". . . "If you only do the easy and useless jobs, you'll never have to worry about the important ones which are so difficult. You just won't have the time. For there's always something to do to keep you from what you really should be doing."

He punctuated his last remark with a villainous laugh.[12]

It's true, isn't it? There's always something to do to keep us from what we really should be doing. The great villain, Satan, wants to distract us, get us off track, confuse our priorities, and keep us so busy that we just won't have time to do what's most important.

Number the following tasks from 1 to 5 with 1 being what you would consider the most important and 5 being the least important task.	Explain why you numbered them the way you did:
_____ Leading a small group Bible Study _____ Watching your kid's volleyball game _____ Finishing a major report for the boss _____ Cleaning the bathroom _____ Having guests over for dinner	

Did you have a tough time ranking which task was the most important? We suspect you did. Done for the glory of God, all of the items on the list can be "good" works . . . even cleaning the bathroom. Giving that toilet a scrub could be one of the most important and godly things you do today. Then again,

finishing the business report might be. It depends on your circumstances. It's not the nature of the task that determines its relative importance. Its importance is determined by your God-given relationships and responsibilities, why you're doing what you're doing, and Who you're doing it for.

The feminist movement taught women to disdain household chores as trivial, unimportant, and demeaning. Read the quotes in the margins on pages 152 and 153.

Generally speaking, what is your attitude toward housework?

You may be young or old; single, married, divorced, or widowed; a student, homemaker, or corporate executive . . . regardless of your particular circumstance, the Lord wants you to recognize the value of the _home_. Your home (whether it's a house, an apartment, condo, or dorm room) isn't just a place to eat, sleep, and hang your purse—it's an important venue for doing good works. The Lord wants you to have a vision for the vital role your home can play in furthering the kingdom of God.

Housework is not an end in itself. Marriage is not an end in itself. Child-rearing is not an end in itself. Home is not an end in itself. None of these things ought to be idolized or upheld as the ultimate goal. They are simply means to a much greater end.

Read the verses in the margin. What ought to be your aim in the "good works" that you do?

The reason we give priority to managing household responsibilities is not that vacuuming, dusting, or cooking are intrinsically valuable or satisfying tasks. It's that we want to create a peaceful, orderly, welcoming environment conducive to nurturing and growing disciples for the kingdom of God. I (Mary) want "Mary's House" to come up on the heavenly Google map when the angels search for "ministry sites in or near Edmonton, Canada."

I (Nancy) want "Nancy's House" to come up when they search for "spiritual lighthouses near Niles, Michigan." Our homes provide a needed and powerful setting for serving others and advancing the work of His kingdom.

As we close this week's lessons, we'd like to leave you with a few thoughts:

- The Lord places great value on the work of the home and so should you.

- Satan will try to distract you from doing what's most important by keeping you busy doing things of lesser importance. You can't do everything. You need to be strategic about how you use your time and energy to invest in eternity.

- It's important to understand the seasonal nature of a woman's life. In the child-rearing season, home management requires significantly more time and energy, and you will do well to adjust your other work commitments accordingly.

- It is an incredible privilege and responsibility to steward the various gifts and relationships the Lord has entrusted to you. Remember that whether in the home, in the marketplace, or anywhere else . . . your aim is to work for God.

→ Review this week's lessons. How do you think the Lord wants you to apply them to your life? Jot down your thoughts and "Personalize It" on page 157.

drawing it out, drawing it in . . .

↓

interior renovation

process

The video for Week Six will help you process this week's lessons. You'll find this week's video, the leader's guide, and additional resources at TrueWoman201.com.

ponder

Think about the following questions. Discuss them with your friends, family, and/or small group:

1. How has our culture's view of work changed since the 19th century, and what challenges has this change created for women?

2. What are some of the most common perspectives about women and work in our culture today?

3. How did you process decisions for your current "work" situation, whether you are a stay-at-home mom, a single woman with a career, a mom with a full- or part-time vocation, etc.?

4. What should govern our decisions about our work life, and what overarching perspective should shape our thinking on this subject?

5. Male and female roles are neither identical nor interchangeable. How does that principle impact your thinking about work both inside and outside the home?

6. Describe what it means to be idle. If there are hours or activities of idleness in your life, what practical steps can you take to redeem that time or those activities for God's kingdom?

7. Our homes provide a powerful setting for serving others and advancing the work of God's kingdom. Do you find joy in that truth? If not, what truths from this week's lessons can help you find joy?

8. Each of us is called to steward the gifts and relationships God has given to us. Does recognizing that primary aim indicate the need for any changes in your day-to-day routine? If so, what practical steps can you take to implement change?

personalize it

Use this page to journal. Write down what you learned this week. Record your comments, a favorite verse, or a concept or quote that was particularly helpful or meaningful to you. Compose a prayer, letter, or poem. Jot down notes from the video or your small group session. Express your heart response to what you have studied. Personalize this week's lessons in the way that will best help you apply them to your life.

drawing it out,
drawing it in . . .

Benevolence

"Practice random acts of kindness and senseless acts of beauty" is a famous quote that supposedly was first scrawled on a paper placemat in a restaurant by California writer and peace activist Anne Herbert in 1982.

According to urban legend, the quote got passed on from person to person for years until someone spray-painted it on a wall in San Francisco. A woman saw the graffiti and copied down the quote to give to her teacher husband, who then posted it on his class bulletin board. One of his students told it to her mother, who wrote about it in a local news column. *Glamour* magazine saw it and urged its readers to practice random acts of kindness, as did *Reader's Digest*. It wasn't long before the quote was on bumper stickers and T-shirts everywhere.[1]

The idea caught on like wildfire. In 1993, Conari Press released *Random Acts of Kindness*, a compilation of quotes and true stories about acts of kindness. Later that year, Chuck Wall, a Bakersfield College professor, assigned his students to "commit random acts of senseless kindness" as a class project. *People* magazine did a story about him and "the kindness movement." In 1995, the Random Acts of Kindness Foundation was established to encourage the practice of kindness in all sectors of society. Even Congress joined in, declaring an entire week in February as National Random Acts of Kindness Week.[2]

*A True Woman is charitable toward others . . . She is "**kind**."*

Gavin Whitsett, the author of a little purple handbook entitled *Guerrilla Kindness*, suggested that people do such things as pay bridge tolls for cars behind them, wave to kids in school buses, send flowers to a convalescent home, or sow nickels in a playground sandbox. He wanted to remind people "that it feels good to act on [kind] impulses."

Though the kindness movement and media attention have waned, the idea still surfaces from time to time. Last Christmas, for example, a "Secret Santa" walked into her local Walmart in Texas and paid off the entire list of layaway accounts.[3]

And not long ago, a young man walked into a local Tim Horton's, a popular Canadian coffee chain, and purchased coffee for the next 500 patrons. His act was replicated in two other Canadian cities. The media used the incidents to remind people what a good idea it is to *practice random acts of kindness and senseless acts of beauty.*[4]

The "random acts of kindness" movement is a powerful commentary on our society. Our lives are so disconnected and so filled with selfish pursuits that we crave those moments when someone breaks out of the norm of self-interest to be kind and considerate toward us.

However, in the type of "random acts of kindness and senseless acts of beauty" that society commends, the benefactor and the beneficiary generally have little if any awareness of each other's deepest motivations and needs. Though the momentary connection may put a smile on their faces, as one writer suggests, the interaction is a paltry "dwarf species" of the rich, God-like type of kindness the Lord wants us to cultivate.[5]

For a believer, kindness is a fruit of the Spirit that is empowered, enabled, and directed by God. When our kindness extends beyond those who deserve or reciprocate our benevolence, when it reaches out to those whose shortcomings and failures we know full well, that is when we reflect the heart of Him who is "kind to the ungrateful and the evil" (Luke 6:35).

The element of design we're studying this week is benevolence: a True Woman is charitable toward others . . . she is "kind." The theme closely ties in to last week's lessons. Both sets of lessons deal with "good works." Last week, we talked about work in a general way, and how a woman decides what kind of work ought to be the focus of her time and attention. We saw that when making decisions about work, the Lord wants women to give high priority to the work of the home.

This week, we'll talk about the type of heart and spirit that produce good works. All the work we do—whether in the home, the marketplace, or other ministry settings—should proceed from a kind heart—a good, benevolent, charitable heart.

A kind-hearted Christian woman is a rare find in this self-centered world where there are far more takers than givers. Christian kindness, expressed in our attitudes and actions, our speech, on the Internet and in social media, in our relationships, and in our homes, churches, and communities, is a powerful means of displaying the amazing kindness of Christ in coming to this world to save sinners. →

great act of kindness

> "When we as God's children are kind to those who don't deserve it, we reflect the gospel, the amazing, undeserved kindness of Jesus Christ."[6]

Nancy

To be kind is to have a *good heart* that is inclined toward doing good things for others.

Several weeks ago, I (Nancy) came down with a bad head cold. I had just had a house full of guests for eight days and was worn out from all the activity. Right at that time, we got hit with a massive snowstorm and record-breaking low temperatures that resulted in things pretty much shutting down for several days. I hunkered down with boxes of Kleenex and megadoses of vitamin C.

In the midst of feeling miserable, I was touched to get a text from a friend who lives nearby and had seen something I posted on Facebook about my cold. She said the Lord had put it on her heart to make me a pot of

chicken noodle soup and would it be okay to drop it by. The humongous pot of homemade soup that showed up at my house that afternoon would have fed a small army through an extended food shortage. I'm still enjoying that delicious soup and being refreshed by the kindness of that sweet couple.

And it's not the first time. That same friend has often texted to ask if she could pick up anything at the store for me while she was out running errands. She has helped cook and clean up dinners I've hosted in my home. She is one of many people who express the undeserved kindness of Christ to me in small and large ways, time and time again.

I (Mary) vividly remember the time I was flat on my back on a gurney in the hospital, being wheeled to an operating room. I was miscarrying twins, and had been cramping and bleeding for several days. Since I was in my second trimester, my gynecologist advised that I have a D&C procedure. For some reason, Brent wasn't there—he had probably returned home to be with our other three children. The young porter pushed the gurney from behind my head. I couldn't see his face, though I could hear the soft thud of his shoes against the polished floor of the empty hallway. I felt so alone. As we reached the elevator, the finality of losing the babies hit me. The tears

flooded my eyes and trickled down into my ears. Wordlessly, the young man handed me a tissue. I felt as though an angel had pressed it into my hand.

That small act of kindness ministered the grace of Jesus to me in a way that is difficult to explain. Even now, more than twenty years later, I can still sense the warm, powerful wave of comfort that gently enveloped me. I don't know if I can think of any other kindness that touched me as powerfully as that simple act.

Describe a time when an act of kindness powerfully ministered to you.

_____

_____

What was it about that act of kindness that made it so meaningful?

_____

_____

Acts of kindness can encourage us, comfort us, provide what we lack, or help us get out of an unpleasant or dangerous predicament. Few things cheer us as much as an act of kindness—whether we're on the receiving or the giving end. I (Nancy) have a friend who has worked as a marriage and family therapist. He has observed that simple kindness is one of the most important ingredients for building a strong, healthy marriage. It's true in other relationships as well.

The element of design we're studying this week, benevolence, is based on the word *kind*, which is the next item on Paul's list of things older women ought to teach younger ones. The Greek word that's translated *kind* means "to be good-natured, to be good and benevolent, profitable, useful, beneficial in its effect, kind, helpful, charitable."[7]

The main challenge in understanding the meaning of the word is the fact that it's one of a series of terms that overlap and are not clearly or consistently distinguishable in meaning—in Greek, Hebrew, or English.[8] Kindness can't be isolated from the qualities of affection, sympathy, friendliness, patience, pleasantness, gentleness, tenderness, generosity, and especially goodness.

In essence, to be kind is to have a *good heart* that is inclined toward doing *good things* for others. In Scripture, *kindness* not only describes the beneficial nature of a deed, but also indicates that the deed is motivated by the godly character of the benefactor. For that reason, the Greek and Hebrew words for kindness are often translated as "good" or "goodness." A kind woman is a good (morally excellent) person whose character moves her to do things that are useful, beneficial, and good.

"Older women likewise are to . . . train the young women to . . . be kind."

Titus 2:3–5

"But when the kindness of God our Savior and His love for mankind appeared, He saved us—not by works of righteousness that we had done, but according to His mercy, through the washing of regeneration and renewal by the Holy Spirit."

Titus 3:4–5 HCSB

Read the second passage in the margin. What are the two phrases Paul uses to identify Jesus? (Hint: They're the phrases that describe what "appeared.")

What did we do to deserve this great kindness of God?

God the Father is infinitely, perfectly kind. How might a deeper understanding of His kindness affect the way you view Him or relate to Him?

Circle the phrase "love for mankind" in Titus 3:4-5 in the margin on page 162.

The Greek word translated "love for mankind" is *philanthrōpia*, from which we get our English word *philanthropy*. In other words, the verse says that Jesus is the perfect expression of the Father's kindness and His philanthropy (benevolence) toward undeserving sinners. Kindness and benevolence originate with God the Father and find their meaning in who He is and what He does—and particularly in and through His greatest, kindest, most philanthropic act—sending His Son to purchase our salvation.

This Great Kindness is a gift. We can't pay for it. We can't demand it. We can't merit it by how good or nice we are, or by our own acts of kindness. No. God saves us because He is eternally and immeasurably kind, good, and merciful. He is the great Benefactor—the great Philanthropist.

So for a child of God, kindness is never truly random or senseless. Instead, it bears witness to the kindness of our heavenly Father and the great redemptive work of Jesus. We are kind because God is kind, and because through Jesus, our hearts are filled to the brim with goodness and kindness. Most people would agree that showing kindness is a nice, decent thing to do. But for a believer, it's the God-thing to do.

Read the verses in the margin. Explain how being a recipient of God's kindness should impact your desire and ability to show kindness to others.

_____

_____

→ **Close in prayer.** Thank the Father for His great kindness and love toward you, which is demonstrated through His Son, Jesus Christ.

"BUT LOVE YOUR ENEMIES, AND DO GOOD, AND LEND, EXPECTING NOTHING IN RETURN, AND YOUR REWARD WILL BE GREAT, AND YOU WILL BE SONS OF THE MOST HIGH, FOR HE IS KIND TO THE UNGRATEFUL AND THE EVIL. BE MERCIFUL, EVEN AS YOUR FATHER IS MERCIFUL."

Luke 6:35–36

"BE KIND TO ONE ANOTHER, TENDERHEARTED, FORGIVING ONE ANOTHER, AS GOD IN CHRIST FORGAVE YOU."

Ephesians 4:32

putting on kindness

"Show kindness and mercy to one another."
Zechariah 7:9

"Put on then, as God's chosen ones, holy and beloved, compassionate hearts, kindness, humility, meekness, and patience."
Colossians 3:12

"Be kindly affectionate to one another with brotherly love, in honor giving preference to one another."
Romans 12:10 NKJV

"To sum up, all of you be . . . sympathetic, brotherly, kindhearted, and humble in spirit."
I Peter 3:8 NASB

Back when I (Mary) was a kid, there was a popular children's chorus about kindness that we often sang in Sunday school:

Be ye kind one to another,
Tenderhearted, forgiving one another
Just as God in Christ hath forgiven you.
Doo-doo-do-do-do-do—do-do-do-do
Ephesians 4:32 (Yeah!)

The "do-do-do-do" part and the "yeah!" part aren't in Scripture, but the rest is a fairly accurate rendition of the verse in Ephesians.

Yesterday, we mentioned that the main challenge in understanding the meaning of the word *kindness* is the fact that it belongs to a cluster of attributes that go together, overlap in meaning, and are even used interchangeably sometimes. It's like the words  *window* and *glass*. They don't mean exactly the same thing. But they're so closely associated that if I were to say, "She peered out through the glass," you'd assume she was looking through a window, and if I said, "She peered out though the window," you'd assume that she was looking through a piece of glass, even though technically, window and glass are two separate things.

Ephesians 4:32 mentions two attributes closely associated with kindness: *tenderheartedness* and *forgiveness*. Use the verses in the margin to complete the "word cloud" by adding the other related attributes.

Kindness Cluster
Tenderheartedness
Forgiveness

The Greek word translated "brotherly" and "brotherly love" is *philadelphos*. It's a combination of *phila*, which means "friendly" or "affectionate," and *adelphos*, which means "brother" or other family member. (I [Nancy] grew up in *Philadelphia*, the city of "brotherly love.")

The word is similar to a word we looked at yesterday. Titus 3:4 says that Jesus revealed God's "love for mankind," or His *philanthrōpia*: phil= friendly/affectionate + *anthrōpos* = humanity.

Can you see the similarity between the two terms? *Philanthropos* (philanthropy) is having a tender heart that's affectionate toward people in general. *Philadelphos* is having a tender, affectionate, and charitable (philanthropic) spirit toward a family member or a specific family—in this case, the family of God.

All the attributes you wrote down in the word cloud contribute to what it means to be kind. Do you want to increase in kindness? Then aim to be more patient. Aim to be more humble. Aim to be more forgiving. Aim to be gentler. Aim to be more sympathetic. As you grow in these related traits, you will grow in kindness.

Examine the attributes in the circles of the following diagram. Think about how each one contributes to kindness.

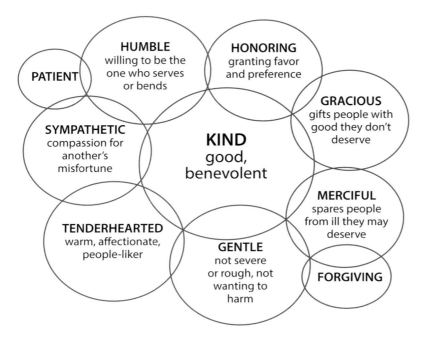

PATIENT

HUMBLE
willing to be the one who serves or bends

HONORING
granting favor and preference

GRACIOUS
gifts people with good they don't deserve

SYMPATHETIC
compassion for another's misfortune

KIND
good, benevolent

MERCIFUL
spares people from ill they may deserve

TENDERHEARTED
warm, affectionate, people-liker

GENTLE
not severe or rough, not wanting to harm

FORGIVING

"Show kindness in your homes, at church, and at work. Show kindness when you rise up in the morning and when you come to the end of your day. Show kindness because God is kind and has been so kind to you."[9]

Lisa Hughes

On the report card, give yourself a grade for how consistently you exhibit each attribute:

A = I'm consistently like this

B = I'm most often like this

C = I'm sometimes like this

D = I'm seldom like this

F = This doesn't describe me at all

Kindness Report Card			
Attribute		Comments	Grade
Tenderhearted	I am warm, welcoming, and compassionate. I genuinely like and care about people.		
Sympathetic	I empathize with people's concerns. I'm patient with their shortcomings.		
Humble	I am willing to be the one who serves, or the one who is inconvenienced.		
Honoring	I grant favor and preference to others. I am eager to see them acknowledged.		
Gracious	I go above and be-yond to treat people well—even if they don't deserve it.		
Merciful	I do not repay evil for evil. I do not harbor resentments. I freely forgive.		
Gentle	I'm not critical. I'm peaceful and genial. I seek to bless, not harm.		

Which attribute is the most challenging for you? Explain why.

_____

_____

Reread Colossians 3:12 on page 164. What are we instructed to do with this cluster of attributes? Circle the correct answer:

A. Casually shrug them off as inconsequential

B. Intentionally put them on like clothing

C. Aim to get a better kindness report card grade

Explain what you think this involves:

_____

_____

The Greek word translated "put on" in Colossians 3:12 means to "envelope in" or "clothe with."[10] Paul admonished his friends to clothe themselves with the type of attitude and behavior that befitted their new life in Christ.

The metaphor of changing clothes was widely used in the ancient world to illustrate spiritual transformation.[11] The apostle wanted them to understand that since they were now saints, they needed to start dressing the part. Their old attitudes would no longer do. They needed to intentionally put on the apparel of Christ and clothe themselves with His kindness.

→ **Close this lesson in prayer.** Are you dressing the part? Confess any lack of kindness the Spirit has shown you. Ask the Lord to soften your spirit and make you kind and tenderhearted.

a kind word

*J*enny was born with a cleft palate. She grew up with the painful awareness that she was different. She never felt as though she fit in. At school, she had to put up with the jokes, stares, and non-stop teasing about her misshaped lip, crooked nose, and garbled speech.

Jenny was convinced that no one outside of her family could ever love her . . . until she met her new teacher, Mrs. Leonard. Mrs. Leonard had a round face, shiny brown hair, a warm smile, and kindness in her eyes.

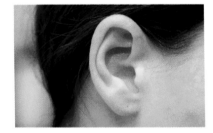

Back then, teachers were required to conduct annual hearing screens. So one day, Mrs. Leonard lined the students up in the hallway for the test. Jenny shifted nervously from foot to foot. In addition to her cleft palate, Jenny could barely hear out of one ear. Determined that her classmates would not know about this deficit—and give them even more reason to tease—Jenny always cheated on the hearing test.

The "Whisper Test" was conducted by having each child stand beside the classroom door, turn sideways, plug the ear closest to the door with a finger, and then repeat the phrase that the teacher whispered from her desk halfway across the room.

Jenny turned her bad ear toward her teacher and pretended to plug her good ear, cupping it so she could hear better instead. She knew that teachers would often say things like, "The sky is blue," or "What color are your shoes?" But not that day. When the "Whisper Test" came, Jenny heard the words: "I wish you were my little girl." Those kind words changed Jenny's life forever.[12]

Proverbs 10:20 says, "*The tongue of the righteous is choice silver; the heart of the wicked is of little worth.*" In other words, the condition of our heart impacts the condition of our speech. If our hearts are filled with kindness, our speech will be filled with kindness too. Unkind words, on the other hand, are a telltale symptom of an unkind heart.

Read Ephesians 4:29 in the margin. The Greek word translated "good" can also be translated "helpful" or "kind." In your own words, describe God's standard for the words we speak.

_____

_____

> "*Let no unwholesome word proceed from your mouth, but only such a word as is good for edification according to the need of the moment, so that it will give grace to those who hear.*"
>
> **Ephesians 4:29** NASB

Good, kind speech benefits, builds, and helps others. It's based on *their* needs and not on our own needs or desires. Kind speech is compassionate, patient, humble, honoring, gracious, merciful, forgiving, gentle, and tenderhearted.

Remind them . . . to speak evil of no one, to avoid quarreling, to be gentle [kind],[13] and to show perfect courtesy toward all people. (Titus 3:1–2)

The Lord's servant must not be quarrelsome but kind to everyone . . . patiently enduring evil. (2 Tim. 2:24)

See that no one repays anyone evil for evil, but always seek to do good [be kind] to one another and to everyone. (1 Thess. 5:15)

She opens her mouth with wisdom, and the teaching of kindness is on her tongue. (Prov. 31:26)

Anxiety in a man's heart weighs it down, but a good word cheers it up. (Prov. 12:25 HCSB)

Use the verses above to complete the following chart:

Characteristics of Unkind Speech	Characteristics of Kind Speech

Is your speech kind? Are you kind toward the clerk who makes a mistake ringing up your order? the fast-food attendant who is anything but fast? the serviceman who is brusque and unhelpful? the coworker who off-loads her work onto your desk? the team member who criticizes your skills? the colleague who constantly feels the need to brag? the friend who is quick to point out your faults? What about in social media, and when posting comments on blogs with which you disagree?

If you were to give yourself a kindness "grade" based solely on your speech in such situations, what grade would you give yourself and why?

Our speech is the fruit of what's in our hearts. According to Ephesians 4:31–32, what attitudes do you need to get rid of and replace with kindness?

It's easy to be kind to people who are nice to us. It's when we're treated unkindly that our true character is revealed. That's when we discover how drastically kindness is lacking in our hearts. If you're deficient in the kindness cluster of attributes, you may respond to injury or offense with:

Bitterness	Uncharitable attitude	You are resentful and have a bad attitude. You feel hurt and defensive, and harden your heart toward the person.
Rage & Anger	Uncharitable feelings	Your thoughts and assumptions emotionally inflame you. You become agitated.
Brawling & Slander	Uncharitable speech	You have difficulty speaking to her civilly (brawling). When you speak about her, you have nothing good to say (slander).
Malice	Uncharitable intentions	You wish evil upon the person who hurt you. You want revenge. You rejoice in your opponent's downfall and gloat over her misfortune. You want to see her fail, be punished, and suffer.

Have you allowed an uncharitable spirit to fester in your heart? Below, identify specific situations in which you've harbored or expressed a lack of charity toward others:

Bitterness (uncharitable attitude):

Rage & Anger (uncharitable feelings):

Brawling & Slander (uncharitable speech):

Malice (uncharitable intentions):

> "When we as God's children are kind to those who don't deserve it, we reflect the gospel, the amazing, undeserved kindness of Jesus Christ."[14]
>
> *Nancy*

A lack of kindness and charity can flare up in the heat of the moment, or it can fester and defile your heart over a period of time. So how can you combat this problem? Ephesians 4:31–32 provides the antidote: replace these unkind attitudes and words with the sort of kindness you've received from God.

→ **Spend some time in prayer**, repenting of your lack of charity. Ask the Lord for grace to demonstrate the kindness of God in your attitude and your speech.

charity begins at home

You've probably heard the slogan "Charity begins at home." It appears to be one of those proverbial sayings with no clear origin. There are various and conflicting explanations as to exactly where this saying originated and what it means.

Some people suggest that the proverb has a negative, self-centered meaning. They claim it originated in 14th-century English literature, in Terence's play *Andria*, when the protagonist sarcastically says, *"Proximus sum egomet mihi"* (the closest one to me is me myself) about a friend he thinks betrayed him and acted selfishly.

Nowadays, the saying "Charity begins at home" is sometimes used in this negative manner by people trying to avoid giving money to charitable causes. For example, if a man is asked for a donation to help flood victims in the Philippines, and he responds with, "Charity begins at home," his

objection is that he needs to look after himself first, and isn't obligated to give money elsewhere.

More often, however, the proverb is used in a positive way, to indicate that a person should be kind and generous to his or her own family first, before worrying about and helping other people. The issue is not one of selfishness, but of being responsible to fulfill one's family obligations.

The great English Reformer John Wycliffe expressed the idea in 1382 when he said, "Charite schuld bigyne a hem-self" ("Charity should begin at himself"). In other words, charity is something that starts in my heart, flows out into my home and closest family relationships, then flows out to the family of God, and finally, in ever-broadening circles, to the world. The idea is illustrated in the following diagram.

"But if a widow has children or grandchildren, let them first learn to show godliness to their own household and to make some return to their parents, for this is pleasing in the sight of God."

I Timothy 5:4

"But you say, 'If a man tells his father or mother: Whatever benefit you might have received from me is Corban'" (that is, a gift committed to the temple), "you no longer let him do anything for his father or mother. You revoke God's word by your tradition that you have handed down. And you do many other similar things."

Mark 7:11–13 HCSB

Look up 1 Timothy 5:8 in your Bible and write it in the space below.

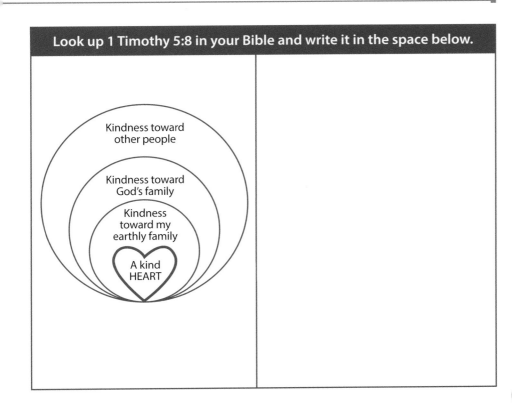

Kindness toward
other people

Kindness toward
God's family

Kindness
toward my
earthly family

A kind
HEART

Explain what you think the verse means by "he has denied the faith."

_____

_____

Read the verses in the margin on page 172. Circle the phrase "first learn to show godliness to their own household." Why do you think it's important to show godliness to our own households first?

_____

_____

Mark 7:11–13 records a confrontation that Jesus had with some religious leaders. Jesus accused them of hypocrisy for coming up with spiritual-sounding excuses for neglecting their family responsibilities.

To declare something "corban" was to legally bequeath it as a gift to God. However, the person could keep using the dedicated item/money. It would only be donated to the temple after his death. A man who declared "corban" on his estate could therefore tell his parents or any other family member who needed his help, "I'm sorry, I can't help you. Everything I have belongs to God."

Jesus condemned this "charity" as hypocritical. On the surface, pledging money to God's work appeared to be a charitable act, but in actual fact, the giver was motivated by self-interest. God commands us to honor our parents and other family relationships. A truly kind heart will be kind to family first. True benevolence begins at home.

In which of the following situations would you find it *easiest* to demonstrate kindness? Put a mark beside the easiest scenario.

- ☐ Serving soup with kindness to the homeless at a soup kitchen
- ☐ Serving soup with kindness to your belligerent child or grumpy husband
- ☐ Serving soup with kindness to a sibling who just berated you
- ☐ Serving soup with kindness to the ungrateful teens at youth group
- ☐ Serving soup with kindness to your family when you're exhausted and no one has offered to help in the kitchen

For most of us, the most difficult place to consistently demonstrate kindness is at home. Kindly making a donation to an agency asking for money for hunger relief is far easier than being kind to a husband, teen, elderly parent, or toddler who is clamoring for you to relieve their hunger.

We don't think it's a coincidence that the directive to cultivate kindness comes immediately after the directive for women to give priority to working

in their homes. Working in the home is often one of the toughest and most thankless jobs. You may be competent and faithful and work hard to manage your home, but Scripture challenges you to consider whether your actions and attitudes in the home flow out of a kind and good heart.

Remember the kindness report card? The Lord wants you to aim to improve your kindness grade, starting with family first—and particularly those family members whom you find the most difficult to love—whether you live under the same roof or not. Which family relationship do you find the most challenging? Do you have a desire to show that person the kindness God has shown you?

Express that desire by writing that family member's initials in the blanks below:

My Heart's Desire	
Tenderhearted	By God's grace, I will be warm, welcoming, and compassionate. I will genuinely like and care about _____.
Sympathetic	I will empathize with _____'s concerns. I will be patient with his/her shortcomings.
Humble	I am willing to be the one who serves _____. I will be happy to be inconvenienced for his/her sake.
Honoring	I will grant favor and preference to _____. I will joyfully put his/her needs above my own.
Gracious	I will go above and beyond to treat _____ well— even when he/she doesn't deserve it.
Merciful	I will not repay evil for evil. I will not harbor resentments. I freely forgive _____.
Gentle	I will not be critical. I will be peaceful and genial. I will seek to bless, not harm _____.

→ Close this lesson by taking some time to pray for God's enabling grace to live out this commitment and to show His kindness to this family member.

with charity for all

O On March 4, 1865, just a few weeks before he was assassinated, President Abraham Lincoln gave his second inaugural address, which ended with these words:

With malice toward none, with charity for all, with firmness in the right as God gives us to see the right, let us strive on to finish the work we are in, to bind up the nation's wounds, to care for him who shall have borne the battle and for his widow and his orphan, to do all which may achieve and cherish a just and lasting peace among ourselves and with all nations.

The address has been identified as the noblest political discourse in history.[16] This is due, in no small part, to its heavy reliance on Scripture. Lincoln challenged a country wracked by civil war to have malevolence toward none and charity toward all; to do good work, have compassion for the brokenhearted, care for widows, orphans, and the needy; to exercise

justice for the oppressed, and have peace and goodwill toward mankind.

Lincoln's challenge is a reflection of God's ongoing challenge to us—to have good, benevolent hearts, and to be instruments of His kindness to our broken world.

Read the verses in the margin. What do you think it means to "love kindness"?

_____

_____

Summarize what the verses teach about "doing good."

_____

_____

_____

"He has told you, O man, what is good; and what does the LORD require of you but to do justice, and to love kindness, and to walk humbly with your God?"
Micah 6:8

"Learn to do what is good. Seek justice. Correct the oppressor. Defend the rights of the fatherless. Plead the widow's cause."
Isaiah 1:17 HCSB

"But be doers of the word, and not hearers only, deceiving yourselves. . . . Religion that is pure and undefiled before God, the Father, is this: to visit orphans and widows in their affliction, and to keep oneself unstained from the world."
James 1:22, 27

All this week we've been studying the design element of benevolence. A True Woman is charitable toward others . . . she is "kind." We've talked about the fact that kindness begins in the heart and shows up in our attitudes and speech, as well as our actions. We've seen that the home is the first place we ought to demonstrate kindness—toward our husbands, children, parents, siblings, and other family members. But kindness doesn't end there. A heart that is truly kind will overflow with compassion for friends, neighbors, colleagues, and those who are poor, oppressed, and downtrodden.

What do the verses in the margin teach about your obligation to extend kindness beyond the walls of your home?

_____

_____

_____

Explain why a woman who withholds kindness "forsakes the fear of the Almighty" and "insults her Maker"?

_____

_____

Jerry Bridges says, "The person who has grown in the grace of kindness has expanded his thinking outside of himself and his interests and has developed a genuine interest in the happiness and the well-being of those around him."[17] A kind heart cannot be contained. It inevitably spills over to minister God's kindness to others.

History is full of examples of women who've demonstrated God's kindness: well-known women like Florence Nightingale, Amy Carmichael, Sarah Edwards, Gladys Aylward, Henrietta Mears, Lottie Moon, and Elisabeth Elliot. Lesser known

"BEHOLD, THIS WAS THE GUILT OF YOUR SISTER SODOM: SHE AND HER DAUGHTERS HAD PRIDE, EXCESS OF FOOD, AND PROSPEROUS EASE, BUT DID NOT AID THE POOR AND NEEDY."
Ezekiel 16:49

"HE WHO WITHHOLDS KINDNESS FROM A FRIEND FORSAKES THE FEAR OF THE ALMIGHTY."
Job 6:14

"THE ONE WHO OPPRESSES THE POOR PERSON INSULTS HIS MAKER, BUT ONE WHO IS KIND TO THE NEEDY HONORS HIM."
Proverbs 14:31 HCSB

"A NOBLE PERSON PLANS NOBLE THINGS; HE STANDS UP FOR NOBLE CAUSES."
Isaiah 32:8 HCSB

women like Mary Clarke, who translated the gospel of Luke into the Limba language; Sarah Martin, a British philanthropist who worked hard for prison reform; and Louise Campbell, who founded the Kwong Yet Girls School in South China. And virtually unknown women, like my (Mary's) friend Charlene, the college student who made chicken soup for an ailing misfit, setting off a chain of events that caused him to come to Christ and forsake his notorious lifestyle of dealing drugs.

We could tell you stories about women we know who rescue girls from the sex trade, minister to women in prison, care for the poor and homeless, take in orphans, foster children, support single moms, rescue abused women, provide hospice for AIDS victims, work to end illiteracy, volunteer at pregnancy counseling centers, minister to girls who suffer from anorexia, bulimia, cutting, and other addictions, provide meals for people in crisis . . . the list of their acts of kindness could go on and on.

The goal of these women is not to become great, but to show how great God is. Acts of kindness, done in the name of Jesus, make the gospel attractive and believable. Ultimately, their purpose is to draw people to accept the  Great Kindness of God found in His Son, Christ Jesus.

As Romans 2:4 points out, God's kindness leads us to repentance. That's why kindness is so important. And that's why we're commanded:

> *Do not let kindness and truth leave you;*
> *Bind them around your neck,*
> *Write them on the tablet of your heart.* (Prov. 3:3 NASB)

Can you think of a time when your kindness or the kindness of another Christian you know drew someone to accept the Great Kindness of God? Briefly describe what happened.

_____

_____

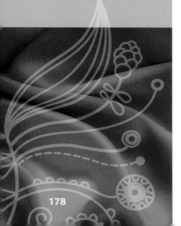

Do you think your family, friends, neighbors, and others would describe you as "kind"? Why or why not?

_____

_____

_____

_____

Read the verses in the margin on page 178. Explain why and how kindness benefits the giver as much as it benefits the receiver.

_____

_____

Scripture teaches that a kind woman is far happier than an unkind one. Are you a kind woman? Do you have a genuine interest in the happiness and the well-being of those around you? Have you bound kindness around your neck and written it on the tablet of your heart?

→ **On page 181, summarize what you have learned about kindness** and explain how the Lord is working in your heart to make you a kind woman.

drawing it out,
drawing it in . . .

interior renovation

process

The video for Week Seven will help you process this week's lessons. You'll find this week's video, the leader's guide, and additional resources at TrueWoman201.com.

ponder

Think about the following questions. Discuss them with your friends, family, and/or small group:

1. How is true Christian kindness different from the kindness offered by those who don't know Christ?

2. What difference has the kindness of God made in your life? How should God's kindness toward us impact how we deal with others?

3. What attributes are related to kindness? Which of these attributes do you find most difficult to express? Would those who are closest to you desribe you as a kind woman?

4. Why are words such a powerful way to demonstrate kindness? Discuss the characteristics of kind speech.

5. Scripture prioritizes the call to demonstrate kindness to family members first. Does that priority indicate a need for some reordering on your part?

6. Why is it sometimes easier to be kind to strangers than to family members and close friends?

7. When we're treated unkindly, our true character is revealed. How did you respond the last time you were poorly treated? As you reflect on that, what does it show you about your heart?

8. Paul's concern in the book of Titus is for the church to make the gospel known and attractive in a dark, lost world. How can Christian kindness contribute toward that end? How does a lack of kindness among believers affect our witness in the world?

personalize it

Use this page to journal. Write down what you learned this week. Record your comments, a favorite verse, or a concept or quote that was particularly helpful or meaningful to you. Compose a prayer, letter, or poem. Jot down notes from the video or your small group session. Express your heart response to what you have studied. Personalize this week's lessons in the way that will best help you apply them to your life.

drawing it out,
drawing it in . . .

disposition

It's a week before Christmas as we are writing this chapter; the nativity scenes with the Babe in the manger remind us of the poignant, powerful, paradoxical way Christ secured our salvation.

Though He existed in the form of God, He did not consider His divine status something to be used for His own advantage. Instead He emptied Himself of His divine prerogatives and took on the form of a servant. He humbled Himself and become obedient to His Father, to the point of death on a cross (Phil. 2:6–10).

Jesus Christ is the epitome of submission. His "not-My-will-but-Yours-be-done" attitude is at the heart of the gospel story. It's the infinitely precious and esteemed mindset that made it all happen. Without Christ's submission to His Father there would be no Babe in the manger and no salvation. We think it's tragic—yet not altogether surprising—that the very disposition that is so embraced by Jesus and treasured by God is so misunderstood and maligned by the world.

Titus 2:5 encourages older women to teach younger ones to be "submissive to their own husbands." What comes to your mind when you hear the word *submissive*? Do you value that disposition? Do you cherish it, and regard it as beautiful and desirable?

Many Christian women hold the trait of submission as far away as possible—like a stinky pair of socks on their way to the laundry bin. Others plug their ears when they hear the word, or roll their eyeballs, or run the other way. Some reject submission outright—by

*A True Woman cultivates a soft, amenable spirit . . . She is "**submissive**."*

redefining what it means, or by maintaining that both parties in a chain of command must submit to each other. Others erroneously think that submission means blind obedience and unquestioning compliance, or that every woman must submit to every man.

Ooooh that "S" word! There's been a great deal of ink spilled and gigabytes blogged about this controversial concept. Stereotypes and misconceptions abound. As we said in *True Woman 101*, we believe that submission to one's husband is the marriage-specific application of having a soft, feminine, amenable disposition. A soft, amenable disposition is integral to what it means to be a woman. Being submissive to one's husband is simply how it's lived out in the context of a one-flesh, covenantal love relationship.

(Before we move on, I [Nancy] would like to say a word to my unmarried sisters: It's important to realize that submission is not exclusive to the marriage relationship—we are all required to submit to the Lord and to the other authorities God has placed in our lives. So please don't tune us out or to think these lessons don't apply to you. We need to cultivate an amenable, submissive spirit just as married women do! We may not have a husband to submit to; but a soft, amenable, submissive disposition is just as vital to our womanhood and femininity.)

So . . . why do so many Christian women have trouble embracing submission? One reason is that we try to understand it apart from its foundational meaning and context. Submission is a concept that goes hand in hand with authority. Both concepts find their origin and meaning in the relationship between God the Father and God the Son. They can't be properly understood apart from that context.

Another reason many struggle with submission is that they confuse it with obedience. Submission and obedience are closely related terms whose meanings overlap but are not identical. Obedience pertains primarily to a person's behavior, whereas submissiveness has more to do with a person's attitude. Being submissive means having a responsive, lead-able spirit that is willing to be obedient to God-ordained authority. Submission is a disposition of the heart that inclines us to bend our knee to God and the authorities He has placed in our lives. As you'll see in this week's lessons, it is entirely possible to have a respectful, submissive heart attitude while at the same time refusing to obey a human authority who is asking us to disobey God.

We'll start off this week's lessons by studying authority and submission in general terms, as they are not exclusive to either gender. Then, we'll tackle some common misconceptions about the two concepts. We'll examine why cultivating a soft, amenable spirit is of particular importance for women—how women are uniquely created to shine the spotlight on the "submissive-to-God" part of the Jesus story, while men are uniquely created to shine the spotlight on the "loving-servant-Head-of-the-church" part of it.

Finally, we'll study the story of Abigail—a steel magnolia who demonstrates how to meld softness with backbone, sweetness with stamina, and gentleness with gumption, and illustrates the beauty and power of a godly, feminine disposition. →

privileged position

> "At the heart of mature femininity is a freeing disposition to affirm, receive and nurture strength and leadership from worthy men in ways appropriate to a woman's differing relationships."[1]
>
> **John Piper**

Salome lived with more privilege than most. Her husband, Zebedee, ran a successful fishing business based at Capernaum, on the north shore of the Sea of Galilee. The family was moderately wealthy, and had important religious-political connections. Their business employed numerous hired workers and associates—strapping young men like Simon Peter, along with his brother, Andrew. Salome's sons, James and John, also worked in the family business.

When they weren't fishing, the two sets of brothers hiked out to listen to John the Baptist, the enormously popular young preacher, whose scruffy cloak made him look like a relic out of the Nevi'im—the annals of the prophets of old. Indeed, many believed that he was the one the ancient prophecies foretold . . . the promised Messiah who would deliver Israel from Roman rule and inaugurate a glorious new kingdom.

The thought made Salome's pulse quicken. The prophecy! Independence! Freedom! She had overheard several women talking about it at the market. The whole countryside was abuzz with anticipation. Her boys were convinced that the time was ripe, and that the rumors about John the Baptist preparing to spearhead a Jewish revolt were true. Talk of politics, religion, and revolution had become the nightly fare around the Zebedee dinner table.

Salome was taken aback one night, when her boys shared some astonishing new information. The fiery preacher had revealed that he wasn't the deliverer—someone else was. And that "someone else" was none other than their own cousin, Jesus!

Jesus! There was no doubt in Salome's mind that Jesus was extraordinary. She had heard all the stories from her sister, Mary.[2] With no small measure

of curiosity, Salome had watched the drama unfold: Mary's report of an angelic visitation. Her extended vacation at Aunt Elizabeth's. Signs of Mary's pregnancy. The hasty marriage. Magi. Gold. A flight to Egypt. The boy confounding teachers in the temple. Salome didn't quite know what to make of it. But now, all the pieces were falling into place.

Salome supported her sons' decision to leave the fishing business to follow Jesus. When Jesus picked up where John the Baptist left off, she generously pitched in with financial support. Herod may have killed the scruffy preacher, but he couldn't stop the revolution. Jesus was wildly popular. Her sons were part of his inner circle. Salome could not have been more proud—or more excited. Jesus had promised that when He was crowned, His disciples would also sit on thrones. The coup was coming soon. She was sure of it. And she wanted to make sure that her sons secured the highest, most privileged positions in Jesus' kingdom.

Read Matthew 20:20–28 in your Bible. Can you think of some reasons why this helicopter mom may have wanted her boys to get the highest positions?

authority & submission

As we said earlier, one reason people have so much trouble with submission is that they try to understand it apart from its foundational meaning and context. Submission is a concept that goes hand in hand with authority. Like two sides of a coin, the two are inseparable. Both find their origin and meaning in the Godhead—in the relationship between God the

Father and God the Son. The concepts cannot be properly understood apart from each other, nor apart from the context of this divine relationship.

Salome was operating under the false premise that a position of authority is the superior, more desirable one. In her mind, ruling involved securing greater position, greater power, greater privilege, and greater prestige to use for one's own benefit—the ruler wins and the chumps under him lose out. Her ideas were sorely mistaken. Scripture paints a radically different picture about the true nature of authority. It teaches that:

"Jesus called them over and said to them, 'You know that those who are regarded as rulers of the Gentiles dominate them, and their men of high positions exercise power over them. But it must not be like that among you. On the contrary, whoever wants to become great among you must be your servant.'"

Mark 10:42–43 HCSB

- Authority is not self-appointed; it's delegated by God.

- Authority is not personally owned; it merely stewards and manages that which belongs to God.

- Authority is not about rights; it's about responsibility.

- Authority is not about seeking prominence; it's about giving prominence.

- Authority is not domineering and dictatorial; it's humble and gentle.

- Authority is not about getting; it's about giving.

- Authority is not about selfish gain; it's about selfless sacrifice.

- Every authority is accountable to a higher authority, and all are accountable to God the Father, who is the ultimate authority.

Read Mark 10:42–43 in the margin. Describe what's wrong with the way "Gentiles" (those who don't know God) rule:

_____

_____

Check the right answer. Jesus wanted his disciples to:

- ☐ reject authority structures
- ☐ overthrow the government
- ☐ hold hands, sing "Kumbaya," and take turns being in charge
- ☐ exercise authority and leadership in the right way

The self-serving, domineering, power-mongering way the rulers of that day exercised authority stood in marked contrast to the way authority functions in the Godhead, and the way God lovingly governs the citizens of His kingdom. Jesus didn't say that authority structures shouldn't exist. But he challenged popular ideas about the true nature of authority and He clarified what leadership actually involves.

Look up the verses below. Draw lines to match each reference to the statement that reflects what it teaches about the true nature of authority.

2 Corinthians 1:24	Godly authority is motivated by love and commitment.
Proverbs 20:28	Godly authority builds up; it doesn't tear down.
Romans 13:4	Godly authority serves as a channel of God's protection and blessing (rulers are God's servants for your good).
Hebrews 13:17	Godly authority watches over your well-being.
2 Corinthians 13:10	Godly authority works with you for your joy.
John 7:18	Godly authority doesn't glorify self; it glorifies God. It puts His character on display.

Would you welcome being under this kind of authority? Explain why or why not.

_____

_____

_____

A proper understanding of authority is critical to our relationship with God and our relationships with one another. Though the ungodly often get it wrong, Jesus wants his disciples to understand the true meaning and get it right.

→ **Close in prayer.** Ask the Lord to show you His perspective on authority and help you overcome any misconceptions you may have.

submission hold

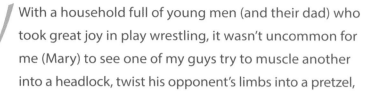

W With a household full of young men (and their dad) who took great joy in play wrestling, it wasn't uncommon for me (Mary) to see one of my guys try to muscle another into a headlock, twist his opponent's limbs into a pretzel, or somehow pin him down to the ground. The bouts were always accompanied by a great deal of grunting, laughing, loud, exaggerated sports commentary, and the occasional tipped-over broken lamp.

"They are . . . to be self-controlled, pure, working at home, kind, and submissive to their own husbands, that the word of God may not be reviled."

Titus 2:4–5

"Oh no!" one would holler, providing the imaginary audience with his own breathless color commentary, "he's got him in the Chicken Wing!" Chicken Wing was the name of one of their favorite moves. Others included the Anaconda Choke, Can Opener, Sharpshooter, and the Boston Crab. All these moves are "submission holds." A submission hold is a combat sports term for a grappling position that is applied for the purpose of forcing an opponent to submit—that is, give in and surrender.

In combat sports, the opponent who dominates and defeats the weaker candidate is the winner. The match determines who the superior fighter is . . . and ultimately, who gets the applause and the medal. The opponent who "submits" loses out on the fame and the prize, and takes the lion's share of abuse in the process.

Submission is undeniably a word with negative connotations. It's commonly viewed as an undesirable position that involves conquest, subjugation, inferiority, and oppression. This idea is so common that it's extremely difficult to root it out of our thinking. The misconceptions—even in the Christian community—are profound. There are few who understand submission's true meaning and view it as the blessing it truly is.

Circle the word *submissive* in the margin on page 188. How do you react to the idea of being submissive? Underline any phrases that describe your feeling:

- I feel mad and resentful that women are singled out this way.

- I'm so sick of the word. It makes me want to hurl.

- I'm not happy about it, but it is what it is.

- Intellectually, I get it. But emotionally, I'm a bit embarrassed that verses like this are in the Bible.

- I've made my peace with it.

- I feel that submission is a privilege and a blessing!

- Other (explain): _____

_____

"As I voluntarily submit to my husband, I am completing him. I am helping him fulfill his responsibilities, and I am helping him become the man, the husband, and the leader God intended him to be.[4]

Barbara Rainey

line up under

The Greek word translated "submissive" is the word *hupotassō* from *hupo* "under, beneath" and *tassō* "to place in order, arrange, or line up." The word is an old military term. It means to arrange under in an orderly fashion—to place in the proper position under rank. In this case, it indicates that the Lord wants a wife to voluntarily line herself up under the headship of her husband.

It's important to note that the word for submission used for the wife's desired attitude differs from the one used for the child's behavior toward his parents and the bondservant's response toward his master. In the case of children and servants, the word is *hupakouō*, from *hupo* "under, beneath" and *akouō* "to hearken, obey." *Hupakouō* means to yield to a superior command or force without necessarily being willing, whereas when Paul tells a wife to *hupotassō* herself, it means to willingly put herself in the proper position.[3]

This is a significant point. Unlike the relationship between a parent and child, where the young child is immature and in need of guidance and correction, the relationship between a husband and wife is a relationship between partners and equals. Parents have a responsibility to bring a child into submission—even if that child is unwilling. At times governing authorities must likewise coerce unwilling citizens to obey. But this pattern does not apply in the marriage relationship. According to the Bible, a wife's submission is her choice alone. A husband has no right to demand it or to try to extract obedience from her. His only responsibility is to love her, woo her, and humbly sacrifice himself for her as Christ did for the church.

The willing submission of a wife to her husband's loving authority mirrors the willing submission of Jesus Christ to the authority of God the Father.

Read the verses in the margins of these two pages. Based on the authority-submission relationship in the Godhead, mark the statements true (T) or false (F):

_____ True equality, partnership, and love can flourish within an authority-submission relationship structure.

_____ Submission involves mindless, robot-like obedience. It means not asking questions or expressing doubts or opinions.

_____ A submissive role prevents someone from making their own choices and decisions.

_____ Those in authority positions should be attentive and carefully listen to their counterpart's appeals and requests.

_____ Authority-submission counterparts can experience profound unity, harmony, communication, cooperation, teamwork, and joy.

Does Christ's submission to God fit the combat sports' definition of *submission*? Explain why or why not.

_____

_____

_____

"I and the Father are one."
John 10:30

"[Jesus] did not count equality with God a thing to be grasped. . . . He humbled himself by becoming obedient. . . . Therefore God has highly exalted him and bestowed on him the name that is above every name."
Philippians 2:6–9

"I lay down my life. . . . No one takes it from me, but I lay it down of my own accord. . . . This charge I have received from my Father."
John 10:17–18

"Do you think that I cannot appeal to my Father, and he will at once send me more than twelve legions of angels?"
Matthew 26:53

Based on what you've learned in today's lesson, come up with your own definition of *submission*.

_____

_____

_____

In the space below, redraw the diagram from page 54 that illustrates the parallel pattern between a husband-wife relationship and Christ's relationships with God and the church:

If a girlfriend asked you why the Bible tells wives to submit to husbands what would you tell her?

_____

_____

_____

 If we were to ask Jesus how He feels about the idea of submission, He'd undoubtedly say, "Submission is a privilege and a blessing." Christ models the true meaning of authority and submission. In His relationship to God the Father, He's the perfect model of submission. In His relationship to the church, He's the perfect model of authority. The husband-wife relationship is a physical, earthly symbol that was created to shine the spotlight on the nature of these relationships.

→ **Close in prayer.** Ask God to give you the mind of Christ and help you value and cherish the trait of submission as He does.

"HE FELL ON HIS FACE AND PRAYED, SAYING, 'MY FATHER, IF IT BE POSSIBLE, LET THIS CUP PASS FROM ME; NEVERTHELESS, NOT AS I WILL, BUT AS YOU WILL.'"

Matthew 26:39

"I DO AS THE FATHER HAS COMMANDED ME, SO THAT THE WORLD MAY KNOW THAT I LOVE THE FATHER. . . . I AM THE TRUE VINE, AND MY FATHER IS THE VINEDRESSER."

John 14:31–15:1

"IN THE SCROLL OF THE BOOK IT IS WRITTEN OF ME: I DELIGHT TO DO YOUR WILL, O MY GOD."

Psalm 40:7–8

"FOR THE FATHER LOVES THE SON AND SHOWS HIM ALL THAT HE HIMSELF IS DOING. AND GREATER WORKS THAN THESE WILL HE SHOW HIM, SO THAT YOU MAY MARVEL."

John 5:20

knuckle under?

"Thus says the Lord GOD: Ah, shepherds of Israel who have been feeding yourselves! Should not shepherds feed the sheep? . . . The weak you have not strengthened, the sick you have not healed, the injured you have not bound up, the strayed you have not brought back, the lost you have not sought, and with force and harshness you have ruled them."

Ezekiel 34:1–4

"Therefore thus says the LORD, the God of Israel, concerning the shepherds who care for my people: 'You . . . have not attended to them. Behold, I will attend to you for your evil deeds, declares the LORD.'"

Jeremiah 23:2

Authority and submission relationships are supposed to display the glory of God and the gospel. They're supposed to be a means of God's protection and blessing. Marriage is supposed to be the relationship that reflects the deepest goodness, unity, love, and delight. But let's be honest. Even the best marriage falls short of the ideal.

Though it's generally a joy for wives to respect and submit to husbands who are seeking to follow Christ and who treat them with sacrificial love and tenderness, it can be extremely difficult to live under the authority of a difficult, sinful man. It's not easy to maintain the right kind of attitude in this situation, and to know how to resist and counter evil in a godly, respectful way.

I (Nancy) often get letters from women who are married to men who are uncharitable, harsh, or even downright evil. Heartbreaking letters like these:

Submissive wife? How so when your husband drinks, smokes, uses porn; when all that is wrong is my fault; when he wants me to arrange for him to have sex with two women at once, and when I won't, says I don't care about his needs? Some say I should just agree with all he says, don't argue or have an opinion, just agree.

I want to forgive but I also don't want to be a doormat or be in denial. Do I ignore these issues and pretend like they don't exist? Do I not voice my opinion about critical issues, like paying the bills, helping out, and getting help for an addiction? I have been in this cycle for three years, and it has robbed my joy and peace. We have gone to counseling, and my husband states bluntly that he doesn't care about my feelings. I have prayed for three years, but now it seems that all that is left is separation or divorce. I have been through hell and back with my marriage, and we have only been married for three years. (Hopeless)

I (Mary) think of the phone conversation I had with a sobbing girlfriend whose critical and demeaning husband constantly quoted Scripture about her obligation to submit and his right to rule over her. I think of the woman whose husband claimed that his authority entitled him to chastise her and lock her in the closet. I think of the acquaintance that came to church wearing sunglasses, to hide the fading bruise around her eye. I think of the times Brent and I have intervened in such circumstances, seeking police and legal protection, offering financial support, and helping women and children flee. Situations like this make my blood boil. The oppression and abuse that happen in the name of "biblical" authority and submission are ugly, deplorable, and profoundly evil. And they are decisively NOT "biblical"!

Some of the Bible's most scathing condemnations are directed toward leaders who fail to exercise authority in a godly manner. The Lord says, *"My anger is hot against the shepherds, and I will punish the leaders; for the* Lord *of hosts cares for his flock"* (Zech. 10:3).

Read the verses in the margin. Why do you think God gets so angry with leaders who fail to lovingly tend to those under their authority?

God gets extremely angry with leaders who are selfish, domineering, and harsh. This type of behavior is an evil, abhorrent misuse of God's authority (as all authority belongs to God), and a serious misrepresentation of His character. The Lord is the King who tends his flock like a shepherd, gathers the lambs in his arms, carries them in his bosom, and gently leads (Isa. 40:11).

We've already addressed several misconceptions about authority and submission, but we want to reinforce a few points before we move on:

- Abuse of authority is an abomination to God (Jer. 23:2; Ezek. 34:1–4; Zech. 11:17). He wants leaders to be shepherds after His own heart.

- People in authority positions will have to give an account to God for how they exercised that authority (Heb. 13:17; 1 Cor. 4:1–5; Ezek. 34:1). They will be judged with greater strictness (James 3:1).

- When authorities are harsh or abusive, we can humbly confront, call them to account, and/or appeal to higher authorities to intervene in the situation (Acts 16:37–38; 25:8–11; 1 Peter 2:23; Eccl. 5:8).

- Our obligation is ultimately to God, our highest authority. We are not bound to obey authorities when they demand submission in matters that clearly depart from biblical truth. In such situations, we are to obey God rather than man (Acts 5:29).

> Selfish, domineering, and harsh leadership is an evil, abhorrent misuse of God's authority and a serious misrepresentation of His character.

We want to be crystal clear that submitting to your husband does not mean submitting to abuse, passively resigning yourself to wrongdoing,

relinquishing your responsibility to take a stand against evil, or failing to speak the truth in love. Submission is not rote obedience. It's about having an amenable, lead-able disposition that desires to honor God's authority by respecting His human authority structures. It's about having the wisdom to discern the best course of action and the courage to do what's right.

It's important to consider a person's responsibility to govern and/or submit in the context of other biblical obligations.

Look up the following verses in the book of Ephesians. Summarize what each verse or passage teaches about our obligations to one another.

4:1–3 _____

4:15–16 _____

4:25–27 _____

4:29 _____

4:31–32 _____

5:11 _____

5:18–21 _____

Ephesians 5:21 instructs us to submit to one another out of reverence for Christ. The passage then identifies three specific relationships that call for a submissive posture: wives to husbands, children to parents, and bondservants to masters. The concept of authority and submission extends into all sorts of other chain-of-command relationships, too—like governments and citizens, bosses and employees, church elders and congregations.

The term *mutual submission* is popular in Christian circles, but "submitting to one another" doesn't mean that both parties in a chain of command are to submit to each other. It means we're to have a respectful disposition that inclines us to submit in all the relationships that call for submission. In some relationships you may have the responsibility to govern, and in others the responsibility to submit.

For the remainder of this week, we'll explore how a submissive spirit contributes to a uniquely feminine soft disposition.

uppity women

The fastest-growing name for a baby girl in 2012 was "Arya," from the wildly popular HBO television series, *Game of Thrones.*[5] The program is known for its graphic sexual content and sexual brutality. We've not watched the show ourselves and we would discourage you from watching it. But we think the phenomenon of women naming their newborn daughters after Arya is telling. The character Arya is a feisty, tough-as-nails preteen daughter of a northern lord. She's a defiant tomboy,

with a fiercely independent streak, and a tongue as sharp as her sword.

Arya's cropped hair and rough-and-tumble manner stand in marked contrast to her older sister, Sansa, who enjoys the traditional pursuits of noblewomen, and is proper, ladylike, and foolishly naive. Sansa exemplifies the old, traditional stereotype of womanhood, whereas Arya exemplifies the current cultural ideal. It's not that Arya prefers the traditional male pursuits of archery, swordplay, and exploring the outdoors over dancing, singing, and sewing. It's that she's got attitude. She's tough, sassy, brash, and defiant.

Many women in our day view toughness, brashness, sassiness, aggressiveness, and fierce independence as desirable character traits. Though some undoubtedly choose the name Arya simply because they like it, we suspect that many view her as a positive role model for their daughters.

Read Proverbs 7:11–12 in the margin. What are the two adjectives Scripture uses to describe a foolish woman?

She is _____ and _____.

What does Proverbs 9:13 say about a woman who adopts this clamorous type of attitude?

_____

_____

she's got attitude!

P Proverbs 7 describes the foolish woman as loud and defiant. The phrase describes her behavior, but more than that, it sums up her state of mind. She's a brash, my-way-or-highway kind of girl. Nowadays, we might describe her by saying, "She's got attitude!"

The Hebrew word translated "loud" means to be tumultuous or clamorous; to murmur, growl, or roar. The description applies to an untameable beast that refuses to bear the yoke. "Like a stubborn heifer" is how the prophet Hosea describes this mindset (4:16). This type of woman *roars*. And it's not so much the volume of her voice, although it definitely can include that. It's her insolence.

Synonyms for this loud type of attitude are sassy, brassy, cheeky, cocky, flippant, mouthy, smart-alecky, brash, or pushy. It's an attitude that is promoted, even admired, by our culture. You can probably think of characters in movies or TV shows, or popular, female news anchors or talk-show hosts, who fit this description. "Girl, you've got attitude!" is considered more of a compliment than an insult.

The second adjective is translated "defiant" (HCSB) or "wayward" (ESV). The Hebrew word means "to be stubborn and rebellious." It reflects a self-willed, obstinate, "nobody tells me what to do" frame of mind. She's *un-leadable*. According to the Bible, an attitude of stubbornness toward people often reflects an underlying attitude of stubbornness toward the Lord (Ezek. 20:38). Ours is a "stubborn and rebellious generation," whose heart is not steadfast, whose spirit is not faithful to God (Ps. 78:8).

Mary

Loud and defiant are like two sides of a coin. *Loud* insists, "You'd better do things my way!" and *defiant* insists, "I'm not doing things your way!"

"Ms. Stupidity" is the equivalent to what the Bible calls a woman who adopts this type of attitude. *The Message* paraphrase calls her "empty-headed." She's foolish, gullible, and knows nothing.

Scripture specifically warns women against having a defiant mindset. It's not liberating and wonderful, as the world would have us believe. It's downright foolish. "Claiming to be wise, they became fools" (Rom. 1:22). Janet attests to the negative effect a rebellious attitude can have on a relationship:

If I were to pick a word to describe my manner toward my husband, it would be "resistant." I was forever resisting him. If he came up with an idea, I suggested a different or better one. If he wanted me to do something, I dug in my heels. If he tried to make a decision, I objected. If he asked me to reconsider, I would refuse. I continually corrected him and put him down. And I always had a sharp comeback ready on the tip of my tongue.

You have to understand that my husband was not a demanding man. He was very kind. But because I believed that compliance was a sign of weakness, and that women should NEVER subject themselves to men, I constantly undermined him. I would not let him lead. Even in the smallest, most insignificant matters, I absolutely refused to follow.

Looking back, I can sadly see how my constant resistance chipped away at his manhood and at our relationship. I resisted and resisted until he gave up and walked away.[7]

The world thinks a sassy, defiant attitude is the epitome of empowered womanhood. It breaks our hearts when we see Christian women fall for this lie. The Evil One has deceived us. A rebellious attitude does not strengthen a woman, nor does it strengthen her relationships. Quite the opposite, in fact. As Janet and countless others have discovered, a spirit of defiance diminishes rather than enhances a woman's life.

Have you been impacted by the popular idea that a defiant or resistant spirit is preferable to a deferential, submissive one? Explain how and why.

The following behaviors may be symptomatic of a loud, defiant spirit. Cross out the behavior in each column that doesn't belong. The first one is done for you.

nag	mock	put-down	snark
badger	explain	bellyache	nix
fault-find	belittle	comment	criticize
cuss out	complain	sneer	appeal
~~discuss~~	ridicule	undermine	discredit

Can you think of other behaviors that are symptoms of defiance? Add them to the list above. Then put a check [√] beside any behaviors you often exhibit.

The world encourages women to cultivate a loud, defiant spirit. But our heavenly Father wants us to cultivate a soft, responsive disposition, the "imperishable beauty of a gentle and quiet spirit" (1 Peter 3:4). This type of disposition is "very precious" to Him.

Why do you think a gentle, submissive spirit is so precious to God the Father?

→ **Close in prayer.** Confess to the Lord any ways in which you've had a rebellious, defiant spirit. Seek His forgiveness and ask Him to help you put on the respectful, submissive character of Christ.

abigail the steel magnolia

R Remember the metaphor of the Steel Magnolia from *True Woman 101*? The image melds beauty with perseverance, softness with backbone, delicacy with durability, sweetness with stamina, and gentleness with gumption. According to 1 Peter 3, the disposition of a truly beautiful woman is gentle, quiet, and amenable (that is, agreeable, submissive, honoring proper authority). That's the soft, delicate part.

At the same time, a True Woman is determined to do what's right and not give in to fear. She isn't swayed by popular opinion or intimidated by what others might say or do. That's the backbone-of-steel part. A godly woman's soft responsiveness is coupled with an uncompromising determination to respond appropriately—to enthusiastically say "yes" to the right things and respectfully say "no" to the wrong things.

In today's lesson, we're going to study the story of Abigail—one of the Bible's foremost steel magnolias. You'll see that submission isn't for wimps. It involves having a soft heart, a sharp mind, and a strong backbone.

Abigail counters many common misconceptions about submission. Her conversation with David is one of the most remarkable and longest female-initiated dialogues between a man and a woman in the Bible. Abigail's story demonstrates that it's possible for a woman's conduct to remain respectful and pure, even when she must say "no" and take a stand against wrongdoing.

In your Bible, read 1 Samuel 25:1–42.

What was Nabal like?

_____

_____

> *"Now the name of the man was Nabal, and the name of his wife Abigail. The woman was discerning and beautiful, but the man was harsh and badly behaved."*
>
> **I Samuel 25:3**

What was Abigail like?

_____

_____

married to a difficult man

Everyone in the region knew David. He was the famed general of Saul's army and the royal son-in-law. The prophet Samuel had anointed David as the next king of Israel. But the current king, Saul, had jealousy issues. He disowned David, gave David's wife Michal (Saul's daughter) to another man, and sought to kill the popular general. That's why David and his band were hiding in the wilderness and neighboring hills of Carmel. Rumor had it that David didn't kill Saul when he had the chance, but was patiently waiting until such time as God established him as king. In the meantime, he and his men protected the shepherds who worked for Nabal, a wealthy rancher, from thugs and thieves.

At the end of the annual sheep shearing festival, Nabal hosted an extravagant feast to celebrate his profits. When David chose the occasion to seek a return favor from Nabal, asking for some food as payment for the protection he had provided Nabal's shepherds, Nabal refused. What's

more, he rudely insulted and belittled the future king and the men who had shown him such kindness. If it weren't for Abigail's swift and effective appeal, David would have retaliated and killed Nabal and all the men on Nabal's estate.

What indicates that Abigail had a humble, submissive spirit, in contrast to Nabal's arrogant, defiant one?

_____

_____

Why do you think Abigail's appeal to David was effective?

_____

_____

In verses 21 to 31, how many times does
Abigail refer to David as "my lord"?   _____ times

How many times does she refer to herself
as his "servant"?   _____ times

How can you tell that Abigail had a strong faith in the Lord and believed
in His promises?

_____

_____

Based on the passage, mark the following statements true (T) or false (F):

_____ Abigail ignored and covered up her husband's sin.

_____ She acted as her husband's helper.

_____ Her actions were for the purpose of benefitting Nabal,
not harming him.

_____ When threatened by her husband's sinful behavior,
she appealed to a higher authority.

_____ She backed up her arguments with Scripture and theology.

_____ She acted defiantly and disrespectfully.

_____ She spoke the truth.

_____ She waited for the right time to discuss issues with her husband.

_____ She took responsibility for her own actions and responses.

_____ She trusted God to deal with Nabal.

We suspect that the reason Abigail was able to effectively appeal to
David, was that she had a genuinely soft, submissive spirit. Over her years of
living with a difficult man, she had managed to avoid becoming hard and
bitter, and had learned how to speak truth in a respectful, winsome way.

People recognized that she was an intelligent, honorable, godly woman—even though she was married to a foolish, dishonorable, boorish guy.

David was "wowed" by this steel magnolia. He could tell she was exceptional. Abigail had a gentle, quiet, amenable spirit. She had intelligence, resolve, and gumption. She had a deep faith and an unwavering commitment to God. She conducted herself with dignity and honor. She was feminine. She was beautiful—inside and out!

Why do you think Scripture emphasizes gentleness, quietness, and amenability as traits that are particularly important for women?

Gentleness, quietness of spirit, and amenability are traits that ought to be cultivated by men as well as women. Yet Scripture identifies these three traits as having a unique importance to a godly feminine disposition. Women are the "soft" ones. That doesn't mean we're to be wimpy or weak. But it does mean that God created us to bear special witness to the goodness and beauty of a soft, submissive spirit in a way that men cannot.

→ **Turn to the "Personalize" section on page 205.** Use the page to summarize what you learned this week. Are you a lead-able woman? Do you have a soft, feminine, steel magnolia–type disposition? How will you apply these lessons to your life?

drawing it out,
drawing it in . . .

interior renovation

process

The video for Week Eight will help you process this week's lessons. You'll find this week's video, the leader's guide, and additional resources at TrueWoman201.com.

ponder

Think about the following questions. Discuss them with your friends, family, and/or small group:

1. Why are many women scornful or fearful of submission in marriage? Describe how this week's lessons have reshaped your understanding of what marital submission is meant to look like.

2. What did Salome misunderstand about authority? Describe what authority is and what it is not.

3. What is the difference between submission and obedience? Give some concrete examples.

4. Review Philippians 2:5–10. How did Jesus demonstrate submission? How is submission in marriage meant to reflect the relationship between God the Father and God the Son?

5. Describe what biblical submission does not include or require.

6. Ephesians 5:21 instructs us to submit to one another. How are those instructions different from the notion of "mutual submission" that's so popular today?

7. Why is a sassy and defiant woman held up as ideal in today's world rather than a woman who has a soft, responsive disposition? What misunderstandings about biblical submission have shaped this new ideal?

8. How does the story of Abigail paint a picture of submission that glorifies God? How does she counter the belief that a submissive woman is a doormat? In what ways would you like to become more like Abigail?

personalize it

Use this page to journal. Write down what you learned this week. Record your comments, a favorite verse, or a concept or quote that was particularly helpful or meaningful to you. Compose a prayer, letter, or poem. Jot down notes from the video or your small group session. Express your heart response to what you have studied. Personalize this week's lessons in the way that will best help you apply them to your life.

drawing it out,
drawing it in . . .

legacy

Basket weaving is one of the oldest-known Native American arts. For thousands of years, the skill was passed down from generation to generation—mother to daughter. The durable baskets were woven from materials readily available in the natural surroundings of each tribe's ancestral homeland.

The Cherokee women harvested river cane, a bamboo-like grass that grew along the banks of streams. They split, peeled, and stripped the cane lengthwise to remove the shiny outer surface. This took considerable skill and strength. The sides were trimmed to a uniform width and the inner surface scraped to reduce thickness and make them more flexible. The pieces were then dried into strips called "straws."

After coloring the strips of cane with natural dyes, the women skillfully wove the cane into colorful, patterned storage containers of various shapes and sizes. The double-weave technique was particularly challenging. The basket is begun at the bottom and woven upward. At the rim, it is turned outward and woven back down to the base. The result is a durable and beautiful basket with double walls.[1]

Over time, native people were displaced from their traditional lands and lifestyles. What's more, commercially available storage containers and the invention of plastic rendered the handwoven baskets nearly obsolete. By the 1940s, there were only a handful of weavers who were skilled in the double-weave technique. The art was in danger of becoming extinct. But Lottie Stamper—a Cherokee woman who came from a long line of basket weavers—helped to spark a revival of the technique.

*A True Woman is a spiritual mother . . . She "**teaches what is good**."*

Lottie began to teach basket making at a Cherokee boarding school. Her students included her niece, Eva Wolfe, along with several other young women, all of whom established careers as basket weavers. Eva Wolfe revived historic patterns of double-weave basketry and became one of the most widely renowned basket makers in the United States. What's more, this group of women intentionally passed on the legacy, so that the ancient art will continue through the coming generations.[2]

Biblical womanhood is an "ancient art" that has been passed down from generation to generation. Titus chapter 2 indicates that a True Woman passes on this legacy through spiritual motherhood. She takes younger, less mature women under her wings, nurtures them, and teaches them what is good. Older women teach younger women, younger women teach their children, and so we pass on the baton of truth from one generation to the next.

In *True Woman 101*, we learned that godly, intentional mothering is integral to womanhood. A woman's physical capacity to give birth points to our spiritual purpose and calling. Bearing and nurturing life is what God has "hardwired" women to do.

Certainly, not every woman is destined to or able to make use of her biological equipment. But motherhood, in a much deeper sense, is at the heart of womanhood. The first woman's name affirms and celebrates this truth: Eve means "life-giver." God's purpose is that every woman—married or single, fertile or infertile—will bring forth life. Regardless of her marital status, occupation, or age, a woman's greatest aim ought to be to glorify God and further His kingdom by reproducing—bearing spiritual fruit. A critical way we do this is through life-to-life, one-on-one nurturing and discipleship of younger women.

Throughout this book, we've studied the elements that Paul identified as essential components of godly womanhood—discernment, honor, family affection, discipline, virtue, responsibility, benevolence, and disposition. Paul told his young pastor friend Titus that these were the "essentials" for women in his congregation to learn. But note that it wasn't Titus' job to directly mentor women in these essentials. Paul gave women the responsibility to teach and

pass on the legacy of godly womanhood from woman to woman, older to younger.

Over the past few decades, the feminist movement has reconstructed ideas about womanhood. Christian women are not unaffected. Most of us have based our ideas about womanhood on cultural norms rather than eternal truth. True womanhood is often maligned and despised. Frequently, our "mothers" don't have the knowledge, the time, or the will to teach, and our "daughters" don't have the time or the will to learn. The light of the ancient art of biblical womanhood has grown dim. Few artisans remain.

It is our prayer that *True Woman 101* and *201* will change all that. We hope that your heart has been stirred by Scripture's beautiful and noble vision of womanhood, and that in this week's lessons you'll accept the challenge to take an active part in passing on the legacy.

mother in Israel

> The challenge of every Christian parent is to bring up children who love God with all their hearts, souls, minds and strength." [3]

Nancy

A recent study in the journal *Human Reproduction* indicates that infertility is on the rise here in Canada where I (Mary) live.[4] In 1984, about 5.4% of couples trying to have children were infertile. By 1992, that statistic had risen to 8.5%. By 2012, the number had skyrocketed up to 16%—and this despite all the advances in fertility treatments and other assisted reproductive technologies.

That means that a staggering one in six couples faces infertility. The rate is even higher for females over the age of thirty-five. By forty years of age, only two in five women who wish to have a baby will be able to do so.[5]

There are few circumstances as potentially difficult for a woman as wanting to have a child but not being able to conceive. Researchers have likened the emotional pain to that of someone with a terminal illness. Those who have not faced infertility can scarcely understand the deep feelings of longing, stress, frustration, anger, sadness, loneliness, envy, failure, grief, and desperation.

I (Mary) once prayed with a woman whose infertility issues had paralyzed her. She had become so depressed with her inability to conceive that she had stopped going to church. She scarcely left the house for fear that she would see a mom pushing a baby in a stroller and burst into inconsolable tears. Her desperation was like that of Jacob's wife Rachel who envied her sister's fertility, and demanded of Jacob, "Give me children, or I shall die!" (Gen. 30:1).

Why do you think most women at some point in their lives desire to be a mom?

There are many reasons women desire children, ranging from selfish to altruistic to idealistic. But the simplest explanation for the urge is that God has wired us that way. The desire to be fruitful is part of what it means to be a woman. That doesn't mean that every woman is aware of the desire, or that she perceives it at every age or stage of life, or in exactly the same way as others do.

Popular culture encourages women to value a good career more than motherhood. Children are often viewed as burdens. Bearing a child is presented as optional—only to be chosen if and when it fits into a woman's overall career, financial, and life plan. When we say that the desire to be fruitful goes hand-in-hand with what it means to be a woman, we are keenly aware that society pressures us to suppress or deny this desire. But it is there nonetheless.

Often, it's only in hindsight, and with the perspective that comes with age, that women recognize that there is no more precious, valuable, and lasting life investment a woman can make than to be a mother. Take Barbara Walters, for example. She was the first woman to co-anchor a US evening news program, a TV personality for more than fifty years, with three Emmy Awards on her mantel. During an interview marking her retirement and extraordinary career success, the 83-year-old Walters was asked to reflect on the moment of her career that brought her the greatest thrill and satisfaction. She got extremely emotional and asked if she could instead express her greatest regret. With tears in her eyes, Walters said, "I regret not having more children. I would have loved to have had a bigger family."[6]

The desire for "motherhood" exists whether or not a woman ever bears biological children. Though I (Nancy) have not had the privilege of giving birth to biological children, one of my greatest joys has been spiritually mothering various children and younger women and couples the Lord has put in my life. I love being called "Mama Nancy" and receiving "Happy Mother's Day" cards from younger women. Over the past few days, I have had the opportunity to encourage and pray with

two young women who are soon to be married, a young mom getting ready to give birth to her third child, and another young woman starting into a new job.

Read the verses in the margin. What is the ultimate aim of both biological and spiritual motherhood?

_____ _____

_____

Identify someone you know who is physically childless, but is a "joyful mother of children." Who are her children, and how does she mother them?

_____

_____

"'Sing, O barren one, who did not bear; break forth into singing and cry aloud, you who have not been in labor! For the children of the desolate one will be more than the children of her who is married,' says the LORD."

Isaiah 54:1

"He gives the childless woman a household, making her the joyful mother of children. Hallelujah!"

Psalm 113:9 HCSB

"I chose you. I appointed you that you should go out and produce fruit and that your fruit should remain."

John 15:16 HCSB

"[We belong] to Him who has been raised from the dead, in order that we may bear fruit for God."

Romans 7:4

Remember Deborah in the book of Judges? The time of judges was a precarious time in Israel's history. Joshua had died, and there was a vacuum of leadership at the national level. All twelve tribes were experiencing invasions and attacks from a variety of enemies and were in constant danger of being overrun. During this volatile time, the Lord raised up "judges" to deliver His people from their enemies and from civil anarchy and spiritual apostasy.

Deborah was a woman from the tribe of Ephraim who walked with God. Her wisdom and prophetic insight were so keen that people came from all over the countryside to seek her counsel and help in settling disputes. So many came that she set up office under "the palm of Deborah," out in the countryside.

At God's direction, Deborah instructed the military general Barak to gather a force of men to fight the king of Canaan. Barak insisted that she travel with him to rally the troops and then to the base camp at Mount Tabor, from where he and his army launched their victorious attack.

Deborah had a long list of impressive credentials. Scripture doesn't tell us how old

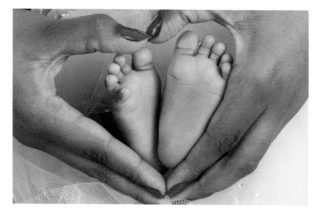

she was or whether she had biological children. We do know that she was married, was prophetically gifted, and that she provided godly judgment and counsel in a chaotic, floundering nation. Deborah could have identified herself as a ruler, judge, prophet, or leader. But she chose a different descriptor.

Look up Judges 5:6–7. How did Deborah describe herself?

_____

_____

Deborah had a God-given nurturing instinct that gave her courage and compassion. She wasn't driven by the things that drive many modern women —power, control, position, or recognition—but by a mother's heart. She saw herself as "a mother in Israel." When she judged disputes and challenged Barak to assume leadership, she was like a mama nurturing her kids. She was a strong, capable woman who never lost sight of her feminine calling to motherhood.

Obviously, if you have children, you are called to mother them well. But there may be other spheres where the Lord wants to use you as a mother.

You can read the story of Deborah in Judges 4 and 5.

Write the name of your church, workplace, school, and/or community in the space below:

I am a mother in: _____

_____

What difference could a mother's heart make in these arenas?

→ **God has fashioned and equipped us as women to be "mothers," to bring forth godly fruit for His glory.** If you are an older woman, ask Him give you a mother's heart for those in your sphere of influence. If you are a younger woman, express your desire to grow into that role as you become an older woman.

old and fruitful

"The righteous flourish like the palm tree and grow like a cedar in Lebanon. They are planted in the house of the LORD; they flourish in the courts of our God. They still bear fruit in old age; they are ever full of sap and green, to declare that the LORD is upright; he is my rock, and there is no unrighteousness in him."

Psalm 92:12–15

"But the path of the righteous is like the light of dawn, which shines brighter and brighter until full day."

Proverbs 4:18

When my (Mary's) kids were young, they begged me to read and reread them an adorable story called *Amos's Sweater* by Janet Lunn. I must have read it about a gazillion times. Amos is a cantankerous old sheep with "angry Amos eyes" who plots to get back his wool, even though it has been knit into a brightly colored sweater.

Decades have passed since I saw that book, and I have no idea what happened to it, but whenever someone in our family is grumpy and reluctant to share or pitch in and contribute, we mockingly quote the opening lines: "Amos was *old*. And Amos was *cold*. And Amos was *tired* of giving away all his wool."

The sad reality is that for many people, getting older goes hand in hand with getting "colder"—and becoming more reluctant to give. Not only that, society promotes the idea that as you age, you have less to offer. Increased age means decreased vitality and productivity.

Have you ever tried to find a birthday card that presents aging as a genuinely positive and desirable thing? When you're getting into your 50s, 60s, 70s, and 80s, you don't tend to think of your life as getting brighter and fuller. You tend to think of it going downhill—that's the way people talk about aging today. But that's not God's perspective on aging.

Read the verses in the margin.

Look up the word *flourish* in a dictionary and write out the applicable definition below:

_____

_____

In the frames below, draw pictures of what the passages say a godly older person is like:

We had you sketch the Psalm 92 image earlier, in Week Two. But the cedar and palm are such powerful metaphors that we wanted to expand and apply them in a different way here.

full of sap and green

Lebanon is famous for its massive cedar forests, which were called "the glory" of Lebanon (Isa. 35:2). The cedar is a magnificent, deep-rooted tree that grows for as many as 2,000 years. It can reach massive diameters and heights (up to 120 feet). Its fragrant wood is red in color and is especially durable and resistant to insects and decay. The wood is highly esteemed for its beauty and durability. Throughout the Old Testament, the cedar tree symbolizes grandeur and majesty (2 Kings 14:9; Ezek. 31:3). The psalmist uses the image of a cedar to indicate that from a spiritual standpoint, people who are godly grow stronger and more beautiful as they age.

The image of the palm tree indicates that they also grow more fruitful. In the Holy Land, date palms were so abundant the Greeks and Romans called it "the land of the

"What do you want your children and friends to remember about you when you've gone to be with Jesus?"[7]

Fern Nichols

palms." Date palm trees grow to forty, fifty, even eighty feet tall. The fibers of the trunk are extremely elastic. A palm tree bends but does not break with the force of the wind. Feathery, green fronds crown the trunk. Palm fronds are a symbol of victory (Rev. 7:9). The crowds waved fronds at Jesus' triumphal entrance into Jerusalem (John 12:13).

The date palm is both beautiful and useful. In antiquity, the fibers from the base of the leaves were woven into ropes and rigging. The leaves were used to make brushes, mats, bags, couches, and baskets. A date palm begins to bear fruit about six years after being planted, and it produces over 300 pounds of dates annually. It continues to be productive for well over a century; and as the tree grows older, the fruit gets sweeter and sweeter.

Use Psalm 92:12–15, Proverbs 4:18, and the explanation about cedars and palms to compile a list describing a godly old woman. (We've included two points to get you started.)

The older she gets, the more she shines.

As the years pass, she gains more wisdom, insight, and clarity.

How does God's perspective on elderly people differ from how society views them?

As you're getting older age-wise, you ought to be maturing spiritually, and bearing more fruit. I (Nancy) love Proverbs 4:18 and often include it on birthday greetings. God's perspective is if you are a righteous person, your life is like the light of dawn—it starts out just like a little glimmer of light, and then as the day progresses and moves closer and closer to noon, the sun gets higher and higher in the sky, until at full noon the light is at its brightest. That's the way we should think of aging.

There should never be a time in your life, no matter how old you are, when you stop flourishing, growing, and being fruitful. There's never a time to retire spiritually; never a time to be put on a shelf spiritually.

A godly old woman flourishes. She's full of spiritual vitality. Her physical body may be diminishing; that's a part of the curse of the fall. But her inner person is being renewed day by day. She never stops growing. She never stops being fruitful. She never stops training younger women. She never stops proclaiming to others the goodness and the wonders of Christ and His gospel.

Do you know a godly old woman who is still bearing fruit and who, like a cedar, is "ever full of sap and green"? Who is she and what do you admire about her?

_____

_____

How about you? Are you flourishing and growing? Are you spiritually more mature and fruitful today than you were five years ago? Or are you growing old and cold and tired of giving away your wool? Explain.

_____

_____

What do you think can help you remain fruitful and flourishing in old age?

_____

_____

Older women are a key component in the Titus 2 formula for biblical woman-hood. It's important that we respect those who are older, and that as we age, we keep becoming more and more like Jesus—until "full day," when we see Him face-to-face.

woman to woman

F ormal education in ancient China was only for the wealthy, and an extravagance reserved for men. Women were excluded from learning how to read and write. Most had their feet bound and were not permitted to work outdoors. So while the men went to school or worked, the women spent their days indoors, in the women's chamber, with other female relatives, friends, and neighbors. Together they cooked meals, made shoes and handcrafts, spun, stitched, and did needlework and embroidery. They sang folk songs, recited poems, and composed their own songs and poems to pass the time. And in one particular region of China, they invented a way to write them all down.

> *"Older women . . . are to teach what is good, and so train the young women."*
>
> **Titus 2:3–4**

The language was called "*nüshu*," which literally means "woman's writing." The wispy, cursive script was used secretly by local women. No man ever learned it. The women wrote their elegant script on fans, embroidered the characters on cloth and handkerchiefs, and wove the letters into quilts. A strong companionship developed between them. Some became "sworn sisters"—which were sisters bound not by blood, but by vows of loyalty.

It was in these sisterhoods that girls grew into womanhood, offering support to one another during foot binding, and learning womanly arts and *nüshu* from their mothers, grandmothers, and aunts.

When it came time for a woman to marry, the bride would leave the female community she knew and loved and move to her husband's house. To ease the sting of separation, the women and sworn sisters carefully crafted a clothbound book, known as a "Third Day Book" for her to open and read on her third day of marriage. The book contained messages embroidered in *nüshu*, expressing the women's hopes and dreams for the bride, as well as their sadness over losing their friend, sister, and daughter. Several pages were kept blank for the bride to use as a journal to embroider her own thoughts.

Nüshu was often used to write letters from mother to daughter or between sworn sisters. It was a private and cherished way for women to keep in touch. It allowed them to support each other and to freely share their joys, struggles, and heartaches—which were many. For over a thousand years the

secret women's language of *nüshu* was passed down from generation to generation, woman to woman, older to younger, mother to daughter, sister to sister. It's truly remarkable that this secret language—written by women for women—was successfully imparted and preserved.

Did you know that God has entrusted us to pass down a special "woman's language"? Unlike *nüshu*, it's not a secret script. But like *nüshu*, it's a uniquely feminine one. It's the language of biblical womanhood, which is the womanly art of living out God's divine design for women. Each generation is challenged to impart the legacy—from woman to woman—from one generation to the next.

from woman to woman

Titus 2:3–4 indicates that every older woman should be a (check all that you think apply):

☐ golfer	☐ teacher	☐ coach
☐ retiree	☐ trainer	☐ mother
☐ CEO	☐ example	☐ mentor

Train is translated from the Greek word *sōphronizō* and *young women* from the Greek word *neos*. Turn back to page 91 for the meaning of these words. Rewrite the definitions below:

Sōphronizō (train): _____

Neos (young women): _____

Did you notice the word *sōphrōn* in *sōphronizō*? We studied *sōphrōn* extensively in Week Four of this study (see page 91). You may remember that it means having a *sound mind*. It's a person who acts like they're in their right mind, spiritually speaking. The word translated *train* literally means "to make of sound mind." It means to instruct or train someone to behave wisely and properly.[8]

In Titus 2:3–4 in the margin on the opposite page, circle the phrase "teach what is good."

The phrase "teach what is good" translates one long Greek word: *kalodidaskalos*, from *kalos—goodness* or *virtue*, and *didaskalos—teacher*. It indicates that every older woman should be a "teacher of virtue."[9] A godly older woman is a teacher of virtue, a trainer, mentor, coach, and example . . . She's a spiritual mother.

If we were to ask you, "Are you an 'older' or 'younger' woman?" you'd likely say you're older than some and younger than others. It's true. To a thirteen-year-old girl, a twenty-five-year-old is an "older woman." Every woman is younger than some and older than others.

When Paul instructed older women to teach the young ones, it's likely that the older women he primarily had in mind were those past child-bear-

ing age. However, his use of the word *neos* indicates that his categories of *older* and *younger* had more to do with experience, life stage, and spiritual maturity than chronological age. A *neos* is a newbie, a "greenhorn"— a fresh, inexperienced novice. It's a woman who is new to the circumstances in which she is placed.

The point is, if you want to be the kind of woman who brings glory to God, you should actively learn from the lives of women who have walked the path before you, and actively teach those who are coming after. Regardless of your age, the Lord wants you to be both a learner and a teacher.

Based on Job 12:12, what advice would you give to younger women?

_____

_____

Based on Psalm 71:18 and Deuteronomy 4:9, what advice would you give to older women?

_____

_____

The advice we would give to **younger women** is this: You can be young and wise, but there are some aspects of wisdom and understanding that you only get with life experience. Remember that. And then remember that God cares about how we treat older believers. They are to be treated with honor and respect (Lev. 19:32). The way you treat older people is an evidence of the way you treat the Lord. Value the life experience of the older women around you. Solicit their input. Receive instruction and correction with humility. Ask questions. Listen.

Older women, you're supposed to be a model. You're supposed to be an example. Your character and your lifestyle should be worthy of respect. You should have a life that younger women will point to and say, "That's what I want to be like when I'm her age." But God wants you to be more than a *model*—He also wants you to be a *mentor*. Does that sound beyond your pay grade? Listen, it simply means drawing on your life experience, in the context of everyday life, to provide encouragement and exhortation to those who are younger. If you stay engaged with the younger generation, you will continue to bear fruit, and your relationships with them will help you stay "ever full of sap and green."

It takes a sisterhood to grow girls up into true womanhood—a godly sisterhood in which every woman learns from the older and mentors the younger. That's God's plan for preserving the language of biblical womanhood.

→ **Close in prayer**, asking the Lord to help you participate in "the sisterhood"—learning from the lives of women who have walked the path before you and teaching those who are coming after.

mentor mama

"Follow the pattern of the sound words that you have heard from me, in the faith and love that are in Christ Jesus."

2 Timothy 1:13

"You, however, have followed my teaching, my conduct, my aim in life, my faith, my patience, my love, my steadfastness . . ."

2 Timothy 3:10

"Remember your leaders, those who spoke to you the word of God. Consider the outcome of their way of life, and imitate their faith."

Hebrews 13:7

Homer's epic poem *The Odyssey* tells the story of Odysseus, king of Ithaca, who left his wife Penelope and infant son Telemachus to fight with the Greek alliance in the Trojan War. Before he left, he placed the responsibility for overseeing his kingdom and raising his son into the hands of his old, trusted friend, Mentor. Knowing it would be years before he returned, Odysseus asked Mentor to oversee Telemachus' growth and development, and to ensure that the boy would be educated, trained, and groomed to fulfill his royal birthright.

It was Homer's story of the relationship between the old Mentor and young Telemachus that first gave rise to the concept of mentorship. By the late 1700s the word *mentor* became a noun in the English language meaning "wise counselor." In modern usage, a mentor is a more experienced (and generally older) person who acts as a trusted friend, teacher, and guide.

One popular website defines mentorship as "a personal developmental relationship in which a more experienced or more knowledgeable person helps to guide a less experienced or less knowledgeable person."[10] It points out that true mentoring is more than just disseminating information. It's about an ongoing relationship of learning, dialogue, and challenge that aims to develop the whole person.

Mentoring has become extremely popular in recent years. People are paying hundreds of dollars an hour for business coaches, executive coaches, career coaches, health coaches, time management coaches, dating coaches, and life cycle coaches. The Life Coaching Institute reports that life coaching is the second fastest growth industry in the world.[11] More than thirty American universities have introduced coaching programs, including Harvard, Yale, Duke, Penn State, and the University of California at Berkeley. What's more, courses offering life coach certification are available online for as little as $69.99.[12] Many life coaches are just in their twenties, prompting the *New York Times* to ask, "Should a Life Coach Have a Life First?"[13]

There are two conclusions we can draw from the life coaching phenomenon. First, people today are hungry for input. They long to have a mentor who can provide wise counsel and guidance. Second, the age-old biblical practice of mentorship is a powerful method for personal growth and development. If life coaching works in secular contexts, just imagine how much more effectual it would be if saturated with the truth of Scripture and the power of the Holy Spirit.

Paul was big on mentorship. Titus was one of his main protégés. Read the verses in the margin on pages 216, 218, 220, and 222, and answer the following questions.

What is the main responsibility of a godly mentor?

_____

_____

What is the main responsibility of someone who is being mentored?

_____

_____

Using the verses, make a list of the types of things a younger woman might learn from an older, godly mentor:

_____

_____

_____

_____

List the ten life coaching elements that are a part of the Titus 2 mentorship curriculum for women, including a phrase summarizing each element. (Hint: You can find a summary in the Table of Contents or Overview of Lessons.)

1. _____

2. _____

3. _____

4. _____

5. _____

6. _____

7. _____

8. _____

9. _____

10. _____

Have you ever benefitted from the example, counsel, and/or input of an older godly woman? Who was she and what did you learn from her?

_____

_____

Our (Mary's and Nancy's) lives are so much richer today because of older people who have modeled godliness for us over the years and have poured into us and mentored us in His ways. We want to challenge you older women to take initiative and reach out to younger people in your community of  faith. One of the things we hear from younger women about the older ones is,

"They just don't want to mentor us." But then we hear older women saying that younger women just don't want to be mentored.

You know what? Whether you're younger or older, take the initiative. Reach out. If you're older, approach and engage with younger women. You don't have to have a PhD in theology. You don't have to have been to seminary. You don't have to be a great Bible teacher. Just open your life, open the Word of God, and come alongside some of these younger women and be willing to share with them, out of your life and His Word.

You may say, "I've blown so much of my life. I've made so many wrong choices. I've failed in so many ways." The older we get the bigger the catalog of failures Satan can throw in our faces. You may think, "I don't have anything to offer." But you can *teach out of your failures as well as your successes*. You can alert younger women to where you blew it, where you didn't trust the Lord, the addictions that you had, about the ways that you failed. When you teach out of your failures, you can help those who are coming behind you to be guarded and protected in their steps.

→ **Your goal as an older woman** (however old that may be), is to be able say to a younger woman, "*Imitate me, as I also imitate Christ*" (1 Cor. 11:1 HCSB).

> "SHE OPENS HER MOUTH WITH WISDOM, AND THE TEACHING OF KINDNESS IS ON HER TONGUE."
>
> Proverbs 31:26

passing the baton

The track-and-field relay events are among the most fast-paced, energetic, and exciting events in the Olympic Games. One misstep can mean the difference between a gold medal and no medal at all. Relay races involve teams of four runners, each running a separate race, known as a "leg." The runners carry a metal baton, and as each runner completes her leg, she passes the baton to the next runner—signifying the end of her run and the start of her teammate's.

The exchange of the baton is critical. It takes place in a specially marked exchange zone. This is the only place where the baton can pass from one runner to the next. It's the part of the race that's the most critical and the most difficult to execute. The exchange is where most teams lose time and position. Fumbling or dropping the baton during an exchange causes a team to slow down, and in some cases, be disqualified. A team with four decent runners can often outrace a faster, more talented team simply by being better at passing the baton.

For many years, I (Nancy) have challenged women with the importance of passing on the "baton of truth." A relay race is an apt metaphor for describing how the Lord wants us to transmit truth from one generation to the

next. Older believers pass the baton on to younger believers, who pass the baton on to the next group of believers. Each generation is responsible for passing on truth to the following generation.

The relay race imagery is particularly meaningful for me (Mary), as my husband, Brent, was a Canadian national 4x400-meter and 4x800-meter gold medalist in college. I loved to watch him practice and race. His team spent a lot of time working on the baton exchange, and had the best timing and execution of any other team. As a result, they held the 4x800-meter Canadian national record for over twenty years.

> "You shall teach them diligently to your children, and shall talk of them when you sit in your house, and when you walk by the way, and when you lie down, and when you rise."
>
> **Deuteronomy 6:7**

> "Only take care, and keep your soul diligently, lest you forget the things that your eyes have seen, and lest they depart from your heart all the days of your life. Make them known to your children and your children's children."
>
> **Deuteronomy 4:9**

> "All Scripture is breathed out by God and profitable for teaching, for reproof, for correction, and for training in righteousness."
>
> **2 Timothy 3:16**

Yet Brent will never forget the one failed exchange that cost him a gold medal. It was a special, prestigious event featuring all-star Olympic athletes and international track-and-field champions, held at the local coliseum in front of a massive cheering audience. Instead of the usual 4x400 race to wrap up the competition, the organizing committee set up a relay with 1x100, 1x200, 1x300, and 1x400 meter legs. Since no one on Brent's relay team was a good sprinter, their slowest runner sat out, and they recruited the best 100-meter sprinter they could find.

The runner they selected was extremely talented, but unaccustomed to running in a team event. Not only that, he had a big ego, and didn't think he needed to practice the baton exchange. On race day, the new team member demonstrated his talent with an explosive start. But his exchange didn't go smoothly, and substantially slowed the team down. In the last leg, Brent came from behind to pull off what appeared to be an electrifying gold-medal finish. But unfortunately, they didn't get the gold. It turned out that the overconfident sprinter had messed up the baton exchange by stepping outside of the exchange zone, so the team was disqualified.

Read the verses in the margin on the opposite page. Why do you think God's plan is that we carefully pass the baton of truth from generation to generation?

_____

_____

Circle the word *diligently*. In what way does a successful baton pass require diligence?

_____

_____

The pattern of passing truth from generation to generation is evident throughout the Old Testament. *"We will not hide them from their children, but tell to the coming generation the glorious deeds of the LORD, and his might, and the wonders that he has done"* (Ps. 78:4). But the New Testament indicates that there's a gender-specific aspect to this transmission. There are gender-specific truths that must be passed down man-to-man and woman-to-woman.

O One example of woman-to-woman influence is found in the story of Naomi and Ruth. Naomi's family moved to Moab because of a severe famine in Judah. There, her son married Ruth. Ruth was a foreigner who worshiped foreign gods. But after her husband's death, she accompanied her mother-in-law back to Judah—adopting both Naomi's nation and her God.

Read Ruth 1:15–17 in your Bible. What do these verses indicate about the relationship between Naomi and Ruth? Why do you think Ruth followed Naomi?

"The wealth of spiritual knowledge and down-to-earth wisdom to be learned from women who have walked through the experiences of life is being lost at a time when, more than ever, young women need someone to come alongside them."[14]

Donna Otto

Due to Naomi's influence, Ruth eventually ended up marrying Boaz. Their son, Obed, was the father of Jesse and the grandfather of King David (1 Chron. 2:12), ultimately making Ruth part of the genealogy of Jesus (Matt. 1:5). That's quite a legacy for both of these women!

Contrast Naomi's legacy to the legacy of two other women: Jezebel and her daughter, Athaliah. Jezebel was the foreign wife of Ahab, king of the northern kingdom of Israel. Jezebel supported large groups of Baal prophets, and tried to exterminate the prophets of God (1 Kings 18:4). Jezebel was such an evil influence that her name became a moniker for a wicked woman (Rev. 2:20). Her corrupt influence spread to the southern kingdom through

her daughter, Athaliah, who married Jehoram, king of Judah, and gave birth to King Ahaziah.

Read about the legacy of Grandma Jezebel and Mama Athaliah in 2 Chronicles 22:2–4. Circle the phrase that indicates that Athaliah was a negative influence in her son's life.

All of us will leave a legacy of one kind or another. It's important that we're diligent to pass on a godly one. We love this challenge by Susan Hunt:

We must recapture the legacy of biblical womanhood and carefully and intentionally pass it to the next generation. If one generation is careless, the next generation suffers. Relinquishing God's design for womanhood has devastating effects on the home, church, and culture.

This battle for biblical womanhood is nothing new. It is simply the reclaiming of what always has been and always will be. But reclaim we must—for the glory of our sovereign King and the advancement of His kingdom.[15]

What part of Susan Hunt's quote strikes you as significant or notable? Why?

_____

_____

Are you carefully and intentionally—"diligently"—passing on the legacy of biblical womanhood? The capacity to reproduce spiritually, to share truth with others, is a sign of spiritual maturity. If you've known the Lord for many years and are not at a place where you can start passing the baton, there's something wrong. That's what the writer of Hebrews says: "By this time you ought to be teachers" (5:12). In other words, you've walked with the Lord long enough. You've been fed enough. You've learned enough. It's time to start passing it on!

You may think that teaching isn't your thing, that it's not your gift. But have you considered that you're always teaching? Your life is always teaching. Your example is always teaching. Your words, your conversations are always teaching. The question is, are you teaching what is good? Are you being intentional about training younger women in the ways of the Lord and in the essentials of godly womanhood?

→ **Are you diligently passing on His truth to the next generation?**
How could you be more intentional about leaving a godly legacy?

_____

_____

drawing it out,
drawing it in . . .

interior renovation

process

The video for Week Nine will help you process this week's lessons. You'll find this week's video, the leader's guide, and additional resources at TrueWoman201.com.

ponder

Think about the following questions. Discuss them with your friends, family, and/or small group:

1. It is God's purpose that every woman bring forth life. How can this truth encourage childless women? What outlook is essential for those seeking to fulfill God's design for women?

2. How does the biblical portrait of older women differ from how they are perceived in our culture?

3. What differentiates an older woman from a younger one? In what category would you place yourself at present?

4. Discuss what Mary and Nancy mean when they say, "It takes a sisterhood to grow girls up into true womanhood."

5. Why has "life coaching" taken hold on our society? How can this trend encourage us in our call to mentor younger women?

6. How wonderful that our failures don't disqualify us from mentoring younger women! How could your past failures be used redemptively to guide and encourage others?

7. What are some truths that can best (or only) be passed on from woman to woman?

8. In what way are we always teaching, even unintentionally? Does the truth of this make you want to reshape anything about your current activities or patterns of speech, and if so, what?

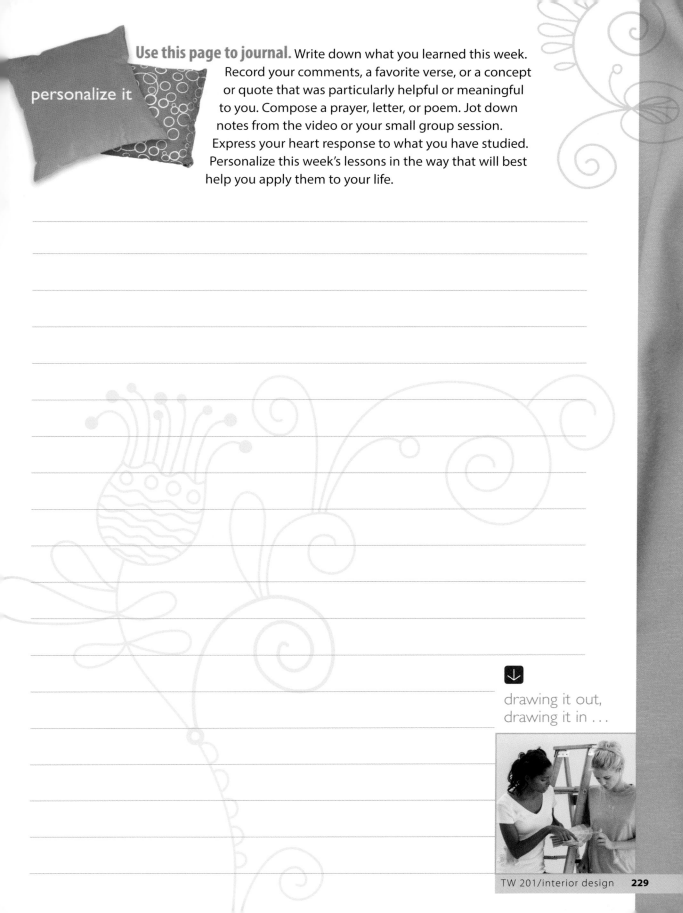

personalize it

Use this page to journal. Write down what you learned this week. Record your comments, a favorite verse, or a concept or quote that was particularly helpful or meaningful to you. Compose a prayer, letter, or poem. Jot down notes from the video or your small group session. Express your heart response to what you have studied. Personalize this week's lessons in the way that will best help you apply them to your life.

drawing it out,
drawing it in . . .

↑

beauty

A True Woman displays the attractiveness of the gospel . . . *"So that the word of God may not be reviled."*

If you hire an interior designer to remodel your home, she'll choose a style and color palette, select appropriate floor and window coverings and lighting, and pick out the perfect furniture, artwork, and décor. She'll put together all the right elements to transform your place from *blah* to *beautiful*. You wouldn't be happy if the end result was a less functional and less attractive space, would you? That's because improving the function and increasing the beauty is the whole point of embarking on a renovation project.

In *True Woman 201—Interior Design*, we've studied the essential design elements for biblical womanhood, as outlined in Titus chapter 2. The Great Designer wants to do an amazing interior renovation in your life. You don't need to worry that He'll get it wrong, or that you won't like the end result. Embracing and celebrating God's design for your womanhood will help you flourish. All the things that make you "you"—your personality, your talents, your gifts, your interests, your intellect, your emotions, even your appearance—will mesh with who God created you to be.

When you invite the Great Designer to renovate your life, you can be assured of two things. First, His design is practical and functional. It works! He'll take that crazy, messy closet filled with garbage—the one you're afraid to open lest you get smacked in the head with falling junk—and organize and clean it up. He'll turn it into a bright, ordered space with hooks and shelves and drawers, and a cubbyhole for every single pair of shoes! It's an apt illustration. Doing womanhood God's way will make your life much more functional. It will improve the way things work.

Second, the renovation will be beautiful. You'll come to love the transformation! And so will others. The Great Designer has a knack for making things breathtakingly beautiful. Just think of the creative genius He pours into every snowflake. Of the billions and billions of snowflakes that have fallen (where we live, anyhow) . . . no two have been exactly, precisely alike. Each snowflake is an artistic, exquisite work of beauty.

In this final week of lessons, we're studying the design element of beauty. A True Woman displays the attractiveness of the gospel. As she matures and grows spiritually, her life becomes increasingly compelling. She's transformed into the image of Jesus, to ever greater levels, from glory to glory (2 Cor. 3:18).

The dictionary defines *beauty* as the qualities in a person or thing that give pleasure to the senses or the mind. Women love beautiful things. They also have an innate desire to BE beautiful—to be seen as pleasing. We believe that this desire is a natural and precious aspect of femininity.

God created us women with a longing to beautify ourselves and to be beheld as beautiful. This womanly desire points to the desire a bride has to make herself as beautiful as she can for her bridegroom. And ultimately, it points to the desire of the church-bride to make herself as

beautiful as she can for Christ, by adorning herself in splendid white garments of righteousness (Isa. 61:10; Jer. 2:32; Rev. 19:7; 21:2).

Sadly, though, we often obsess over the type of beauty that fades, while we neglect the type that lasts— the unfading beauty of the heart, which is of great value in God's eyes (1 Peter 3:4).

Our Titus curriculum outlines the things that make women truly beautiful. A woman who cultivates the elements of godly discernment, honor, affection, discipline, virtue, responsibility, benevolence, and a

submissive disposition and who seeks to leave a godly legacy is a beautiful woman. She "adorns" the gospel (Titus 2:10). Her life showcases the jaw-dropping beauty of redemption. Her life makes the story believable and attracts people to Jesus. →

beautifying it

"To the pure, all things are pure, but to the defiled and unbelieving, nothing is pure; but both their minds and their consciences are defiled. They profess to know God, but they deny him by their works. They are detestable, disobedient, unfit for any good work."

Titus 1:15–16

Have you ever noticed those big, square power transformer utility boxes sitting on concrete pads at ground level? They're often found near sidewalks, roads, and alleyways and are usually painted a dull green or gray color. Because the metal surfaces are monotone, smooth, and accessible, these boxes are often targets for vandalism. The vandals tag the blank canvas-like surfaces with spray-painted graffiti messages, names, and profanities. It costs communities considerable time, effort, and money to keep the graffiti cleaned off.

Some communities have come up with a way to combat the problem. They've hired artists to paint the transformer boxes and cover them with intricate, colorful artwork. The beautiful art covers each surface and leaves no room for graffiti. It discourages vandals from tagging the boxes, because their message would be virtually unreadable. It would be overpowered by the pattern of the commissioned art. Cities that hire artists to paint transformer boxes, such as the city of Fort Collins, Colorado, estimate that they save up to $130,000 in cleanup costs over the life of each box.[1]

In a sense, our lives resemble those transformer boxes. We can choose to cover them in beautiful artwork, or let them be defaced by things that are offensive, crass, and profane.

Throughout the book of Titus, Paul identifies two types of people: those who choose to beautify their lives by living the way God says, and those who don't. The former are "sound in faith," while the latter "turn away from the truth" (1:13–14). The former are "pure," while the latter are "defiled and unbelieving" (1:15).

Read Titus 1:15–16 in the margin on the previous page. What are the primary observable characteristics of those in the "defiled and unbelieving" category? Make a list in the space below:

denying Him by their works

The interesting thing about these categories is that both groups in Titus' day professed to know God. In contemporary terms, both were church-goers; both listened to the messages, sang on the worship team, taught Sunday school, and went to Bible studies. But what differentiated one group from the other was their willingness to obediently apply truth to their lives.

The defiled and unbelieving group was unwilling to deal with their short-comings. They were quite satisfied being arrogant, quick-tempered, violent, greedy, envious, undisciplined, insubordinate, rebellious, dishonest, lazy, gluttonous, slanderous, quarrelsome, impure, self-indulgent, and slaves to all sorts of addictions. Essentially, their lives were no different from people outside the church. And they didn't care to change.

It's supposed to be obvious to anyone who's looking that there's a huge difference between those who believe in Jesus and those who don't. The difference should be crystal clear. Unfortunately, that's not always the case.

I (Nancy) recently came across a survey of sixteen- to twenty-nine-year-old church outsiders who make no profession of faith. Eighty-four percent of them said, "I'm not a Christian, but I know somebody who is." However, of those 84% who knew a Christian, only 15% said they could see any lifestyle difference between themselves and those Christians.[2]

There's something wrong with that picture. The difference should be obvious. The gospel is powerful. The gospel is transformational. But the gospel will not be heard and received by our culture, by our generation, by your children, by your neighbors, or by the people in your workplace if it cannot be seen in the lives of those of us who profess to believe it.

In Titus chapter 2, Paul gives instructions to believers in various seasons and stations of life—to men, women, older and younger believers, and to employees. In each case, the apostle says, "Here's what the gospel should look like in your life." He also gives a number of "purpose" clauses, to explain *why* it's important that it look that way.

Turn to the book of Titus in your Bible. For each verse below, write down the "purpose clause" that Paul cites as the reason believers ought to behave a certain way. (Hint: The clauses usually start with the words "that" or "so that.")

Titus 2:5 _____

Titus 2:8 _____

Titus 2:10 _____

Paul gives similar instructions in his letter to Timothy. Write down the "purpose clauses" he cites in the following verses:

1 Timothy 5:14 _____

1 Timothy 6:1 _____

Summarize why Paul wanted the various groups of believers to pay attention to the way they lived. What was his primary concern?

_____

_____

_____

_____

As Christian women, we're to cultivate the elements of godly womanhood in our lives, "that the word of God may not be reviled" (Titus 2:5). That word *reviled* in the Greek is *blasphēmeō*. Does that sound familiar? It's the word from which we get our English word *blasphemy*. And it means just that—to blaspheme, to defame, to dishonor or speak evil of.

When we claim to follow Christ and to believe the Bible, but we don't live out the implications of God's Word, we cause the Word of God to be reviled. You see this concept in Romans 2, where Paul says, "As it is written, the name of God is blasphemed among the Gentiles"—or unchurched/unbelievers—"because of you" (v. 24). Now, what did they do that caused the name of God to be blasphemed? If you read that whole paragraph in Romans 2, starting at verse 17, you see that they are hypocrites. They profess to know one thing—they even teach it to others—but they don't live it. There's been no change in the way they talk and behave.

A Christian woman whose life doesn't bear witness to the transformative power of the gospel causes the gospel to be blasphemed, defamed, and dishonored—it's as though she invites vandals to deface it with foul graffiti.

If, on the other hand, she cooperates with God and allows Him to change her, she "adorns" the gospel. To adorn means to beautify it and make it attractive. Outsiders will look at her life and say, "Wow! Her life makes me think the Bible is true!" We can't just tell them it's true. They need to see and feel and experience that it really is true through our lives.

Can you identify any areas in which the beauty of Christ in your life has been defaced by sin or hypocrisy?

_____

_____

→ **If it reflects the desire of your heart**, pray and ask the Lord to forgive and cleanse you so you can adorn the gospel.

beauty alert

"How great is his goodness, and how great his beauty!"
Zechariah 9:17

"Splendor and majesty are before him; strength and beauty are in his sanctuary."
Psalm 96:6

"Oh, worship the Lord in the beauty of holiness! Tremble before Him, all the earth."
Psalm 96:9 NKJV

". . . that I may dwell in the house of the Lord all the days of my life, to gaze upon the beauty of the Lord."
Psalm 27:4

*I*n 2012, Israel passed legislation to combat the rise of anorexia and bulimia, especially among young girls. The first part of the legislation outlawed underweight fashion models. Models in Israel are now required to get a doctor to state that their body mass index is at least 18.5% before they're allowed to pose for photos professionally.

Adi Barkan, a prominent modeling agent who helped write the law, said that ultrathin models look "like dead girls." Barkan estimated that around half of the 300 professional models in the country would have to gain weight in order to work.[4] Under the conditions of the new law, a model who is 5'8" must weigh at least 119 pounds. Although that's still super skinny, at least her organs will have the minimum body fat needed to function properly.

The second part of the new Israeli legislation has been dubbed the "Photoshop law." Politicians argued that regulating the skinniness of models wasn't enough when photo editors have this magic wand called Photoshop that can erase blemishes, lengthen a neckline, slim a waistline, or remove half a thigh.

So the second part of the legislation places strict limitations on how much the photos of models can be edited in advertisements. Any ad that makes a model look thinner is now required to be clearly labeled as "photoshopped" or "enhanced." Similar to the warning labels on cigarettes, the labels on photoshopped ads imply that ingesting the images could be bad for a woman's self-image and emotional health.

It can be dangerous to base our ideas about beauty on the wrong model. But unfortunately, most of us look to Hollywood and fashion magazines to define beauty and to tell us how we might become more beautiful.

As we said in the introduction to this week's lessons, the dictionary defines *beauty* as the qualities in a person or thing that give pleasure to

the senses or the mind. This definition places beauty squarely in the eye of the beholder. Something is only beautiful to the extent that it gives pleasure to *my* mind or *my* senses. So if popular opinion doesn't regard something as beautiful, chances are that I won't either.

The Bible presents a model of beauty that is far more objective. It tells us who defines beauty, where it comes from, and exactly what it is that makes someone beautiful.

Based on the verses in the margins (pages 236 and 237), come up with a biblical definition of *beauty*.

The Bible teaches that beauty is:

_____

_____

_____

fashion statement

Like many women today, the women in ancient Israel were *fashionistas*. They used cosmetics, perfume, hairdos, jewelry, and the latest designer fashions and accessories to beautify themselves. They outlined their eyes in black, using lead sulfide. They painted on eye shadow using the mineral of green malachite (Jer. 4:30; Ezek. 23:40). Eyebrows were darkened by applying a black paste. Red ochre served as rouge for coloring cheeks and as lipstick base.

Henna was applied in patterns to the hands and feet, and used to darken fingernails and toenails. Henna was also used for hair dye. Perfumed oils were commonly used on the hair and skin.[5]

In Mesopotamia, the Sumerians and Babylonians introduced the use of yellow and red ochre to powder the face and cover imperfections. Archaeologists' findings

"HE HAS MADE EVERYTHING BEAUTIFUL IN ITS TIME."

Ecclesiastes 3:11

"FOR THE LORD TAKES PLEASURE IN HIS PEOPLE; HE WILL BEAUTIFY THE HUMBLE WITH SALVATION."

Psalm 149:4 NKJV

"CHARM IS DECEPTIVE AND BEAUTY IS FLEETING, BUT A WOMAN WHO FEARS THE LORD WILL BE PRAISED."

Proverbs 31:30 HCSB

"HOW BEAUTIFUL UPON THE MOUNTAINS ARE THE FEET OF HIM WHO BRINGS GOOD NEWS, WHO PUBLISHES PEACE, WHO BRINGS GOOD NEWS OF HAPPINESS, WHO PUBLISHES SALVATION, WHO SAYS TO ZION, 'YOUR GOD REIGNS.'"

Isaiah 52:7

corroborate the importance of cosmetics in daily life. They've dug up ancient cosmetic palettes, kohl tubes and sticks, spoons, rods, rouge pots, hairpins, combs, cosmetic dishes, tweezers, brushes, picks, and mirrors.[6] In one excavation, an object was discovered that appears to be a curling iron and is dated about 1400 B.C.[7]

The coquettish Hebrew ladies mentioned in Isaiah 3:18–24 undoubtedly picked up on these or other fads. They flocked to the market to discover the latest trends, fashions, and cosmetics, much as women today flock to Pinterest or the Mall of America.

What are some of the limitations and problems that can result from relying on things like this to make you beautiful?

_____

_____

_____

Use 1 Peter 3:3–5, Isaiah 3:18–24, and the verses in the margin of today's lesson to compile a list of the things that contribute to each type of beauty:

Things that contribute to the type of beauty that fades	Things that contribute to the type of beauty that lasts

Which column do you pay more attention to on a daily basis and why?

_____

_____

enthralled by her beauty

P Psalm 45 is a messianic psalm that foreshadows the relationship between King Jesus and His church-bride. Verse 11 says, "The King will greatly desire your beauty" (NKJV).

The Lord is enthralled by your beauty. It's not the fading beauty of youth, of clear unwrinkled skin, or of a trim, shapely figure that attracts Him. Nor is it the

transient beauty of carefully applied cosmetics or the latest style of clothing. The type of beauty that appeals to Him is the lasting beauty of someone who truly believes in God . . . someone who clothes herself in the spectacular garments of salvation, holiness, humility, faith, submission, gentleness, and quietness. This type of beauty adorns the gospel, making it attractive and believable to outsiders. Even more importantly, it pleases the Lord.

A bride is meticulous about her appearance. On the big day, she wants to look as lovely as possible for her groom. Do you have that kind of desire to be beautiful for Jesus? Explain.

_____

_____

→ **What aspect** of your "appearance" could use some attention? Close in prayer, asking the Lord to give you the right perspective on beauty and to increase your heart's desire to be beautiful for Him.

_____

_____

beautiful things

"A voice says, 'Cry!' And I said, 'What shall I cry?' All flesh is grass, and all its beauty is like the flower of the field. . . . The grass withers, the flower fades, but the word of our God will stand forever."

Isaiah 40:6–8

"[Wisdom] will place on your head a graceful garland; she will bestow on you a beautiful crown."

Proverbs 4:9

*L*earning about biblical womanhood has been a journey for us. Thankfully, we've grown and we're both at a different place in our understanding than we were ten, twenty, or thirty years ago.

I (Mary) grew up in a German immigrant family with five brothers, and was somewhat of a tomboy. I was determined to prove that anything my brothers could do, I could do better. The only fistfight I've ever gotten into was when one of my older brothers derided me with, "You're just a girl!" While all the girls in my school took home economics, I took shop. While they studied cosmetology, I studied drafting. While they participated in dance club, I led the Christian club. I was good at leading. I was good at sports. And I had a strong aversion to anything pink or girly.

After I finished high school at the age of sixteen, I was the first woman in my region ever hired by Hudson's Bay—a major Canadian department store, like Macy's—as a night janitor. I outdid all my older male colleagues, proving that I could handle the heavy work and equipment. I earned four times as much as any other person my age. I started my own business. I started my own rock band. I was the only one of my siblings to put myself through university and earn a professional degree. But at some point, I had to reconcile my tomboyish demeanor, fierce independence, and desire to outdo the guys with what the Bible says about womanhood.

I (Nancy) am a firstborn, type A daughter of two firstborn, type A parents. I have always had strong opinions and tons of vision and drive.

I was a serious-minded child who loved school and dreaded recess, weekends, and vacations. (Strange, I know!) I also wanted to be in charge of pretty much everything. The only two things I enjoyed playing with my younger siblings were "school" or "church"—and invariably I wanted to be the teacher or the preacher!

I loved the Lord and wanted to please and serve Him. From elementary school on, I was always eager to take advantage of ministry opportunities. But I struggled to reconcile my strong, outspoken, take-charge personality with what I understood to be a biblical perspective on womanhood. A meek and quiet spirit? I thought I'd have to have a personality transplant for that to ever be possible.

If you would have told either of us when we were twenty that we would one day be writing about biblical womanhood and would be helping to lead a counterrevolution to reclaim it, we probably would have laughed at the thought.

In our desire to understand God's design for us as women, we both started from the premise that what God says is "right." After all, He is God and we are not. But it took years for us to grasp that His design for women is not only *right* but it is also *good* . . . and even longer to truly delight in the magnificence and beauty of it. Admittedly, there are times when we still struggle with some of the concepts. But the more we grasp and say yes to His ways, the more we love them!

good and beautiful truths

Throughout this *True Woman 201* study, we've looked at things that "accord with sound doctrine" (Titus 2:1). The elements of womanhood we've studied are true. They are right. But there's a phrase in our Titus passage that indicates that not only are these things true and right, but they are also beautiful.

The phrase is at the end of verse 3, where it says that older women are to "teach what is good." In last week's lessons, we learned that this phrase is

translated from one long Greek word: *kalodidaskalos*, from *kalos—goodness* or *virtue*, and *didaskalos—teacher*. It indicates that older women are to be teachers of virtue. But there's another nuance contained in this word; it's the idea of beauty. The word *kalos* refers to good, virtuous things that are **beneficial**

and also incredibly **beautiful**.[8] *Kalodidaskalos* could be translated as "teaching good and beautiful things."[9] We've spent the past nine chapters talking about good and beautiful things:

Discernment—learning how to think correctly about womanhood, in accordance with sound doctrine—is a good and beautiful thing!

Honor—reverently making much of Christ, and always living like you're in a temple—is a good and beautiful thing!

Affection—loving husbands and children (especially your own) and esteeming God's family plan—is a good and beautiful thing!

Discipline—making wise, intentional, self-controlled choices—is a good and beautiful thing!

Virtue—cultivating goodness and purity in every area of your life—is a good and beautiful thing!

Responsibility—maintaining the right work priorities and giving priority to the work of the home—is a good and beautiful thing!

Benevolence—being kind and charitable toward others—is a good and beautiful thing!

Disposition—cultivating a soft, amenable, submissive spirit—is a good and beautiful thing!

Legacy—teaching and spiritually mothering younger women—is a good and beautiful thing!

Are there any of the above elements of womanhood that you know are right but do not yet perceive as good and beautiful? Which ones? Explain why.

_____

_____

Turn back to page 238 and circle the word *imperishable* in 1 Peter 3:3–5.

"To give them beauty for ashes, the oil of joy for mourning, the garment of praise for the spirit of heaviness; that they may be called trees of righteousness, the planting of the LORD, that He may be glorified."

Isaiah 61:3 NKJV

"Out of Zion, the perfection of beauty, God shines forth."

Psalm 50:2

"You are altogether beautiful, my love; there is no flaw in you."

Song of Solomon 4:7

Read all the verses in the margins of this lesson. Why is the beauty of biblical womanhood an imperishable beauty? (Check all that apply)

- ☐ Because it's based on the wisdom of God
- ☐ Because it's based on the Word of God
- ☐ Because it's based on the character of God
- ☐ Because this type of beauty is bestowed by God
- ☐ Because all earthly beauty will one day be eclipsed by the eternal beauty to which it points

According to Isaiah 61:3, what is the ultimate reason God works in our lives to make us beautiful?

_____

_____

So many women struggle with issues of personal appearance and self-worth. They look in the mirror, and the reflection they see doesn't appear beautiful to them—not according to the world's standard, anyhow. All they see are the

physical imperfections—the nose that's too long; the eyes that are too squinty; the skin that's plagued with bumps, pits, or zits; the sags, the bulges, the folds, and the wrinkles.

The Bible presents a grace-soaked, spectacular vision for female beauty. It insists that the King is enthralled—ENTHRALLED!—with the beauty of *every* woman who puts her faith in Him. We've been talking a lot about the things that make a woman radiate with the beauty of Christ. We've challenged you to examine various areas of your life, and to work at change. But it's important for you to realize that cultivating spiritual beauty isn't meant to be another onerous guilt-inducing item on your endless to-do list. No. The type of beauty God wants in you is the beauty that *He* will bestow on you as you allow His Spirit to conform you to the image of Jesus. It's a gift of grace.

→ **Pray and thank the Lord that the King is enthralled with your beauty.** Ask Him to make your life a reflection of His beauty and grace.

feminine beauty

*A*s I (Nancy) edited parts of this study, the Sochi Winter Olympics were on my television screen, playing in the background. I stopped to watch the figure skating performance of Korean skater "Queen" Yuna Kim—the highest-paid female athlete in the world. I was mesmerized by her grace and beauty. Apparently, others are too. The commentator noted that it's "her gentleness and her softness" that have caused the world to be so endeared to her.

What a lovely illustration of the power of true femininity! I don't know whether Yuna Kim is a follower of Christ. But I do know that "gentleness" and "softness" are traits that Scripture identifies as beautiful aspects of woman-hood. These feminine traits are "very precious" in God's eyes (1 Peter 3:4). And though they are often rejected by the world, they are attractive nonetheless.

Review the ten elements of True Womanhood. Summarize what Scripture teaches about each element. Then, reflect on how our culture promotes a different message. As you do the exercise, we suggest that you turn to the applicable section of the book to help you recall what you've learned.

> "A God-centered woman lives to reflect the beauty and wonder of His ways and to join every created thing in heaven and earth in glorifying and worshiping Him eternally."[10]
>
> *Nancy*

Design Element One: Discernment (pages 14–37)

A True Woman is characterized by right thinking . . . She knows "*what accords with sound doctrine.*"

What Scripture teaches about this:	What popular culture says:

Design Element Two: Honor (pages 38–61)

A True Woman makes much of Christ . . . She is *"reverent in behavior."*

What Scripture teaches about this:	What popular culture says:

Which design elements do you find the most challenging, and why?

Design Element Three: Affection (pages 62–85)

A True Woman values the family . . . She *"[loves husband] and children."*

What Scripture teaches about this:	What popular culture says:

Design Element Four: Discipline (pages 86–109)

A True Woman makes wise, intentional choices . . . She is *"self-controlled."*

What Scripture teaches about this:	What popular culture says:

Design Element Five: Virtue (pages 110–133)

A True Woman cultivates goodness . . . She is *"pure."*

What Scripture teaches about this:	What popular culture says:

Design Element Six: Responsibility (pages 134–157)

A True Woman maintains the right work priorities . . . She values *"working at home."*

What Scripture teaches about this:	What popular culture says:

Design Element Seven: Benevolence (pages 158–181)

A True Woman is charitable . . . She is *"kind."*

What Scripture teaches about this:	What popular culture says:

To what extent do you think your ideas about womanhood are impacted by popular culture?

How can you ensure that your ideas are informed by Scripture instead?

Design Element Eight: Disposition (pages 182–205)

A True Woman cultivates a soft, amenable spirit . . . She is "*submissive.*"

What Scripture teaches about this:	What popular culture says:

Design Element Nine: Legacy (pages 206–229)

A True Woman is a spiritual mother . . . She "*teaches what is good.*"

What Scripture teaches about this:	What popular culture says:

Design Element Ten: Beauty (pages 230–253)

A True Woman displays the attractiveness of the gospel . . . "*So that the word of God may not be reviled.*"

What Scripture teaches about this:	What popular culture says:

beautiful pillars

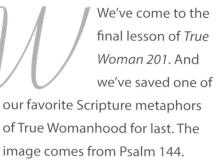We've come to the final lesson of *True Woman 201*. And we've saved one of our favorite Scripture metaphors of True Womanhood for last. The image comes from Psalm 144.

In this psalm, David mingles prayers with praise. He starts out by confidently asking God to give him victory and deliver Israel from her enemies (vv. 1–11). Then he envisions what a time of God's blessing and peace would look like: The nation's sons and daughters would grow up and flourish as men and women, the nation would prosper economically, and crime would be virtually nonexistent (vv. 12–14). At the end of the psalm, David acknowledges that such a paradise could only come from God, and be experienced by people whose God is the Lord (v. 15).

Read Psalm 144 in your Bible, paying special attention to the figures of speech David uses to describe Israel's sons and daughters. What does he envision that Israel's sons will be like as they grow into manhood (v.12)?

What does he envision that Israel's daughters would be like as they grow into womanhood?

> "A God-centered woman embraces the supreme purpose for which she was created. She lives to reflect the beauty and wonder of His ways and to join every created thing in heaven and earth in glorifying and worshiping Him eternally."[11]
>
> *Nancy*

King David envisioned that God's blessing would make the nation's sons grow into mature, strong, stable, productive plants. He envisioned that it would make her daughters be "like corner pillars cut for the structure of a palace." Another version says, "like corner pillars that are carved in the palace style" (HCSB). But what does the image mean?

David is making reference here to the caryatide columns that were common in Egyptian architecture. Their appearance was doubtless familiar to the Hebrews.[12] A caryatide is a marble statue carved into the shape of a tall, beautiful woman, and used like a pillar, as an architectural support. The female statue typically stood on a small pedestal, and was dressed in an elegantly draped, floor-length gown. Her long hair was elaborately plaited and styled. A crown rested on top of her head, and on top of that rested the weight of the structure.

Palaces typically featured numerous caryatides standing in a row. The best-known example is from ancient Greece, the six-figured *Caryatid Porch of the Erechtheion*, which has been preserved on the Acropolis at Athens.

But the metaphorical "pillars" pictured in this psalm aren't standing in a row, holding up the porch of a palace. They're standing at the corners of homes, and are supporting the structure of the nation.[13]

Draw a picture of David's metaphor of womanhood in the frame below.

The metaphor presents a powerful image of the beauty, dignity, strength, and influence of godly womanhood, doesn't it? It reminds us of the quote we cited in *True Woman 101* by the 19th-century British pastor John Angell James. Here again is a portion of that quote:

> *Every woman, by her virtue or her vice, by her folly or her wisdom, by her levity or her dignity, is adding something to our national elevation or degradation. . . . A community is not likely to be overthrown where woman fulfills her mission, for by the power of her noble heart over the hearts of others, she will raise that community from its ruins and restore it again to prosperity and joy.*[15]

Pastor James believed that true womanhood was so vital that the strength and success of a nation depended on it. Without godly womanly influence, its moral fabric would unravel, families would fail, and it would certainly sink into degradation and ruin. It appears from Psalm 144 that King David would agree.

We are so encouraged by reports from around the world about how God is using the True Woman movement to raise up women as pillars in their homes and communities. Here's one from a young wife in Austria whose marriage has been radically changed as she has come to discover and delight in Christ and His good plan for her life:

> *At one point our relationship was so broken, that my then fiancé had no strength to move on, because I tore him down with my words. God finally opened my eyes and began to change me. My husband says this message has transformed me and our relationship. Where there was quarreling and shouting, there is now peace. You have instilled a burning desire in me to be a True Woman of God and to pass on what I learn from His Word to other women and the next generations!*

And another from a Spanish-speaking sister in the Dominican Republic:

> *He took me from being a feminist young woman—selfish and with earthly desires— to a new young woman. I didn't want to get married or have kids. I was studying medicine with the intention of just being rich and economically powerful. I was pretty opposite of God's design for me.*

After digging in His Word, everything began to change. My desires, goals in life, purpose—everything! Now He made me love my design and I can't stay quiet about this with other girls. Here I am giving up medicine for studying the Bible. It looks like craziness to people, but I know Whom I believe.

Whatever your past, your limitations, your needs, or your season of life, you can be like a beautiful pillar to adorn and uphold your marriage, family, church, workplace, and community. May it be so, by His grace and for His glory!

Read the Elisabeth Elliot quote in the margin of page 250. Explain how knowing Christ ought to make you "a different kind of woman."

_____

_____

We are so grateful that you have joined us on this journey. We hope this study has helped you come to a better understanding of God's plan and calling for us as Christian women. We pray that the Lord will continue to change you from the inside out, as you discover and embrace His divine design, and that He will use your life to point those around you to the beauty of Christ.

→ **Take time to reflect on what you've learned in *True Woman 201*.** Use the Personalize It section on page 253 to record how it's impacted your life.

drawing it out,
drawing it in . . .

interior renovation

process

The video for Week Ten will help you process this week's lessons. You'll find this week's video, the leader's guide, and additional resources at TrueWoman201.com.

ponder

Think about the following questions. Discuss them with your friends, family, and/or small group:

1. How has this ten-week study better enabled you to "throw out the cookie cutter" when it comes to your understanding of biblical womanhood?

2. Why do we have nothing to fear when we entrust ourselves to God's renovating work in our lives and hearts?

3. Discuss the variety of ways a True Woman displays the attractiveness of the gospel.

4. How can our God-given desire for beauty best be fulfilled? What truths have you learned in this study that inspire you to pursue true, spiritual beauty?

5. What are the characteristics both of those who choose to beautify themselves God's way and those who don't? Ground your answer in Titus 1:13–15.

6. Why is it vital that our lives reflect our profession of faith? What results if the transforming impact of the gospel cannot be seen in the lives of Christan women?

7. Discuss the various ways women clothe both their outward and their inward person. What sort of adornment brings pleasure to the Lord? Does God's pleasure motivate you to "dress" biblically? If so, how?

8. Why is biblical womanhood as described in Titus 2 so attractive? How is God glorified and His kingdom advanced when we display His beauty?

personalize it

Use this page to journal. Write down what you learned this week. Record your comments, a favorite verse, or a concept or quote that was particularly helpful or meaningful to you. Compose a prayer, letter, or poem. Jot down notes from the video or your small group session. Express your heart response to what you have studied. Personalize this week's lessons in the way that will best help you apply them to your life.

drawing it out,
drawing it in . . .

We hope this study has helped you better understand your mission and calling as a woman. As we said at the outset, our intention has been to present timeless biblical principles that apply to women of all cultures, personalities, ages, and stages of life. As we allow Him to give us an interior makeover, it's critical that the foundation of our womanhood is rock solid. If you haven't yet had a chance to study *True Woman 101: Divine Design*, we'd encourage you to do so. In that eight-week study we explore the fact that God created women with a divine design that differs from men. He also created us different from one another. We are different by design.

throw away the cookie cutter

The Bible doesn't give us a simplistic, prescribed set of rules about what womanhood must "look" like. It doesn't tell us, for example, how long our skirts should be, or whether we should pursue advanced education, or that women must be the ones who clean the toilets and cook all the meals, or that we should never work outside of the home, or that all women should get married, or that we must educate our children a certain way. The Bible doesn't contain such cookie-cutter checklists.

That's not to say that our decisions don't matter. God has given us some clear principles about womanhood in His Word. It's important that we wrestle with how to implement these principles. We need to rely on the Holy Spirit's guidance to help us figure out how to apply them in our particular situation. But we must avoid a cookie-cutter mentality. We are all unique. Every woman's circumstances are distinct. We each need to carefully discern how to apply God's principles in our own lives. We can encourage one another in that process, but it's not up to us to determine how they must be applied in other women's lives.

delight in the differences

W We encourage you to delight in the diversity and to avoid the temptation to compare yourself with others. Cling firmly to core biblical convictions; hold less tightly to matters of application and preference. In both, be gracious and humble. Allow God to express His many-splendored grace through the various gifts and sensitivities He has given to different women who love Him and desire to honor Him.

It's also important to remember that true womanhood is a journey. It certainly has been for both of us. The Lord has challenged and changed our thinking and behavior over time. We are at a different place in our understanding and application of True Womanhood now than we were twenty or thirty years ago. And we're still learning and growing!

Further, it's important to remember that though we aim for the ideal, we live in a less-than-ideal world. Because of the reality of sin, experiencing and expressing the biblical ideal for womanhood will be difficult in some circumstances. We are sinners. Men are sinners. God's grace can enable us to walk with Him and please Him in every situation, but we need wisdom to discern how to reflect God's heart and ways in a broken world.

True Women are not haughty, self-righteous, or condemning. They are encouragers rather than critics. They know they are hopeless and helpless apart from God's grace. And they are generous in giving grace to others. They extend grace to those who do not have the same convictions about what the Bible teaches

about womanhood. They extend grace to those who make alternate decisions about how to apply biblical principles. They extend grace to those who are at a different stage of their journey. They extend grace to those who are dealing with tragic, formidable circumstances. They extend to others the same kind of grace they themselves have received from God.

marvel at the meaning

In closing, we want to remind you that as important as the elements of biblical womanhood are, their greatest significance is in that to which they point. True Womanhood is not an end in and of itself. Our womanhood exists to put the story of Jesus Christ on display. Its purpose is to draw attention to the beauty and wonder of the gospel.

There's nothing quite as compelling as a really good romance, is there? We're all familiar with the storyline. The dashing hero fights to rescue the lovely princess from evil. She falls head over heels in love with him. He proposes. Then they ride off into the sunset to live happily ever after.

Have you ever wondered why so many stories follow this basic plot? Or why participating in a real-life version is the dream of so many women? It's not because Hollywood came up with such a fantastic script, or because movie stars make romance so attractive. No. It's because God wanted people to know and participate in the greatest love story of all time— the amazing, pursuing love of Christ for undeserving sinners.

Our Father God created male and female, sex and marriage, to give us a physical picture of what a spiritual relationship with Jesus is all about. Jesus Christ, the sinless Son of God, came to earth to rescue His Bride (the church)

from the terrible consequence of sin—separation from God, spiritual and physical death. Christ loved His Bride so much that He died on the cross to bear the punishment of sin in her place. He rescued her from evil and made a covenant commitment to her.

In response to His initiative, she cannot help but love Him and has responded favorably to His proposal. Spiritually, she is betrothed (engaged) to Him.

She keeps herself for Him and readies herself for the day they will be forever united. It's a love story like no other. It's the story of the gospel. Christ's story is the story that earthly romance was created to tell.

We trust that by God's grace you have become a part of that great story. The fact is, it's impossible to be a True Woman apart from having a personal relationship with Christ and having His Spirit living within you. Apart from Him, you may strive and struggle to perform or to gain His favor; you may be able to conform to some external standard or to impress others with how "good" you are—but you will never have the grace and the power you need to be the woman He designed you to be, from the inside out.

We hope you've responded to Jesus' call, that you have repented of running your own life and going your own way, and that you have accepted His free gift of forgiveness and salvation. If you haven't, you can do that right now by praying and telling the Lord that you recognize His right to rule in your life, that you are turning to Him from your sin and rebellion against Him, that you receive by faith the death He died in your place on the cross, and that you want to enter into an eternal relationship with Him.

In the end, saying "yes" to Jesus is what True Womanhood is all about. We hope this study has inspired you to marvel, embrace, and delight in God's spectacular plan, and that you've begun to discover the beauty, joy, and fulfillment of being exactly who He created you to be. He wants you to be so much more than what the world upholds as the ideal. He wants you to be a True Woman!—a woman who says "Yes, Lord!"; a woman who by His grace patterns your life according to His grand, interior design for your life!

aim to make a difference

Make It a Movement

In the 1970s, there was an advertising campaign that featured commercials with a young woman who cheerfully chirped that she *"told two friends about Faberge Organic Shampoo, who told two friends, who told two friends, and so on, and so on . . ."* while her image multiplied over and over again on the screen.

The potential of exponentially spreading a message by word of mouth is amazing. We did the math: If you tell two friends each week, who in turn tell two friends each week, then the message will spread to over half a million people in three months!

If every woman who does this study invites two other women to do it, and they invite their friends to do it, and we all begin to live out the call to True Womanhood, by God's grace, we could be used to turn the tide and make a profound difference in the lives of the next generation.

As we shared in the introduction, the goal of the True Woman Movement is to help women:

- *Discover and embrace* God's design and mission for their lives
- *Reflect the beauty* and heart of Jesus Christ to their world
- *Intentionally pass* the baton of Truth on to the next generation
- *Pray earnestly* for an outpouring of God's Spirit in their families, churches, nation, and world

If that sounds like something you'd like to be a part of—or even if you're just curious to learn more—we encourage you to take the next step and consider what you can do to get involved.

you can make a difference

To get to know more of the heartbeat of the True Woman Movement, visit us online at TrueWoman.com. You'll find links there to many helpful resources.

Here are ten ways you can get involved and make a difference:

1. **Grow and interact with others on the True Woman Blog**—Sign up for this and other great, daily content at ReviveOurHearts.com.

2. **Take the 30-Day True Woman Makeover Challenge**—Find this and other challenges at ReviveOurHearts.com/Challenges.

3. **Sign, Share & Study the True Woman Manifesto**—We're praying for 100,000 women to join us in a personal and corporate declaration of belief about what the Bible teaches about womanhood. Learn more about it on TrueWomanManifesto.com.

4. **Host a True Woman 101 or 201 Bible study**—Study this series with your sisters, daughters, coworkers, neighbors, relatives, and friends.

5. **Host your own Event**—Everything you need to pull off an effective True Woman Event is available on TrueWomanEventKit.com.

6. **Share the True Woman Movement with your friends and followers**— "And she told two friends, and she told two friends, and so on, and so on . . . ." Spread the word; we're on Facebook, Twitter, Instagram, and Pinterest!

7. **Gift a True Woman book to a friend**—We have lots of recommended resources available in our online store on ReviveOurHearts.com for you to choose from, including:

   • *Girls Gone Wise—in a World Gone Wild* by Mary Kassian

   • *Lies Women Believe: And the Truth That Sets Them Free!* by Nancy Leigh DeMoss

   • *Lies Young Women Believe: And the Truth That Sets Them Free!* by Nancy Leigh DeMoss and Dannah Gresh

   • *Fierce Women: The Power of a Soft Warrior* by Kimberly Wagner

   • *Radical Womanhood* by Carolyn McCulley

8. **Make a donation**—Every dollar counts. Your donation helps keep the website, the blog, and True Woman conferences going.

9. **Attend a True Woman conference**—Check out the schedule for the next True Woman conference. Plan to attend, and encourage your friends to join you.

10. **Do another recommended Bible study or book study**—Visit ReviveOurHearts.com/RecommendedStudies.

becoming God's true woman

We hope this study has made a difference in your life and that you will continue on the journey toward True Womanhood. Most of all, we pray you will continue to get to know the One to whom the story of True Womanhood points—our Savior and friend, Jesus Christ. It's in saying "yes" to Him that your life will reflect God's beautiful work of art and others will be drawn to Him!

→ True Woman Manifesto

*A personal and corporate declaration of belief,
consecration, and prayerful intent—
to the end that Christ may be exalted
and the glory and redeeming love of God
may be displayed throughout the whole earth*

SCHAUMBURG, IL
OCTOBER 11, 2008

We believe that God is the sovereign Lord of the universe and the Creator of life, and that all created things exist for His pleasure and to bring Him glory.[1]

We believe that the creation of humanity as male and female was a purposeful and magnificent part of God's wise plan, and that men and women were designed to reflect the image of God in complementary and distinct ways.[2]

We believe that sin has separated every human being from God and made us incapable of reflecting His image as we were created to do. Our only hope of restoration and salvation is found in repenting of our sin and trusting in Christ who lived a sinless life, died in our place, and was raised from the dead.[3]

We realize that we live in a culture that does not recognize God's right to rule, does not accept Scripture as the pattern for life, and is experiencing the consequences of abandoning God's design for men and women.[4]

We believe that Christ is redeeming this sinful world and making all things new, and that His followers are called to share in His redemptive purposes as they seek, by God's empowerment, to transform every aspect of human life that has been marred and ruined by sin.[5]

As Christian women, *we desire to honor God* by living countercultural lives that reflect the beauty of Christ and His gospel to our world.

To that end, we affirm that . . .

Scripture is God's authoritative means of instructing us in His ways and it reveals His holy pattern for our womanhood, our character, our priorities, and our various roles, responsibilities, and relationships.[6]

We glorify God and experience His blessing when we accept and joyfully embrace His created design, function, and order for our lives.[7]

As redeemed sinners, we cannot live out the beauty of biblical womanhood apart from the sanctifying work of the gospel and the power of the indwelling Holy Spirit.[8]

Men and women are both created in the image of God and are equal in value and dignity, but they have distinct roles and functions in the home and in the church.[9]

We are called as women to affirm and encourage men as they seek to express godly masculinity, and to honor and support God-ordained male leadership in the home and in the church.[10]

Marriage, as created by God, is a sacred, binding, lifelong covenant between one man and one woman.[11]

When we respond humbly to male leadership in our homes and churches, we demonstrate a noble submission to authority that reflects Christ's submission to God His Father.[12]

Selfish insistence on personal rights is contrary to the spirit of Christ who humbled Himself, took on the form of a servant, and laid down His life for us.[13]

Human life is precious to God and is to be valued and protected, from the point of conception until rightful death.[14]

Children are a blessing from God; women are uniquely designed to be bearers and nurturers of life, whether it be their own biological or adopted children, or other children in their sphere of influence.[15]

God's plan for gender is wider than marriage; all women, whether married or single, are to model femininity in their various relationships, by exhibiting a distinctive modesty, responsiveness, and gentleness of spirit.[16]

Suffering is an inevitable reality in a fallen world; at times we will be called to suffer for doing what is good—looking to heavenly reward rather than earthly comfort—for the sake of the gospel and the advancement of Christ's Kingdom.[17]

Mature Christian women have a responsibility to leave a legacy of faith, by discipling younger women in the Word and ways of God and modeling for the next generation lives of fruitful femininity.[18]

Believing the above, we declare our desire and intent to be "true women" of God. *We consecrate ourselves* to fulfill His calling and purposes for our lives. *By His grace and in humble dependence on His power, we will:*

1. Seek to love the Lord our God with all our heart, soul, mind, and strength.[19]

2. Gladly yield control of our lives to Christ as Lord—we will say "Yes, Lord" to the Word and the will of God.[20]

3. Be women of the Word, seeking to grow in our knowledge of Scripture and to live in accord with sound doctrine in every area of our lives.[21]

4. Nurture our fellowship and communion with God through prayer—in praise, thanksgiving, confession, intercession, and supplication.[22]

5. Embrace and express our unique design and calling as women with humility, gratitude, faith, and joy.[23]

6. Seek to glorify God by cultivating such virtues as purity, modesty, submission, meekness, and love.[24]

7. Show proper respect to both men and women, created in the image of God, esteeming others as better than ourselves, seeking to build them up, and putting off bitterness, anger, and evil speaking.[25]

8. Be faithfully engaged in our local church, submitting ourselves to our spiritual leaders, growing in the context of the community of faith, and using the gifts He has given us to serve others, to build up the Body of Christ, and to fulfill His redemptive purposes in the world.[26]

9. Seek to establish homes that manifest the love, grace, beauty, and order of God, that provide a climate conducive to nurturing life, and that extend Christian hospitality to those outside the walls of our homes.[27]

10. Honor the sacredness, purity, and permanence of the marriage covenant—whether ours or others'.[28]

11. Receive children as a blessing from the Lord, seeking to train them to love and follow Christ and to consecrate their lives for the sake of His gospel and Kingdom.[29]

12. Live out the mandate of Titus 2—as older women, modeling godliness and training younger women to be pleasing to God in every respect; as younger women, receiving instruction with meekness and humility and aspiring to become mature women of God who in turn will train the next generation.[30]

13. Seek opportunities to share the gospel of Christ with unbelievers.[31]

14. Reflect God's heart for those who are poor, infirm, oppressed, widows, orphans, and prisoners, by reaching out to minister to their practical and spiritual needs in the name of Christ.[32]

15. Pray for a movement of revival and reformation among God's people that will result in the advancement of the Kingdom and gospel of Christ among all nations.[33]

Who knows whether you have

come into the kingdom

for such a time as this?

Esther 4:14 NKJV

1. 1 Cor. 8:6; Col. 1:16; Rev. 4:11

2. Gen. 1:26-27; 2:18; 1 Cor. 11:8

3. Gen. 3:1-7, 15-16; Mark 1:15; 1 Cor. 15:1-4

4. Prov. 14:12; Jer. 17:9; Rom. 3:18, 8:6-7; 2 Tim. 3:16

5. Eph. 4:22-24; Col. 3:12-14; Titus 2:14

6. Josh. 1:8; 2 Tim. 3:16; 2 Pet. 1:20-21; 3:15-16

7. 1 Tim. 2:9; Titus 2:3-5; 1 Pet. 3:3-6

8. John 15:1-5; 1 Cor. 15:10; Eph. 2:8-10; Phil. 2:12-13

9. Gen. 1:26-28; 2:18; Gal. 3:26-28; Eph. 5:22-33

10. Mark 9:35; 10:42-45; Gen. 2:18; 1 Pet. 5:1-4; 1 Cor. 14:34; 1 Tim. 2:12-3:7

11. Gen. 2:24; Mark 10:7-9

12. Eph. 5:22-33; 1 Cor. 11:3

13. Luke 13:30; John 15:13; Eph. 4:32; Phil. 2:5-8

14. Ps. 139:13-16

15. Gen 1:28; 9:1; Psalm 127; Titus 2:4-5

16. 1 Cor. 11:2-16; 1 Tim. 2:9-13

17. Matt. 5:10-12; 2 Cor. 4:17; James 1:12; 1 Pet. 2:21-13; 3:14-17; 4:14

18. Titus 2:3-5

19. Deut. 6:4-5; Mark 12:29-30

20. Ps. 25:4-5; Rom. 6:11-13; 16-18; Eph. 5:15-17

21. Acts 17:11; 1 Pet. 1:15; 2 Pet. 3:17-18; Titus 2:1, 3-5, 7

22. Psalm 5:2; Phil. 4:6; 1 Tim. 2:1-2

23. Prov. 31:10-31; Col. 3:18; Eph. 5:22-24, 33b

24. Rom. 12:9-21; 1 Pet. 3:1-6; 1 Tim. 2:9-14

25. Eph. 4:29-32; Phil. 2:1-4; James 3:7-10; 4:11

26. Rom. 12:6-8; 14:19; Eph. 4:15, 29; Heb. 13:17

27. Prov. 31:10-31; 1 Tim. 5:10; 1 John 3:17-18

28. Matt. 5:27-28; Mark 10:5-9; 1 Cor. 6:15-20; Heb. 13:4

29. Ps. 127:3; Prov. 4:1-23; 22:6

30. Titus 2:3-5

31. Matt. 28:19-20; Col. 4:3-6

32. Matt. 25:36; Luke 10:25-37; James 1:27; 1 Tim. 6:17-19

33. Chron. 7:14; Ps. 51:1-10; 85:6; 2 Peter 3:9

Now is the time!

I desire to be a part of a countercultural,
spiritual revolution among Christian women in our day.

I have read and personally affirm the True Woman Manifesto,
and I hereby express my desire to join other women in living out and
reproducing its message—to the end that Christ may be exalted
and the glory and redeeming love of God may be
displayed throughout the whole earth.

_____

NAME   DATE

Go to www.TrueWoman.com/Manifesto to add
your signature to the True Woman Manifesto.

NOTES

Introduction: Elements of Design

1. Susan Hunt, *By Design: God's Distinctive Calling for Women* (Franklin, TN: Legacy Communications, 1994), 17.
2. John Piper, "God Created Man Male and Female: What Does It Meant to Be Complementarian?," sermon, accessed March 29, 2014, http://www.desiringgod.org/sermons/god-created-man-male-and-female-what-does-it-mean-to-be-complementarian.
3. Mary A. Kassian, *The Feminist Mistake: The Radical Impact of Feminism on Church and Culture*, rev. ed. (Wheaton, IL: Crossway, 2005), 299.
4. Quoted in Donna Tersiisky, "The Elements and Principles of Visual Design," accessed November 27, 2012, http://nwrain.net/~tersiisky/design/design.html.

Element One: Discernment

1. "Interior Design Element: Five Elements of Interior Design," Imago Interiors website, accessed November 28, 2012, http://www.imagointeriors.com.au/pages/interior-design-elements.html.
2. Theodore J. Passon, "Sick-building syndrome and building-related illness," Environmental Exprt website, accessed November 30, 2012, http://www.environmental-expert.com/articles/sick-building-syndrome-and-building-related-illness-51823.
3. Richard Dawkins, "Richard Dawkins Quotes," *Brainy Quote* website, accessed December 4, 2012, http://www.brainyquote.com/quotes/authors/r/richard_dawkins_3.html.
4. Tim Challies, *The Discipline of Spiritual Discernment* (Wheaton, IL: Crossway, 2007), 16.
5. Ibid., 61.
6. Nancy Leigh DeMoss, *Lies Women Believe: And the Truth That Sets Them Free* (Chicago, IL: Moody, 2001), 35.
7. "Know Your Money," United States Secret Service, accessed December 11, 2012, http://www.secretservice.gov/know_your_money.shtml.
8. DeMoss, *Lies Women Believe*, 32.
9. Challies, *Discipline of Spiritual Discernment*, 61.

Element Two: Honor

1. See http://architecture.about.com/od/greatbuildings/ig/Monuments-and-Memorials/The-USS-Arizona-Memorial-.htm and http://www.nps.gov/valr/upload/press_kit.pdf.
2. Clement of Alexandria, in *The Letters to Timothy, Titus, and Philemon*, ed. W. Barclay, The Daily Study Bible Series (Philadelphia, Westminster: 1975), 249.
3. Richard Eden, "The Queen Tells the Duchess of Cambridge to Curtsy to the 'Blood Princesses'," *Telegraph*, June 24, 2012, http://www.telegraph.co.uk/news/uknews/theroyalfamily/9351571/The-Queen-tells-the-Duchess-of-Cambridge-to-curtsy-to-the-blood-princesses.html.
4. Kenneth S. Wuest, *Word Studies from the Greek New Testament*, 3 vols. (Grand Rapids, MI: Eerdmans, 1980), "Tt. 2:3." See also H. D. M. Spence, ed. *Titus*, The Pulpit Commentary, vol. 24 (London: Funk & Wagnalls, 1909).
5. Jane Taber, "Tory MP's Bill Gets Tough with War-Memorial Vandals," *Globe and Mail*, September 9, 2012, http://m.theglobeandmail.com/news/politics/ottawa-notebook/tory-mps-bill-gets-tough-with-war-memorial-vandals/article619271/?service=mobile; Jenny Yeun, "Vandalizing War Memorials Won't Be Tolerated: Feds," *Ottawa Sun*, September 13, 2012, http://www.ottawasun.com/2012/11/13/vandalizing-war-memorials-wont-be-tolerated-feds-2.
6. Mary A. Kassian, "A True Woman Chooses Wisdom," *True Woman* blog, accessed May 16, 2013, http://www.truewoman.com/?id=1339.
7. Amos Bronson Alcott, "Reverent Quotations," *Brainy Quote* website, accessed August 1, 2013, http://www.brainyquote.com/words/re/reverent213057.html.

Element Three: Family Affection

1. W. Hendriksen and S. J. Kistemaker, *Exposition of Ephesians*, vol 7, New Testament Commentary (Grand Rapids, MI: Baker, 1953–2001), 167–69.
2. See Mary A. Kassian, *Girls Gone Wise in a World Gone Wild* (Chicago: Moody, 2010), 138–44.
3. Dr. D. A. Carson points out that there is more overlap in the use of these words than often thought. See his Exegetical Fallacies, 2nd ed. (Grand Rapids, MI: Baker Academic, 1996).
4. J. Strong, *Enhanced Strong's Lexicon* (Bellingham, WA: Logos Bible Software, 2001).
5. "Macmillan Changes Marriage Definition to Include Gay Couples," *Business Standard*, August 23, 2013, http://www.business-standard.com/article/pti-stories/macmillan-changes-marriage-definition-to-include-gay-couples-113082300952_1.html.
6. Ibid.
7. John Piper, "Let Marriage Be Held in Honor: Thinking Biblically about So-Called Same-Sex Marriage," *Desiring God* blog, accessed August 26, 2013, http://www.desiringgod.org/sermons/let-marriage-be-held-in-honor-thinking-biblically-about-so-called-same-sex-marriage.
8. W. Hendriksen and S. J. Kistemaker, *Exposition of the Pastoral Epistles*, vol. 4, New Testament Commentary (Grand Rapids, MI: Baker, 1953–2001), 147.
9. G. W. Knight, *The Pastoral Epistles: A Commentary on the Greek Text*, New International Greek Testament Commentary (Grand Rapids, MI: Eerdmans, 1992), 297.
10. Lauren Sandler, "Having It All Without Having Children," *Time*, August 13, 2013, http://content.time.com/time/magazine/article/0,9171,2148636,00.html.
11. Corrine Maier, *No Kids: 40 Good Reasons Not to Have Children* (Ontario: McClelland & Stewart, 2009), Kindle edition, Loc. 1345.
12. Ibid., loc. 1,346.

13. Debi Martin, "On Being Christian and Childfree," blog, accessed August 13, 2013, http://twiga92.wordpress.com/on-being-christian-and-childfree/.

14. Stan Guthrie, "The Childfree Life: A Christian and Personal Response," Crosswalk.com, accessed September 4, 2013, http://www.crosswalk.com/faith/spiritual-life/the-childfree-life-a-christian-and-personal-response.html.

15. Sandler, "Having It All."

16. Ibid.

17. Ibid.

18. John Piper, "The Ultimate Meaning of True Womanhood," message given at True Woman 2008, http://www.truewoman.com/?id=336#session_text.

19. Mary. A Kassian, "The ABC's of True Womanhood," message given at True Woman 2012, http://www.truewoman.com/?id=221.

20. Simone de Beauvoir, *The Second Sex: The Classic Manifesto of the Liberated Woman* (repr. New York: Vintage, 1974): "The oppression of woman has its cause in the will to perpetuate the family and to keep the patrimony intact, woman escapes complete dependency to the degree in which she escapes from the family" (p. 100); "All forms of socialism, wresting woman away from the family, favor her liberation" (p. 126); "The Revolution is impotent as long as the notion of family and of family relations continues to exist" (p. 143).

21. Betty Friedan, *The Feminine Mystique*, (New York: Norton, 1997), 423-28.

22. Betty Friedan, *The Feminine Mystique*, Twentieth Anniversary ed. (New York: Norton, 1983), 337, 385.

Element Four: Discipline

1. Dietrich Bonhoeffer, cited in "Quotes About Self Control," GoodReads website, accessed September 18, 2013, http://www.goodreads.com/quotes/tag/self-control?.

2. Maia Szalavitz, "The Secrets of Self Control: The Marshmallow Test 40 Years Later," *Time*, September 6, 2011, http://healthland.time.com/2011/09/06/the-secrets-of-self-control-the-marshmallow-test-40-years-later/#ixzz2eQwVpA19.

3. Jonah Lehrer, "Don't! The Secret of Self-Control," *New Yorker*, May 18, 2009, http://www.newyorker.com/reporting/2009/05/18/090518fa_fact_lehrer.

4. Nancy Leigh DeMoss, *Lies Women Believe: And the Truth That Sets Them Free* (Chicago: Moody, 2001), 94.

5. Kelly McGonigal, *The Willpower Instinct: How Self-Control Works, Why It Matters, and What You Can Do To Get More of It* (New York: Penguin, 2012), Kindle edition, locs. 54–55.

6. "What percentage of people fail the resolutions they make on New Year's Day?," Answers.com, accessed September 12, 2013, http://wiki.answers.com/Q/What_percentage_of_people_fail_the_resolutions_they_make_on_New_Year's_Day.

7. W. E. Vine; John R. Kohlenberger III, Ed., *The Expanded Vine's Expository Dictionary of New Testament Words* (Minneapolis, MN: Bethany House, 1984).

8. Spiros Zodhiates, *The Complete Word Study New Testament* (Chattanooga, TN: AMG Publishers, 1991), 947.

9. Tim Challies, Blog post: "The Lost Virtue of Self-Control" (August 29, 2014) http://www.challies.com/christian-living/the-lost-virtue-of-self-control.

10. Brent Jang, "The Equation of a Disaster: What Went Wrong in Lac-Mégantic," *Globe and Mail*, July 14, 2013, http://www.theglobeandmail.com/news/national/the-equation-of-a-disaster-what-went-wrong-in-lac-megantic/article13214911/.

11. Don W. King, "Narnia and the Seven Deadly Sins," http://cslewis.drzeus.net/papers/7sins.html Dr. Don W. King Department of English Montreat College© 1984 Don W. King A version of this essay first appeared in Mythlore 10 (Spring 1984): 14-19. Reprinted with permission of the author.

12. Louw, J. P., & Nida, E. A. (1996). Greek-English lexicon of the New Testament: based on semantic domains. New York: United Bible Societies. Newman, B. M., Jr. (1993). *A Concise Greek-English dictionary of the New Testament*. Stuttgart, Germany: Deutsche Bibelgesellschaft; United Bible Societies.

13. Michel de Montaigne, cited in "Quotes about Self Control," *GoodReads* website, accessed September 18, 2013, http://www.goodreads.com/quotes/tag/self-control?.

Element Five: Virtue

1. C. Brand, C. Draper, et al., eds. *Holman Illustrated Bible Dictionary* (Nashville: B&H, 2003), s.v. "Lye."

2. Becca Rawson, "It Floats! The Rise of Ivory Soap as an Enduring Consumer Brand," Exhibition Concept Prospectus Submitted to Dean Cloke and Professor Johnson, Georgetown University" (blog), accessed October 18, 2013, https://blogs.commons.georgetown.edu/rlr32-amst/files/2009/06/beccarawson_ivorysoap_finalproject1.pdf.

3. G. Kittel, G. Friedrich, and G. W. Bromiley, *Theological Dictionary of the New Testament* (Grand Rapids, MI: Eerdmans, 1985). See also J. Strong, *The New Strong's Dictionary of Hebrew and Greek Words* (Nashville: Thomas Nelson, 1996).

4. Alexander Nazaryan, "Love Canal's Toxic Legacy," *Newsweek*, October 20, 2013, http://www.newsweek.com/love-canals-toxic-legacy-589. Randy Alfred, "Love Canal Calamity Surfaces," *Wired*, November 21, 2008, http://www.wired.com/2008/11/nov-21-1968-love-canal-calamity-surfaces/; http://en.wikipedia.org/wiki/Love_Canal; http://www.nytimes.com/1988/08/05/nyregion/after-10-years-the-trauma-of-love-canal-continues.html.

5. *Voices of the True Woman Movement: A Call to the Counter-Revolution* (Chicago, IL: Moody, 2010), 135.

6. Thomas C. Oden, *Interpretation: A Bible Commentary for Teaching and Preaching. First and Second Timothy and Titus* (Louisville, KY: John Knox Press, 1989).

7. Spiros Zodhiates, *The Complete Word Study New Testament* (Chattanooga, TN: AMG Publishers, 1991), 884.

8. Albrecht Classen, *The Medieval Chastity Belt: A Myth-Making Process*, (New York: Palgrave Macmillan, 2007). See also "The Secret Histories of Chastity Belts: Myth and Reality," Semmelweis Museum exhibition, July 23–October 24, 2010, Library and Archives of the History of Medicine, accessed November 18, 2013, http://www.semmelweis.museum.hu/muzeum/kiallitasok/erenyov/reszletes_en.html. See also Nancy Koerner, "Chastity Belts Reveal Fascinating Mindset both Inside and Outside the Iron Underpants," *Examiner*, July 20, 2010, http://www.examiner.com/article/chastity-belts-reveal-fascinating-mindset-both-inside-and-outside-the-iron-underpants.

9. Alison Harris, "Fact or Fiction – Chastity Belts?," accessed September 4, 2013, http://blogs.law.harvard.edu/houghtonmodern/2013/05/10/fact-or-fiction-chastity-belts/.

10. Source unknown. "The Refiner's Fire" illustration was contributed to Sermon Central by Tim Harrison and is cited on numerous websites. Retrieved November 19, 2013 from http://www.sermoncentral.com/illustrations/illustrations-about-silver.asp.

11. William Shakespeare, Bartleby.com, accessed November 19, 2013, http://www.bartleby.com/348/1441.html.

12. D. A. Case and D. W. Holdren, *1–2 Peter, 1–3 John, Jude: A Commentary for Bible Students* (Indianapolis, IN: Wesleyan), 158.

Element 6: Responsibility

1. Nancy Leigh DeMoss, *Revive Our Hearts*, "The True Value of Your Home", radio program, https://www.reviveourhearts.com/radio/revive-our-hearts/the-true-value-of-your-home/.

2. Carolyn McCulley, *The Measure of Success: Uncovering the Biblical Perspective of Women, Work, and the Home* (Nashville: B&H, 2014), 36.

3. J. D. G. Dunn, *Romans 9–16*, vol. 38B, Word Biblical Commentary (Dallas: Word, 1998), 889.

4. W. Hendricksen and S. J. Kistemaker, *Exposition of the Acts of the Apostles*, vol. 17, New Testament Commentary (Grand Rapids, MI: Baker, 1953–2001), 614.

5. Tim Challies, "Work That Makes a Difference," *Challies.com*, January 30, 2014, http://www.challies.com/christian-living/work-that-makes-a-difference.

6. Leonardo da Vinci, Good Reads website, accessed November 27, 2013, https://www.goodreads.com/quotes/tag/work?page=5.

7. Mary A. Kassian and Nancy Leigh DeMoss, *True Woman 101: Divine Design* (Chicago: Moody 2012), 188-89.

8. Ibid., 49.

9. T. D. Lea and H. P. Griffin, *1, 2 Timothy, Titus: An Exegetical and Theological Exposition of Holy Scripture*, vol. 34, New American Commentary (Nashville: Broadman, 1992), 300–301.

10. Simone de Beauvoir, *The Second Sex: The Classic Manifesto of the Liberated Woman* (New York: Knopf, 1952), 510.

11. As cited at *Goodreads* website, accessed December 2, 2013, http://www.goodreads.com/author/quotes/21798.Betty_Friedan.

12. Norton Juster, *The Phantom Tollbooth* (New York: Random House, 1961), 212.

13. As cited at *Dictionary.com*, "Quotes," accessed December 2, 2013, http://quotes.dictionary.com/Housework_is_work_directly_opposed_to_the_possibility.

14. As cited at the *CWLU Herstory* website, accessed December 2, 2013, http://www.uic.edu/orgs/cwluherstory/CWLUArchive/polhousework.html.

Element Seven: Benevolence

1. Leslie Barker, "The Kindness Movement," *Kindness* website, accessed December 5, 2013, http://www.kindnessusa.org/kindnessmovement.htm.

2. http://www.kindnessusa.org/preparingtheproclamation.htm.

3. http://www.theindychannel.com/news/good-news/secret-santa-pays-off-walmart-layaway-bills.

4. "Caffeine Copycat? 500 Free Coffees Given Away in Ottawa, Calgary, Edmonton," CTV News website, accessed December 5, 2013, http://www.ctvnews.ca/canada/caffeine-copycat-500-free-coffees-given-away-in-ottawa-calgary-edmonton-1.1383473#ixzz2mW2rsnlb.

5. Philip D. Kenneson, *Life on the Vine: Cultivating the Fruit of the Spirit in Christian Community* (Downers Grove, IL: InterVarsity Press, 1999), 34.

6. Nancy Leigh DeMoss, *Revive Our Hearts*, "A Lasting Kindness," radio program, https://www.reviveourhearts.com/radio/revive-our-hearts/a-lasting-kindness/.

7. J. Cathey, *Holman Illustrated Bible Dictionary* (Nashville, TN: Holman Bible Publishers, 2003), Kindness.

8. Baker's Evangelical Dictionary of Biblical Theology, ed. Walter A. Elwell (Grand Rapids, MI: Baker, 1996), s.v. "kindness."

9. *God's Priorities for Today's Woman* (Harvest House, 2011), Kindle edition, loc. 3330 [Found at GoogleBooks.com].

10. K.S. Wuest, *Wuest's Word Studies from the Greek New Testament: for the English Reader* (Grand Rapids, MI: Eerdmans, 1997), Col 3:9–12.

11. B.B. Thurston, *Reading Colossians, Ephesians, and 2 Thessalonians: A Literary and Theological Commentary* (Macon, GA: Smith & Helwys Publishing, 2007), 50.

12. Names have been changed. Illustration from *Sermon Illustrations* website, accessed December 9, 2013, http://www.sermonillustrations.com/a-z/s/speech.htm.

13. The Greek translated as "gentle" in Titus 3:2 is epiekeis. According to the *Exegetical Dictionary of the New Testament* (ed. H. R. Balz and G. Schneider [Grand Rapids, MI: Eerdmans, 1990]), epiekeis can be translated as "gentle" or "kind," s.v. "ἐπιεικής."

14. DeMoss, "A Lasting Kindness."

15. C. H. Spurgeon, "Christ's People--Imitators of Him," sermon delivered on April 29, 1855; accessed at: http://www.spurgeon.org/sermons/0021.htm.

16. Abraham Lincoln, "Second Inaugural Address" (1865), *Abraham Lincoln Online* website, accessed December 10, 2013, http://www.abrahamlincolnonline.org/lincoln/speeches/inaug2.htm.

17. Jerry Bridges, *The Practice of Godliness* (Colorado Springs, Co: NavPress, 1983), 232.

Element Eight: Disposition

1. Quoted in *Becoming God's True Woman* (Wheaton, IL: Crossway, 2008), 25.

2. While Scripture does not specifically identify Salome and Mary of Nazareth as sisters, church tradition and many commentators and theologians agree that it is possible the two were siblings and that Salome was the sister of Mary referred to in John 19:25. See: Hall, D. R. (1996). Salome. In D. R. W. Wood, I. H. Marshall, A. R. Millard, J. I. Packer, & D. J. Wiseman (Eds.), *New Bible dictionary* (3rd ed., p. 1046). Leicester, England; Downers Grove, IL: InterVarsity Press. Easton, M. G. (1893). In *Easton's Bible dictionary*. New York: Harper & Brothers.

3. S. Zodhiates, *The Complete Word Study Dictionary: New Testament* (Chattanooga, TN: AMG), s.v. See also A. T. Robertson, *Word Pictures in the New Testament* (Nashville: Broadman, 1933), "Eph 5:21."

4. Barbara Rainey, "What Should Be a Wife's 'Role' in Marriage?" http://www.familylife.com/articles/topics/marriage/staying-married/wives/what-should-be-the-wifes-role-in-marriage#.VGO0OsmM-lg.

5. Aly Weisman, "'Arya' Is the Fastest-Growing Baby Name Thanks to 'Game of Thrones,'" *Business Insider*, May 13, 2013, http://www.businessin-sider.com/arya-is-the-fastest-growing-baby-name-thanks-to-game-of-thrones-2013-5. See also http://www.wetpaint.com/game-of-thrones/articles/2013-05-14-arya-is-fastest-growing-baby.

6. Mary A. Kassian, "A True Woman Chooses Wisdom," message given at True Woman 2008, http://www.truewoman.com/?id=1339.

7. This letter and parts of this section are taken from Mary Kassian, *Girls Gone Wise in a World Gone Wild* (Chicago: Moody, 2010), 60–62.

Element Nine: Legacy

1. Cherokee Traditions: Lottie Stamper. http://www.wcu.edu/library/DigitalCollections/CherokeeTraditions/People/Baskets_LottieStamper.html, accessed November 14, 2014.

2. Susan C. Power, Art of the Cherokee: Pre-History to the Present (Athens, Georgia: University of Georgia Press, 2007. p. 137-138). accessed online on November 14, 2014 at http://books.google.ca/books?id=ZPVEos7PKIgC&pg=PA137&lpg=PA137&dq=lottie+stamper&source=bl&ots=J5ElAu ZOp5&sig=JisH5Wutk81f_bsra2qU2S9l6Bo&hl=en&sa=X&ei=KGxmVJDoAc7IsQTLg4KQCw&ved=0CCUQ6AEwADgK#v=onepage&q=lottie%20 stamper&f=false.

3. Nancy Leigh DeMoss, *Lies Women Believe: And the Truth That Sets Them Free* (Chicago: Moody, 2001), 173.

4. Sharon Kirkey, "Infertility on the Rise in Canada: Study," Nationalpost.com, February 15, 2012, http://news.nationalpost.com/2012/02/15/infertili-ty-on-the-rise-in-canada-study/.

5. "Your Age and Fertility," BabyCentre Medical Advisory Board website, July 2013, http://www.babycentre.co.uk/a6155/your-age-and-fertility.

6. Piers Morgan interview with Barbara Walters, transcript, December 17, 2013, CNN.com, http://piersmorgan.blogs.cnn.com/2013/12/17/barbara-walters-reviews-her-career-and-life-i-regret-not-having-more-children-i-would-have-loved-to-have-had-a-bigger-family/?hpt=pm_t5.

7. Quoted in *Voices of the True Woman Movement* (Chicago: Moody, 2010), 139.

8. D. C. Arichea and H. Hatton, *A Handbook on Paul's Letters to Timothy and to Titus*, UBS Handbook Series (New York: United Bible Societies, 1995), 284.

9. H. G. Liddell, *A Lexicon: Abridged from Liddell and Scott's Greek-English Lexicon* (Oak Harbor, WA: Logos Research Systems).

10. "Mentorship," *Wikipedia*, accessed February 19, 2014, http://en.wikipedia.org/wiki/Mentorship.

11. "About Life Coaching," Life Coaching Institute website, accessed February 22, 2014, http://www.lcia.com.au/about-life-coaching.aspx.

12. "Life Coach Certification," the website of Expert Rating Certified Professional, accessed February 22, 2014, http://www.expertrating.com/certifi-cations/Life-Coach-Certification/Life-Coach-Certification.asp.

13. Spencer Morgan, "Should a Life Coach Have a Life First?," NYTimes.com, January 27, 2012, http://www.nytimes.com/2012/01/29/fashion/should-a-life-coach-have-a-life-first.html?scp=1&sq=should%20a%20life%20coach%20have%20a%20life?&st=cse&_r=0#.

14. Donna Otto, *Finding a Mentor, Being a Mentor* (Harvest House, Eugene, OR, 2001), 13.

15. Susan Hunt and Barbara Thompson, *The Legacy of Biblical Womanhood* (Wheaton, IL: Crossway, 2003), 12.

Element Ten: Beauty

1. "Fort Collins Artists Paints Transformer Boxes to Reduce Graffiti," CTVNews, April 24, 2013, accessed February 25, 2014, http://www.youtube.com/watch?v=YCA2vDQ3WKg.

2. David Kinnaman, *unChristian: What a New Generation Really Thinks about Christianity . . . and Why It Matters* (Grand Rapids: Baker Books, 2007), 15, 48.

3. Mary A. Kassian, "Exposed," *True Woman* blog, accessed February 25, 2014, http://www.truewoman.com/?id=672.

4. "New Model Restriction Law a Major Victory for Body Image," *Skeptikai* website, April 3, 2012, http://skeptikai.com/2012/04/03/new-model-restriction-law-a-major-victory-for-body-image/.

5. W. A. Elwell and P. W. Comfort, eds., *Tyndale Bible Dictionary* (Wheaton, IL: Tyndale, 2001), s.v. "Cosmetics."

6. K. A. Kitchen, "Cosmetics and Perfumery," in New Bible Dictionary, ed. I. H. Marshall, A. R. Millard, J. I. Packer, and D. J. Wiseman (Downers Grove, IL: InterVarsity, 1996).

7. D. R. Gautsch, "Cosmetics," in C. Brand, C. Draper, A. England, S. Bond, E.R. Clendenen, & T.C. Butler (Eds.), *Holman Illustrated Bible Dictionary* (Nashville, TN: Holman Bible Publishers, 2003), 350.

8. L. O. Richards, *The Bible Reader's Companion*, electronic ed. (Wheaton, IL: Victor, 1991), 849.

9. A. T. Robertson, *Word Pictures in the New Testament*, "Tt. 2:3." (Nashville: Holman Reference, 2000).

10. *Voices of the True Woman Movement* (Chicago: Moody, 2010), 40.

11. Ibid.

12. J. M. Freemanand H. J. Chadwick, *Manners and Customs of the Bible* (North Brunswick, NJ: Bridge-Logos, 1998), 326–27.

13. Ibid.

14. Elisabeth Elliot, *Let Me Be a Woman* (Wheaton, IL: Tyndale, 1976, 2004), 43.

15. John Angell James, *Female Piety: The Young Woman's Friend and Guide through Life to Immortality* (Morgan, PA: Soli Deo Gloria, 1995), 72–73.

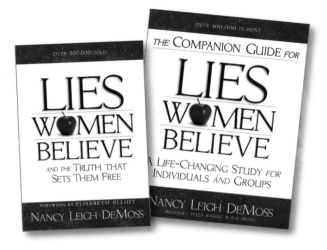

lies women believe

More resources for you, women's study, or teen study

Resources to hand out

- *Free From Lies*—25-pack of leaflets
- *The Truth That Sets Us Free*—25-pack of bookmarks

Lies Women Believe & Companion Guide

- DVD
- Audio book
- Available in Spanish

Lies Young Women Believe & Companion Guide

- *Lies Young Women Believe—Conversation with Dannah*
- CDs
- Audio book
- Available in Spanish

To place your order,
visit us online at
ReviveOurHearts.com

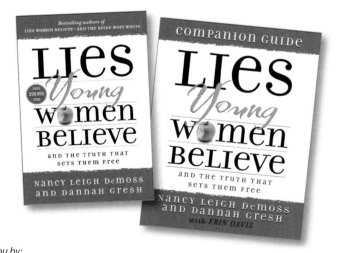

Brought to you by:

 |

Girls GONE Wise

More resources for Girls Gone Wise!

You'll find videos, a forum, and many other resources to help you learn how to walk wisely on the GirlsGoneWise.com website. And make sure to follow Girls Gone Wise on Facebook and Twitter too!

Also available: *Girls Gone Wise* **gear! Get the bag, mug, and buttons.**

MOODY
Publishers™

From the Word ***to*** *Life*

the true woman line of books
For Truth. For Joy. For Life.

true woman 101
divine design
an eight-week study in biblical womanhood

mary a. kassian
nancy leigh demoss

FOREWORD BY NANCY LEIGH DeMOSS

Together
Growing Appetites For God
by Carrie Ward
an Experiment in Life

Becoming God's True Woman
...WHILE I STILL HAVE A CURFEW

SUSAN HUNT
MARY A. KASSIAN

THE POWER OF A SOFT WARRIOR
FierceWomen
KIMBERLY WAGNER

Erin is a fresh, clear voice with a timely message, developed in the laboratory of life with God's Word in hand.
—Nancy Leigh DeMoss

If you have swallowed the pop culture Kool-Aid, you need to read this book and consider if the hand that rocks the cradle does, in fact, rule the world.
—Mary A. Kassian

BEYOND BATH TIME
Embracing Motherhood as a Sacred Role
ERIN DAVIS

FOREWORD BY DANNAH GRESH
confessions of a boy-crazy girl
ON HER JOURNEY FROM NEEDINESS TO FREEDOM
paula hendricks

MOODY Publishers
From the Word to Life

heartfelt thanks . . .

We are both blessed to be surrounded and supported by a host of like-minded, servant-hearted friends and colleagues, apart from whose encouragement, help, and prayers undertakings such this resource would never come to fruition.

Of the many who played a part in the birthing and development of True Woman 201, special gratitude is due to:

Paul Santhouse, *Erik Peterson*, and *René Hanebutt*, along with our other friends at Moody Publishers. Only eternity will reveal all the fruit borne by this many-year partnership.

Numerous *Revive Our Hearts* team members whose servant-hearted efforts were invaluable, notably:

>   *Mike Neises*, Senior Publishing Director, project coordinator
>
>   *Paula Hendricks*, editorial assistant
>
>   *Dawn Wilson*, research assistant
>
>   *Hannah Kurtz*, formatting and endnotes
>
>   *Sandy Bixel* and *Martin Jones*, administrative support
>
>   *Lydia Brownback*, editorial input

Dawn Wilson, *Kim Wagner*, and *Lydia Brownback*, help with discussion questions

Dr. Chris Cowan, Greek language review

Friends who reviewed and provided helpful input on parts or all of the manuscript: *Leslie Bennett* (who also conducted a beta test with a small group of women), *Tim Challies*, *Carrie Gaul*, *Paula Hendricks*, *Jennifer Lyell*, *Carolyn McCulley*, *Lindsay Swartz*, and *Dawn Wilson*.

Our dear *Praying Friends* who faithfully lift us up to the Throne of grace and whose support and encouragement on this project helped us persevere through the prolonged "labor and delivery" process.

Above all, may *Christ* be magnified!